Contents

Foreword

Diagnosis of any allergy or intolerance can be a daunting prospect for the home cook, and dietary information can be difficult to come by, especially finding tempting everyday recipes, which have to omit some basic ingredient. This useful and informative book with its combination of sound nutritional advice and collection of delicious, interesting family dishes will prove an invaluable guide to those individuals and parents who are having to cater, perhaps for the first time, for themselves or members of their family, diagnosed as lactose intolerant. This cookery book is a collaboration between Emily White, trained chef, restaurateur and cook and Miller Rogers, a nutritional therapist with a London practice.

Emily White is the daughter of two well-known restaurateurs in Suffolk. She trained at Prue Leith's cookery school and this was followed by several years working as a chef in London at various wine bars and restaurants. In the early 1990s she moved back to Suffolk and set up a small catering company. Eventually she took over as manager of her parents' busy restaurant in Colchester – The Warehouse Brasserie and then cooked and managed their next venture, The Red Onion Bistro in Sudbury. She is presently helping her brother with his popular pub/restaurant The Treble Tile in West Bergholt. With a husband and two young school-age children to cook for she has become increasingly interested in centring her cooking around nutritious, healthy food and believes it to be a sensible step to cut down on the intake of dairy produce. She has used her experience of commercial and domestic catering to create these dairy-free recipes which should help you stay on your elimination diet without feeling deprived.

Miller Rogers was brought up in a household where eczema, asthma and hay fever were prevalent. She became interested in the effects of food on the body when she was diagnosed with allergies and intolerances and as a result was brought up with the strong smell of goat's milk emanating from the fridge. She had the idea of setting up a health food shop or restaurant that would cater for those with food restrictions and so studied for a degree in Catering and Retail Management. After gaining experience in retail catering outlets such as Cranks, she was drawn into film production. Eight years later as a Production Manager having problems eating a restricted diet on location, she went to see a nutritional therapist. When she finally stopped eating dairy products there was a significant improvement in her condition. As her allergies started to improve and she saw the benefit of a nutritional understanding she decided to study, firstly part-time and then full-time, nutritional therapy, herself. She now has her own practice (www.difficultdiners.com) and is presently setting up a programme of nutritional education for teenagers at a local health centre.

THE
EVERYDAY
DAIRY-FREE
COOKBOOK

Recipes for Lactose Intolerants

MILLER ROGERS AND EMILY WHITE

GRUB STREET · LONDON

Published by Grub Street
4 Rainham Close
London SW11 6SS
Email post@grubstreet.co.uk
www.grubstreet.co.uk

Reprinted 2006, 2008, 2010, 2011

British Library Cataloguing in Publication Data
Rogers, Miller
  The Everyday Dairy-Free Cookbook
  1. Milk-free diet – recipes
  I. Title II. White, Emily
  641.5'63

ISBN 1 902304 73 X

Cover design: Hugh Adam
Cover photograph: Simon Smith
Photography: Michelle Garrett
Typesetting by Pearl Graphics, Hemel Hempstead
Printed and bound in Great Britain by
MPG, Bodmin, Cornwall

The publishers would like to thank TTC
(01773 520205, sales@tctabletop.com)
for kindly supplying china, linen and cutlery for photography

Note: When making any of the recipes in this book, only
follow one set of measures at a time (i.e. metric or imperial).

Grub Street uses FSC (Forestry Stewardship Council) paper for its books

INTRODUCTION

How this book will help

The word 'allergy' is bandied around so often and appears to be the root cause of so many symptoms that it seems we have been overtaken by an epidemic of allergies. People claim to be allergic to anything from sunlight, pollution, mobile phones, any and all foods, and even their bosses! Some reactions are more obvious like a peanut allergy causing anaphylactic shock, but if the symptoms are more obscure how do we know if we are allergic to it? Are we actually more allergic than we used to be or are we more aware of allergic symptoms and consequently notice them more? There has certainly been an increase in magazine and newspaper articles about allergies.

As a milk allergy is one of the top two most common allergies[1], this book has been designed to help anyone beginning (or needing encouragement to maintain) a dairy- or lactose-free diet. We will start by explaining what a milk allergy actually is, and how it differs from a lactose intolerance, then we will go through the different symptoms before describing what following a dairy- and lactose-free diet involves. We will look at foods that can be used to replace dairy products, and what non-dairy eaters need to be aware of with calcium and protein levels in their diet. We have put together some handy hints for eating out, lunch at work, or dinner at a local restaurant; and a Replacement Ingredients section for help with shopping and advice on the many different products that have grown up around the non-dairy market. There are some more vulnerable groups in the population, for example babies, children, teenagers and pregnant women, who need to make sure they are getting an adequate nutritional intake, so if this is relevant to you please read the notes about calcium intake. There are also people who follow a dairy-free diet but are not allergic to dairy nor lactose intolerant, so we have added a few comments about fat content and a list of the benefits of avoiding dairy produce. Lastly, we have included some suggested meals and notes on cooking and preparing recipes.

This book aims to show that dairy-free meals need not be dull or boring, but can be every bit as tasty as a meal that includes dairy products. However, we do need to be realistic; we are missing out a whole food category, so whilst some recipes use dairy alternatives, others are designed to stimulate imaginative cooking without the use of dairy substitutes. If you have any concerns about following a dairy-free diet or have a condition that may be affected by your diet, it is important you consult your doctor before starting the diet.

Incidence and Increase of Dairy Allergy and Intolerance

In 1997 the brewers Guinness, advertised that '88.2% of statistics are made up on the spot'. In actual fact it was a quote from Vic Reeves, but nonetheless it is with great trepidation that I pass on any statistics at all. As a Nutritional Therapist I have been taught to question statistics that are surprising, unexplained or newsworthy. Had the full trial been published? Had it been conducted properly? Was there something left unreported that would explain the statistic?

---

[1] Brostoff J & Gamlin L, THE COMPLETE GUIDE TO FOOD ALLERGY AND INTOLERANCE 1998, Bloomsbury Publishing.

Although the government has not got exact figures, the National Diet and Nutrition Survey produced by the Stationery Office in April 2000 found that 9% of boys and 13% of girls reported having an allergy to one or more foods; whilst 4% and 6% (boys and girls respectively) were reported to have their allergies diagnosed by a doctor. In the US dairy allergy and intolerance is estimated to have an incidence of 5% of the population, and as they have a fairly similar ethnic mix to us, our figures are likely to be similar.

HealthScreening is the UK's biggest tester of food sensitivities and they have seen an increase from 20,000 customers a year to 40,000 over the last five years. A report in August 1999 showed a staggering 62% of all their customers had tested sensitive to dairy. Another testing centre York Labs has reported similar findings, as has a manufacturer of non-dairy products.

The Severe and Brittle Asthma Unit at the NHS Birmingham Heartlands Hospital has reported their findings of a double-blind, placebo-controlled, food challenge programme. In January 2001, over 50% of patients had a confirmed food allergy and dairy products were a trigger in 50% of them. Although not everyone gets tested for food allergies and sensitivities it is clear there is a greater awareness of the effect food has on our bodies, and that some foods might trigger particular problems.

So what is a milk allergy?
An allergy is an abnormal reaction by the immune system to specific substances (known as allergens). An allergy to milk is usually caused by a reaction to proteins contained in the milk, such as casein.

And a lactose intolerance?
A lactose intolerance is an inability to digest lactose fully. Lactose is digested by the enzyme lactase which splits it into two sugars; the monosaccharides – glucose and galactose. If lactose is not broken down properly then the normal channels of absorption for the monosaccharides cannot be used. Instead the lactose remains in the intestinal tract and feeds specific bacteria that multiply and can cause the characteristic symptoms of lactose intolerance (*see* Symptoms below).

What is a food sensitivity?
The term 'food sensitivity' is an umbrella term that covers an allergy and intolerance as well as other reactions such as false food allergies; they are sometimes hard to distinguish from each other.

Primary Lactose Intolerance
The condition Primary Lactose Intolerance is a complete lack of lactase production, rather than diminished production; it tends to occur in early adolescence and stays throughout life.

Secondary Lactose Intolerance
Secondary lactose intolerance is usually short term and occurs if the lining in the intestines has become damaged such as after an illness or infection. Diarrhoea and some medicines (nonsteroidal anti-inflammatory drugs, antibiotics and aspirin) can inhibit lactase production for a few weeks.

Congenital Lactose Intolerance
Congenital lactose intolerance is the term used for a child born with no lactase production and therefore who cannot tolerate any amounts of milk or milk products.

Galactosaemia
Galactosaemia is a rare hereditary disease; it is the inability to metabolise the galactose part of lactose.

Symptoms
Although the symptoms listed below are caused either by an allergy to milk or a lactose intolerance please bear in mind that they are not specific to these conditions, and therefore are not necessarily an indicator of a milk allergy or lactose intolerance.

Allergy to milk
The symptoms of an allergy have three categories; skin reactions; stomach and intestinal reactions; and nose, throat and lung reactions. They can have a quick onset after contact with the allergen or offending item. These symptoms are not specific to a *milk* allergy – they are indicative of an immune reaction, so if any of these symptoms persist after excluding milk from your diet, you should consult a professional who could help you identify any other allergies (*see* Diagnosis below).

Skin Reactions:
• Itchy red rash
• Hives
• Eczema
• Swollen lips, tongue, mouth, face and or throat
• Allergic eyes, black eyes ("Shiners")

Stomach and intestinal reactions:
• Abdominal pain
• Abdominal bloating
• Gas or wind
• Cramps
• Diarrhoea (usually very runny)
• Vomiting

Nose, throat and lung reactions:
• Coughing
• Wheezing
• Runny nose
• Sneezing
• Eyes, watering or itchy
• Short of breath

Lactose Intolerance
When lactose is not digested properly it remains in the intestine and cannot be

assimilated. The conditions within the intestine encourage this fermentation process and create gases; these are usually the cause of the pain and flatulence associated with lactose intolerance.

The symptoms associated with lactose intolerance tend to be:
- Abdominal pain and bloating
- Stomach cramps
- Cramps
- Gas or wind
- Diarrhoea (starting 1/2 – 2hrs after lactose consumption)
- Nausea and vomiting

Usually there is a correlation between the amount of lactose ingested and the severity of the symptom; so the more lactose eaten the worse the symptoms. Someone suffering a severe lactose intolerance may well end up with malnutrition and weight loss. Some of the symptoms for lactose intolerance are similar to allergy symptoms; if the symptoms have a quick onset then they are more likely to be an immune response and therefore an allergic reaction.

Diagnosis
If you suspect you are allergic to milk or are lactose intolerant, you should get the diagnosis confirmed by your local GP. A blood test will verify your allergy but if your doctor is checking for a lactose intolerance then there are also breath and stool tests.

If, however, your suffering falls on unsympathetic ears contact your nearest qualified nutritional therapist and they will be able to help you. They are unlikely to give you the above tests but will ask hoards of questions about your health, lifestyle, and symptoms and should be able to settle your suspicions. Many people eliminate dairy from their diet to see if they feel better. I would suggest writing down what and when you eat for a week in a food diary and see if this correlates with your symptoms. I would still recommend seeking professional advice, as it may be something in addition to or in conjunction with dairy foods that may be causing the problem. Do not eliminate foods from a child's diet without professional advice.

Treatment
Unfortunately for those who love creamy pasta sauces and crumpets dripping with butter the treatment for a dairy allergy or lactose intolerance is to follow a dairy-free diet. The good news is that as soon as you eat less food containing dairy or lactose you should start to feel better. Sometimes the allergy or intolerance does improve, particularly if it has only shown itself due to a poor immune system; but generally the treatment of eliminating the offending food items is long term. What you can do to help is change your attitude, try not to be really negative, focusing only on what you can't eat. Instead look at all the hundreds of ingredients you can have and remind yourself how much better you feel without all the allergic or intolerant symptoms you used to suffer. Learn to appreciate the taste of food made with fresh ingredients instead of shop bought processed meals; swap dried herbs for fresh ones and notice the flavours coming out; add hummus to cooked dishes before serving to give them a slightly creamy edge; and master using substitutes such as Oatly or

Rice Dream. As a small form of consolation, if you are strict you may get so accustomed to non-dairy foods, that anything with dairy in it starts to taste strange, in fact I think my taste buds have adjusted as I would really rather not have cow's milk at all.

If you have secondary lactose intolerance, the more temporary variety, even when you have attended to the original cause of the illness, it is still advisable to remove all lactose from the diet for a while to allow time for the lactase enzyme production to re-establish itself.

If you have a lactose intolerance rather than an allergy to milk products, you may find it helps to alleviate the symptoms if you take one of a number of products on the market containing lactase. These products provide the missing lactase enzyme and can either be added to milk to reduce the amount of lactose or taken with a meal containing lactose. There are both lactose enzyme caplets and drops that should be available at your local health food shop, or they could order them in for you. Common products are: Lifeplan 'Lactase Enzyme', Lactaid 'Lactaid Drops', and Solgar 'Lactase 3500'.

Probiotics International manufacture ProtexinLacta, this is a product containing gut flora that are present in a healthy intestine. The combination of probiotics in the capsule usually enables a gradual increase in acceptance of lactose, but should be taken for at least a week before experimenting with different foods.

I have not had any experience with these supplements but would recommend that if you are intolerant to lactose you should avoid eating it. As the symptoms for a dairy allergy and lactose intolerance are so common it is hard to be sure that there is not any other underlying problem that might be covered up by adding lactase into the equation.

In indigenous cultures where milk drinking is not customary, the ability to digest lactose disappears early on in life, usually after weaning. So it would appear that we continue to produce lactase in response to dietary intake, and 'experiments have shown ... that both humans and laboratory animals can develop a tolerance to lactose if it is taken consistently in gradually increasing amounts'.[2] However, this is not recommended, as any course of action such as this must be carefully monitored to avoid aggravating symptoms.

What is a dairy-free diet?

A dairy-free diet excludes any product that is made from animal's milk; strictly this is not just cow's milk but goat's and sheep's milk too. These include the many derivatives of milk, such as cream, butter and yoghurt, but also less obvious ones that the manufacturers use, such as whey and casein (the thin fluid remnants of cheese making, and a milk protein respectively). It is important that all these derivatives are recognised as dairy products, as they can all cause adverse reactions. All of the following are dairy products.

- Whole milk
- Pasteurised milk
- Sterilised milk
- Homogenised milk
- Long life milk
- Skimmed milk
- Semi-skimmed milk

---

[2] Ballentine R, DIET AND NUTRITION 1978 Himalayan International Institute.

- Evaporated milk
- Condensed milk
- Milk solids
- Dried milk
- Powdered milk
- Cream
- Butter
- Buttermilk
- Margarine
- Cheese
- Whey
- Cottage Cheese
- Yoghurt
- Casein
- Caseinates
- Lactose
- Lactic Acid

What you will have to stop eating

Apart from the products that are listed above like milk, cream and cheese, or foods that are easily spotted like ice cream or milk chocolate you will need to be aware that many prepared foods are made with milk. Milk derivatives are often added to breads, cereals, sandwich spreads, salad dressings, cakes, biscuits, and ready meals whether fresh or frozen. Start by familiarising yourself with the list of milk derivatives above and when you are buying a processed product make sure you read the label. You may well find that your favourite snack or pudding is dairy free anyway but the worse your symptoms are the quicker you will find reading the label comes naturally.

Substituting with goat products?

Depending on the reason for avoiding dairy products, goat's milk, cheese, and butter may be included in the diet. There are many differences between goat's and cow's milk but the following have been identified as possible reasons that some people who are allergic or intolerant to cow's milk may be able to tolerate goat's products.

- Casein, one of the milk proteins, occurs in different forms, and the one most prevalent in cow's milk is absent in goat's milk.
- The casein molecules in goat's milk group together in smaller clusters than in cow's milk.
- The fat globules in goat's milk are smaller than those in cow's milk.
- The fat globules tend to clump together less in goat's milk.

Other animal products

Sheep's milk is now available both fresh and in powdered form, while the number of different sheep's cheeses produced continues to grow. Some who cannot eat cow's products may be able to tolerate these.

Buffalo mozzarella is also readily available, but buffalo are bovine, so it should be treated carefully by those allergic to cow's milk.

Yoghurt

People who are lactose intolerant can sometimes tolerate yoghurt. This is because the bacteria added to the milk in order to turn it into yoghurt breaks down some of the lactose before it is eaten. Cow's yoghurt is not suitable for a dairy-free diet, but goat and sheep yoghurt may be permitted in less strict regimes

Cheese

Apart from goat and sheep cheeses that have been mentioned in the paragraphs above, some people with a lactose intolerance find they are able to digest the harder cheeses, such as Cheddar and Cheshire. The reason for this is that much of the lactose is removed during production. Aged Gouda and Edam are even lower in lactose, as is cottage cheese.

Milk

There is also a reduced-lactose milk available.

Soya

Soya products are often used as dairy substitutes. They come in many different forms and seem to help bridge the gap between a dairy-free diet and eating a slightly different diet. There are soya milks, drinks, yoghurts, puddings, tofu (fermented soya) and TVP (textured vegetable protein). The soya bean is hailed as a highly beneficial ingredient, but it is also claimed that it can be detrimental to health. At the moment there is a great deal of research being undertaken to try and determine the effects of including soya in your diet. There are many articles being written about these effects, and as more information is uncovered it is important for you to be able to make your own judgement. Please bear in mind that there is usually an angle from which the author is writing; for example they may have been paid by the farming lobby to increase their sales; or they may be staunch vegetarians trying to push the benefits of not eating meat. Here are some of the topics that are often covered in articles on soya, and some countering comments.

- *Protein Content:* Soya is said to be beneficial to us as it has a good quality protein content. Admittedly, the protein content of soya beans is high at 36%[3], but as I have explained in the Protein section, the Western diet often includes too much protein, which adds an unnecessary digestive strain on the body. More importantly though, we can only benefit from the protein in soya if it is combined with a grain such as rice or oats, as soya protein is what is known as an 'incomplete' protein. There are twenty-two amino acids that can make up a protein, but only eight of them are essential in our diet. Soya protein does not contain enough of the essential amino acids to make a 'complete' protein, so in order to gain the benefit of the protein in soya it must be eaten with a grain that adds the missing amino acids and turns it into a first class protein.
- *Easy To Digest:* Soya beans are claimed to be an easy to digest alternative to dairy, but it is actually harder to digest than other pulses, such as black-eyed beans or red lentils that contain 23.5 and 23.8% protein respectively.
- *Phytoestrogens:* The phytoestrogens contained in soya are said to prevent breast and prostate cancer but these are available in supplement form and would avoid other negative effects of eating soya.

---

[3] Protein percentage is for dried raw soya beans as a wet weight. McCance, & Widdowson, COMPOSITION OF FOODS (5th edition) 1991, Royal Society of Chemistry, Cambridge.

- *Isoflavones:* Soya contains the isoflavones, genistein and daidzein, which mimic the effects of oestrogen in the body and have been claimed to increase the risk of cancer. Some soya products such as TVP actually have the isoflavones concentrated during their manufacture.
- *Phytic Acid:* Soya contains phytic acid, this binds to nutrients in the gut and makes them unavailable for absorption, but other whole grain foods such as rice or oats also contain phytic acid.
- *Cancer Link:* Soya has been linked with stomach cancers, but so have a copper deficiency (Wales), low vitamin A and calcium intake (Japan), and many other poor diet constituents.
- *Enzyme Inhibitors*: Soya contains enzyme inhibitors: the trypsin inhibitor is destroyed by heat so would only affect raw soya bean eaters. On the other hand eating raw broccoli or cauliflower can inhibit the thyroid gland.

With such a question mark lying over the effects of soya beans, the answer must lie in low or at least moderate consumption. Vegetarians could easily end up eating soya yoghurt for breakfast, tofu sausages for lunch and moussaka made with TVP for supper. This clearly is a high soya intake, so it is recommended that you limit your intake of soya to no more than once a day, thus not overly restricting your diet, whilst gaining the beneficial properties of the soya bean.

Other products available as an alternative to dairy foods
There are a number of alternatives to milk and dairy on the market. See the section on Replacement Ingredients on page 16 for a list of some foods that can be used as alternatives and their suitability for substitution. Shopping for a dairy-free diet can involve endless label reading, but to make it easier some supermarkets have compiled lists of their dairy-free foods, see the section of References at the back for addresses of UK supermarkets' customer service departments. There is also a list of relevant societies and other organisations.

Calcium
As milk is high in its calcium content it is often thought that a dairy-free diet will leave people with an inadequate calcium intake. Calcium is used for the building and maintenance of healthy bones and teeth, and muscular contraction, among many other functions. It is important that we eat adequate calcium levels as this can avoid bone diseases that have been linked to low calcium levels or calcium mishandling, for example osteoporosis.

The recommended daily amount (RDA) of calcium for an adult is 700 mg. This level has been set to avoid deficiency symptoms for 80% of the population, assuming an average weight of 70 kg, but this is not always suitable for everyone. Groups such as the elderly, and pregnant or lactating women have a higher RDA, whilst others have lower demands for example anyone who is underweight. Children have different RDAs dependent on their age; see the Children section on page 193.

Calcium is not a scarce mineral in our food, so most people should be able to get an adequate calcium intake even if they omit dairy produce from their diet. It is the amount of calcium absorbed that is more important, or endless supplements can be taken only to be flushed out of the body in what is often referred to as expensive urine. If you are eating a restricted diet (other than dairy) or are concerned about your nutrient intake make sure you seek professional advice. It is important to note that not all forms of calcium in food are equally available to the body, for example spinach contains oxalic acid which binds to the calcium and inhibits absorption in the intestines, similarly phytic acid binds the calcium in whole grain products. This does not give a good excuse to avoid the healthier wholegrain foods, but means that the calcium is less available so your intake should take account of this and be a bit higher.

The table below lists various foods with their calcium intake. Without advocating processed foods, you can see that some of them still contain good quantities of calcium.

Food	Calcium content mg per 100 g (wet weight)
Oatmeal	52
Wheat Flour – fortified	130-140
Mince pies (individual)	75
Tomato Purée	48
Watercress – raw	170
Spinach – raw	170
Celery – raw	41
Chick peas – whole, dried, raw	160
Chick peas – canned, re-heated, drained	43
Potato waffles – frozen, cooked	32
Baked beans – canned, reheated	53
Prawns – boiled	150
Mussels – boiled	200
Anchovies and Pilchards	300
Partridge and Pheasant	46-49
Apricots – raw	73
Oranges	47
Tahini Paste (Sesame seed paste)	680
Chocolate Nut Spread	130
Kit Kat	200
Chicken egg – boiled	57

Figures taken from *Composition of Foods*[4]

Studies have shown that in cultures without dairy herds, there is no prevalence of calcium deficient diseases, such as osteoporosis associated with the Western diets, and interestingly it has been reported that there is a 75-100% incidence of lactose intolerant adults in these non-dairy-dependent populations. This is one of the reasons many nutritionists recommend a considerably lower RDA of calcium. In Sri Lanka, India and Peru an intake around 300 mg/day was shown to be adequate. In other studies Westerners were also able to adapt to a much lower daily intake than our RDA.

[4] McCance & Widdowson COMPOSITION OF FOODS (5th Edition) 1991, Royal Society of Chemistry, Cambridge.

Protein

Foods such as meat, fish and milk are often prized for their high protein content, but the reality is that Western diets are rarely short of protein, so this idolatry seems unnecessary. Over recent years the RDA has fallen and is currently 21-65 g/day for a 70 kg adult, leaving an average of around 45 g/day.

Alternative nutritionists usually recommend an even lower intake (30-35 g/day) as any protein excess to requirements puts an added strain on the body, for many reasons, for example:

- Calorie for calorie, protein uses up more energy to digest than other calorie sources.
- During protein digestion waste products build up and must be excreted, if too much protein is eaten then this causes an extra burden on the liver.
- Current farming techniques often add to the metabolic load of digestion particularly animal protein, which is in itself harder to digest than vegetable protein.

As milk and its derivative products are commonly relied upon as a source of protein, it is important to make sure the dairy-free diet is still providing sufficient protein. This is crucial for vegetarians who are often dependent on dairy foods for their protein intake. Vegetable protein sources do not provide all the essential amino acids required in our diet, but if beans or pulses are combined with grains then the result is a better quality protein than if they were eaten separately, and the protein is nearly as good in quality as that in meat. Protein complementation occurs naturally in our diet with examples such as beans on toast, rice and lentils, or hummus on pitta, but vegetarians need to monitor their intake. If your body is in good health, even less protein is needed as it is digested, absorbed and utilised more efficiently, although during illness protein requirements actually increase.

Eating out

Eating out on a restricted diet is not easy; waiters with poor English and unsympathetic chefs can make it much harder. If your allergy or intolerance is severe the first thing to mention to the waiter is how important it is for you not to have any dairy produce whatsoever. Taking a moment to explain your allergy seems to get better results than just appearing to be fussy, and when you are no longer 'being difficult' people are more helpful and understanding.

Breakfast: If you are staying away from home, it is pretty safe to assume there will not be a supply of dairy-free alternatives for your breakfast, although increasingly hotel restaurants stock soya milk so it is worth asking. If there is no suitable substitute you do not have to go without your breakfast. Just leave the butter off toast and if you can't bear tea or coffee without milky substitutes, have a herbal tea or hot water with lemon. Try pouring fruit juice over your cereal instead of milk, but this may be something you grow to like, as it does taste very different! For cooked breakfasts have fried or poached eggs with oil or try porridge made with water and add fresh fruit for flavour. If away for longer trips it may be easier to take supplies with you.

Lunch and Dinner: If it is a one-off lunch or somewhere you eat regularly such as work, think about taking lunch with you as then you have complete control over what you eat and will probably end up with something much more tasty; this does require time in advance to prepare. Otherwise many supermarkets and delicatessens do a range of ready prepared foods that are suitable for dairy-free lunch-time eating. Try the ever expanding range of sushi boxes, and there are a variety of dairy-free salads available now such as pasta, roasted vegetable, and beans or carrots; just make sure you read the labels thoroughly.

Many people on a restricted diet think it is easier to give restaurants a wide berth, than antagonising waiters by sending them running backwards and forwards from the kitchen answering questions about ingredients. You don't have to avoid eating out, but it is best to avoid a scene so it is probably easier to assume most dishes have a dairy base. Try suggesting what you would like rather than getting a waiter to choose your meal, after all you are more used to a dairy-free diet than they are. For example, assuming that most sauces are made with butter or cream, try ordering fish or meat without the sauce or with it on the side; perhaps ask for meat or fish to be grilled with oil rather than butter. I have found chefs tend to respond better to a specific request than a cover all "No dairy please".

Chinese restaurants may be an easier target, as they tend not to cook using dairy products. In Indian restaurants most dishes are made with ghee or clarified butter, but the process of clarifying the butter breaks it down into a substance many people with a dairy allergy can tolerate; many of their dishes are both yoghurt- and cream-free. Slightly less common on the high street is the Mongolian barbeque-style restaurant, they are great for those on a restricted diet as you can choose what ingredients to include in your meal. Otherwise you could ask for a pizza with just the tomato sauce and other favourite dairy-free toppings, such as pepperoni, mushrooms, olives or pineapple.

Babies, Children, and Teenagers
As there are so many children who cannot tolerate dairy products, a section has been included for meals children will enjoy, as well as teatime treats so they don't feel so deprived. Most other recipes are also suitable for children, but be wary of high salt content, as young children should not eat adult-sized salt portions. For parents who are worried about their children's calcium intake, here are the recommended intakes for different aged children.

Reference Nutrient Intake for Calcium (mg/day)

Age	RNI
0-6 months	525
7-12 months	525
1-3 years	350
4-6	450
7-10	550
11-14	M: 1000
	F: 800
15-18	M: 1000
	F: 800

Figures taken from *Human Nutrition and Dietetics*[5]

[5] Garrow JS & James WPT HUMAN NUTRITION AND DIETETICS (9th Edition) 1998, Churchill Livingstone.

Pregnancy and Lactation

During pregnancy there is a significant transfer of minerals from mother to foetus, and similarly during lactation from mother to baby; so the mother's diet must make up for this added depletion by increasing her intake. We don't know quite to what extent our absorption and assimilation rates become more efficient but the National Research Council Recommended Dietary Allowances have issued a list of recommended dietary allowances for pregnancy and lactation. The calcium requirement recommended is 1200 mg/pd or a 50% increase above the levels for non-pregnant non-lactating women.[5]

Protein requirements also increase and although the extra amount required varies throughout pregnancy it is estimated that an increase of 6 g/day is sufficient. During the first 6 months of lactation an extra 15 g/day is adequate, whilst this reduces to 12 g/day for subsequent months.[5]

Following a dairy-free diet but not allergic or intolerant?

Some people choose to follow a dairy-free diet for reasons other than being allergic or intolerant. These reasons may be a desire to lose weight; a concerted effort to be health conscious; a change from vegetarian to vegan; or simply a suspicion that dairy foods may be making them feel uncomfortable.

Fat content

Although cow's milk contains only 3.9 g of fat per 100 g, it is made up of 87% water and therefore derives 53% of its calories from fat. When milk is used to make butter and cream, the fat is concentrated so double cream ends up containing 48 g/100 g fat or rather getting 96% of its calories from fat. Avoiding dairy products or even just the full fat derivatives can cut out unwanted calories and help people lose weight, provided they are following a sensible healthy eating plan.

Dairy product fat and calorie composition*
(per 100 g wet weight)

Item	Fat g/100 g	Kcal/100 g	Kcal from fat
Milk, full fat	3.9	66	53%
Milk, semi-skimmed	1.6	46	31%
Milk, skimmed	0.1	33	3%
Cheese, Cheddar	34.4	412	75%
Cheese, Edam	25.4	337	69%
Cream, single	18	188	86%
Cream, double	48	449	96%

* Figures taken from *Composition of Foods*[6]

What are the benefits of avoiding dairy products?

For whatever reason you have chosen to eliminate dairy products from your diet, the result can benefit your health in many ways.

---

[6] McCance & Widdowson, *op. cit.*.

- *Lower cholesterol and fat intake:* The high levels of cholesterol and fat contained in milk have been linked to coronary thrombosis, strokes, angina pectoris and other circulatory diseases.
- *Less mucus problems:* Catarrh, hay fever and sinus problems often occur where there is a high dairy consumption. This is because milk tends to produce excessive mucus in the intestines, and other parts of the body.
- *Better protein digestion:* Milk consumption neutralises stomach acid and as proteins are digested in the acid stomach environment this results in proteins being only partially digested often causing discomfort.
- *Better nutrient absorption:* Milk consumption builds up mucus in the intestines, and when it mixes with food residue it forms a hard material coating the intestinal wall. This blocks movement through the intestinal wall, both nutrient absorption and enzyme secretion that further aids digestion. Excluding dairy products from your diet will stop encouraging alkali-forming (unfriendly) bacteria from colonising in your intestines; these inhibit mineral absorption.
- *Healthier cells, Potassium:* Our body has a mechanism to maintain the correct balance of potassium and sodium ions within our cells. It is known as the sodium-potassium pump and works to drive the sodium ions out whilst holding on to the potassium ions, and keeping the cells healthy. In babies the requirements in the cell are reversed, and milk has the clever capability of actively encouraging sodium into the cells against the force of the sodium-potassium pump. As a baby changes into a child, so too the body changes, and at around a year and a half we no longer need so much intracellular sodium. As adult requirements are for higher intracellular potassium the ability for milk to aid sodium entry to the cell is not appropriate. It has been found that excess sodium in the cells increases susceptibility to chronic disease as high sodium concentrations have been found in many diseased organs, for example cancer. Avoiding dairy produce stops actively encouraging sodium to enter your cells.
- *Healthier cells, Magnesium:* Despite containing high levels of calcium, milk products can actually deplete the body of calcium. This is because magnesium is required to regulate calcium metabolism and keep the body's calcium in the right place such as the bones. Unfortunately milk has a low ratio of magnesium to calcium (1:10). Unless we eat enough foods with high levels of magnesium to counteract the poor magnesium content of milk we cannot utilise the calcium properly. Although we are all told we need to drink our milk to avoid osteoporosis later on in life, we actually need to make sure we have enough magnesium with our calcium rather than just eating dairy products. What makes it worse is that dairy produce not only decreases the body's calcium, but also depletes the magnesium stores. Unsurprisingly, recent studies have shown that bone-related problems such as osteoporosis and hip fractures are only prevalent in milk consuming societies. In the UK we consume a great deal of dairy produce and osteoporosis is a problem on the increase. A dairy-free diet will help keep your calcium-magnesium ratio in better balance.
- *Less colic in babies:* Not a huge advantage to everyone, but if you live with or even next door to a baby with colic encouraging the mother not to have dairy products while she is breastfeeding might just help you up your sleep quota. This is because the cow's proteins and antibiotics get absorbed into the mother's blood stream where they are passed on to the baby via the breast milk.[7] Furthermore studies have shown that

7 JOURNAL OF THE AMERICAN DIETETIC ASSOCIATION. Lust *et al*, 96 (1996) 46-48.

bottle-fed babies with colic tend to have their condition improve if dairy is removed from their diets.
- *Healthier arteries:* You will avoid eating the enzyme, xanthine oxidase present in milk, which is believed to attack the coronary arteries, and is particularly a problem in homogenised milk.
- *Other associated diseases:* Increasingly research is finding that there are many other diseases linked to dairy consumption. Health problems in children that have been positively identified with cow's milk are insulin dependent diabetes mellitus (IDDM), anaemia, diseased arteries, autism, hyperactivity, learning difficulties, lead poisoning, bedwetting, insomnia, recurrent pneumonia and pulmonary disease, nephrosis, and eczema.

If that isn't enough to encourage you to keep off your dairy then there are organisations around the world that are specifically anti-milk with plenty of literature explaining reasons why milk is not good for adult consumption. Try www.nomilk.com or join a relevant internet newsgroup.

There are also two very good sites that contain up-to-date information about dairy allergies and milk intolerances (www.lactose.co.uk, or www.lactoseintolerance.co.uk).

Maintaining a healthy balanced diet without eating dairy products
Whether you are eating a restricted diet or not, the general guidelines for healthy eating still apply. These are low fat; no added salt; at least five portions of fresh fruit and vegetables daily; and whole grain foods should replace refined foods where possible. Furthermore all foods should be free of contaminants, so where possible try to find organic foods.

Vegans need to watch that they have an adequate vitamin B12 intake, as this is only available from animal sources and will need supplementing.

Some Suggested Meals

	MONDAY	TUESDAY	WEDNESDAY	THURSDAY
Breakfast	Cornflakes with apple juice	Toast with vegan margarine and a fruit spread	Porridge made with Oatly (leave it soaking overnight for added creaminess) and add a chopped banana	Alpen with Rice Dream
Lunch	Hummus, chilli and crisp vegetable wrap	Risotto of artichoke hearts and mushrooms	Smoked salmon and spinach quiche	Chicken, avocado and watercress salad with pitta bread
Evening Meal	Grilled fillet of sea trout with creamy watercress sauce Steamed carrots Roasted garlic and olive oil mashed potato * * * Baked chocolate and almond torte	Lamb tagine French beans à la Greque Spicy potato wedges * * * Blackcurrant ice cream	Puy lentil and mushroom moussaka * * * Raisin and almond ground rice pudding	Mushroom and nut pâté * * * Seared calves liver with bacon, sage and sherry vinegar sauce Sesame noodles Piquant vegetables * * * Grilled honey glazed pineapple and fig kebabs served with an orange sabayon

	FRIDAY	SATURDAY	SUNDAY
Breakfast	Toast with olive oil fresh marjoram and tomato slices	Poached eggs on wholemeal toast (use olive oil)	Bacon sandwich with fresh tomato slices
Lunch	Potato, bean and corn frittata	Warm sweet potato and artichoke salad Polenta bread rolls	Roasted leg of duck with ginger and honey Potato and celeriac boulangere Crunchy stir-fry cabbage and carrots with caraway * * * Fresh strawberry and vanilla roulade
Evening Meal	Salmon and king prawn brochette Onion, tomato and rosemary focaccia Green salad with tarragon French dressing * * * Tangy citrus cheesecake	Thai seafood soup * * * Creamy chilli chicken with basil and coconut Basmati rice Cumin spiced cauliflower * * * Banana and cashew nut ice cream	Spaghetti carbonara-style Mixed leaves with sun-dried tomato, and basil dressing * * * Hot chocolate

Cooking and preparing recipes

If you pick up a cookbook and find a recipe that you would like to make but it includes dairy products, don't feel that you can't make it. As you get used to your new way of eating you will find that you are more able to spot substitutions. There are a few basic replacements that will make your life easier and as your confidence grows with your cooking repertoire you may well suddenly feel that a dairy- or lactose-free diet isn't that restrictive whilst you have control over your own kitchen. Replace butter with vegan margarine for spreading, frying, baking; olive oil for quick frying or lard for pastry or other baking. Try the various milk substitutes listed in the back with different recipes, Rice Dream is slightly sweet so is better in puddings, and Oatly is the most heat stable so is better in soups. You will see that hummus has been added to a number of recipes and it adds a creamy feel, try it at home with tomato-based sauces; or use any of the soya yoghurts or creams available in health food shops.

General

If you are cooking for someone else who is allergic or intolerant MAKE SURE YOU DO NOT EXPERIMENT ON THEM, if you are in any doubt whatsoever check with them whether to include an ingredient. It is not worth the risk of causing them any discomfort or harm. If you haven't already got one, a blender is a worthwhile investment, as the puréed texture always feels creamier, a taste that is often missed in a dairy-free diet. Unless otherwise marked all recipes have been made with size 3 eggs, and all spoonfuls are level. The information contained in this book is correct at the time of writing but intended for general reference purposes only. It is not a substitute for professional medical advice or a medical examination. Always seek the advice of your GP if you believe you are suffering from the symptoms of a milk allergy, a lactose intolerance or any other medical condition before starting any new treatment. No information in this book should be used to diagnose, treat, cure or prevent a dairy allergy or lactose intolerance or any other medical condition without the supervision of a GP or other medical doctor.

REPLACEMENT INGREDIENTS

When starting a dairy-free diet, most people do not know where to start looking to find food that doesn't make them feel deprived, so I have put together a list of products that are either dairy free or low in lactose. The following products are all available in the UK and if your local health food shop does not stock the item you are after, ask them to order it in for you – but do check ingredients if your diet is restricted further than just dairy products. I have not included biscuits, soya milk or soya milk drinks as there are so many different varieties and all readily available.

Now that supermarkets have so many own brand products, some of them produce a list of their dairy-free goods. Contact the relevant head offices listed in the references section.

Basic Ingredient	Brand / Supplier	Replacement Product Name	Category
Butter			
(see Margarine)	Delamere Dairy	Goat's butter	Low lactose
Cheese	Biddy Merkins	Vegerella:	
		Italian	
		Mexican	
	Bute Island Foods	Cheddar	All vegan
		Cheshire	
		Stilton (Blue)	
		Cheddar/Chives	
		Hickory Cheddar	
		Gouda Style	
		Edam Style	
		Mozzarella	
	Florentino	Parmezano	
	La Fonte Della Vita	Vegan Cheese Alternative	
	Galaxy Foods	Soya slices:	Vegan
		Cheddar Style	
		Mozzarella Style	
	Redwood Company	Cheezly Dairy Free Cheddar Cheese:	Vegan
		Red Cheddar Singles	
		White Cheddar Singles	
	Tofutti	Tofutti Soya Cream Cheese:	Vegan
		Original (plain)	
		Garlic and Herbs	
		Herbs and Chives	
		French Onion	
	Woodlands Dairy Park	'Nannies' Goat's Cheddar	Low lactose
Chocolate and Carob Bars	The Booja-Booja Co	Cognac flambéed banana truffles	Vegan
		Around midnight expresso truffles	
		Ginger wine truffles	
		Hazelnut crunch rochers	

	Plamil	Chocolate & Hazelnut Bar	Vegan
		Martello Chocolate Bar	
		Chocolate Bar Plain	
		Chocolate Bar Mint	
		Carob Bar	
		Carob Bar No Added Sugar	
		Carob Bar with Hazelnuts	
		Orange Carob Bar	
		Carob Drops No Added Sugar	
		Organic Chocolate	
		Organic Mint Chocolate	
		Organic Orange Chocolate	
	Silhoutte, distributed by Allergycare	Dark Carob Bar, and Golden Wrapped Mini Eggs	Vegan
	By Whizzers	Chocolate Beans	Dairy free
	By D&D Specialist Chocolates	All sorts	Dairy free
Desserts	Yosa	Probiotic Snack Food: Pineapple	Vegan
		Apple & Banana	
		Peach & Passion Fruit	
		Fruits of the Forest	
	Clearspring	Imagine – Non-Dairy Desserts	
		Chocolate Dessert	
		Lemon Dessert	
		Butterscotch Dessert	
		Banana Dessert	
	Organic Valley	Organic Rice Pudding Dairy Free	
	Plamil	Rice Pudding with Sultanas – Sugar Free	Vegan
	Provamel	Soya Desserts	Vegan
		Chocolate	
		Vanilla	
		Hazelnut	
Desserts (Frozen)	Sunrise	Ice Dream	Vegan
		Carob Chocolate Ice Cream	
		Vanilla Non Dairy Ice Cream	
		Raspberry Ripple Ice Cream	
	Tofutti	American Soya Desserts – Supreme Range	
		Vanilla Fudge	
		Belgian Chocolate	
		Madagascan Vanilla	
		Wildberry Supreme	
		Chocolate Cookies	
		Better Pecan	
		4 Vanilla Fudge Tube	
		Rock and Roll P.M.P.	

Ice cream	Swedish Glace Winner Iced	Non Dairy Dessert Raspberry Flavour Vanilla Flavour Strawberry Flavour Chocolate Flavour	
	Blissful Buffalo	Buffalo Ice Cream	
Margarine	Granose Foods	Vegetable Margarine Sunflower Margarine Soya Margarine Olive Grove Margarine	
	Matthews Foods	Organic 'Pure' Dairy Free Vegetable Margarine	Vegan
	Rakusens	Tomor Kosher Margarine	Dairy free
	Vitaquell	Vitaquell Extra Cuisine Vegetable Margarine Organic Margarine Vitacult Vitaquell Omega 3	Vegan
	Supermarket own brand	Various – but check it says vegan or dairy free on the label or there will be hidden ingredients	
Milk and Non-Dairy drinks	Skane	Mill Milk Classic Oat Drink	Vegan
		Mill Milk Oat Drink Oatly Oat Drink	
	Recipe leaflets avail from manufacturer	Rice Dream: Original Vanilla Chocolate Carob	Dairy free
	Evernat	Organic Almond Drink Organic Hazelnut Drink	
	Provamel	Provamel Rice Drink	
	Various	Soya Milk Lactolite – Lactose reduced Whole UHT Milk	Dairy free
	Delamere Dairy	Fresh Goat's Milk Whole Semi-skimmed	
	Blissful Buffalo	Buffalo Milk	
Milk (powdered)	Allergycare	Goat's Milk	Low lactose
		Rice Milk	Dairy free
		Sheep's Milk (skimmed)	Low lactose
		Soya Milk	Dairy free

Milk (frozen)	Shepherds Purse	Frozen Sheep's Milk	Low lactose
	Suttons Dairies	Frozen Goat's Milk	Low lactose
Stock	Kallo	Cubes:	
		Knorr	Dairy free
	Marigold	Vegetable Bouillon	
		Vegan	
		Dairy Free	
		Organic	
	Shop's own brand	Various	Variable so check label
Yoghurt	Granose	Soya Yoghurts	
		Strawberry	
		Apricot	
		Peach Melba	
		Blackcurrant & Apple	All vegan
	Haldane	"So Good" Soya Yoghurts	Vegan
		Natural Soya	
		Peach & Passion Fruit	
		Black Cherry	
		Strawberry	
		Pineapple	
	Provamel	Desserts:	Vegan
		Organic Yofu Red Cherry & Peach/Mango	
	Sojasun	Soya Desserts	Vegan
		Natural B.A.	
		Raspberry & Passion Fruit	
		Apricot & Guava	
		Vanilla Dessert	
		Chocolate Dessert	
	Woodlands Park Dairy	Live Goat's Yoghurt	
		Natural	
		Strawberry	
		Apricot	
		Live Greek Style Sheep's Yoghurts	
		Natural	
		Apricot	

SPECIALITY FOOD MANUFACTURERS
(all available as mail order)

Blissful Buffalo Belland Farm Tetcott, Holsworthy Devon EX22 7RG	✆ 01409 271253 www.blissfulbuffalo.fsnet.co.uk	Buffalo milk, cheese and yoghurt
Booja Booja Company Hall Farm Bungay Road, Hempnall Norfolk NR15 2LJ	✆ 01508 499049	Organic, gluten, dairy and low-sugar chocolates
D & D Chocolates 261 Forest Road Loughborough LE11 3HT	✆ 01509 216400	Dairy free and no added sugar chocolates
Delamere Direct Delamere Dairy Yew Tree Farm Bexton Lane Knutsford Cheshire WA16 9BH	✆ 01565 632422 sales@delameredairy.co.uk www.delameredairy.co.uk	Range of chilled ready-meals made with goat's milk, butter, cheese, yoghurt and cream, which they also sell
Goodness Direct South March Daventry Northants NN11 4PH	✆ 0871 871 6611 info@goodnessdirect.co.uk www.goodnessdirect.co.uk	Online special diet shop
Lifestyle Healthcare Centenary Business Park Henley on Thames Oxfordshire RG9 1DS	✆ 01491 570000 orders@glutenfree.co.uk www.glutenfree.co.uk	Variety of dairy-free foods
Neals Yard Dairy 6 Park Street Borough Market London SE1 9AB	✆ 0207 645 3550 mailorder@nydairy.co.uk	Sheep and goat cheeses
Sillfield Farm Endmoor, Kendal Cumbria LA8 0HZ	✆ 01539 567609 www.sillfield.co.uk	Unpasteurised sheep cheeses
Sussex High Weald Dairy Putlands Farm Duddeswell, Uckfield East Sussex TN22 3BJ	✆ 01825 712647	Sheep's milk, cheese, yoghurt, and fromage frais
Taste of the Wild Cottage No 3 Saltoun East Mains Haddington East Lothian EH41 4HR	✆ 01875 341949 www.tasteofthewild.co.uk	Special dietary, organic and natural foods

Soups, Dips, Starters and Snacks

Chunky Leek, Potato and Puy Lentil Soup

Thai Seafood Soup

Cream of Spinach and Nutmeg Soup

Smoked Haddock Chowder

Creamy Carrot and Coriander Soup

*Miso Soup with Tofu, Noodles
and Wakame Seaweed*

Hummus Dip

Chive Cream Cheese Dip

Tahini and Lemon Dip

Herbed Olive and Anchovy Dip

Avocado and Prawn Empanadas

Crab Rösti Cakes

Crisp Garlic and Leek Stuffed Mussels

Fish Fritto Misto

Herb and Kipper Soufflé

Herb Crumbed Fresh Sardine Fillets

Niçoise Tartlets

Smoked Salmon Roulade with Smoked Trout Mousse

Squid with Chillies and Tomatoes

Chinese-Style Crispy Pork Strips

Marinated Lime and Sesame Chicken Sticks

Smoked Duck Salad with Spiced Walnuts

Mushroom and Nut Pâté

Roasted Cherry Tomato Bruschetta

Crispy Spinach and Pine Nut Filo Parcels

Hummus, Chilli and Crisp Vegetable Wrap

Bacon, Tomato and Watercress Wrap

Never cook pulses in salted water. They will become tough. Try this recipe using red lentils or brown lentils, vary the cooking time accordingly.

Chunky Leek, Potato and Puy Lentil Soup

Puy lentils are easy to cook and do not require pre-soaking. They also provide an excellent source of protein and fibre. I usually have plenty of onions, potatoes and lentils in my cupboard, and quite often make this soup when everything else has run out and I want a quick and nutritious soup for lunch.

6 oz	puy lentils	175 g
2	medium leeks	2
10 oz	potatoes (weight after peeling)	275 g
1 tbsp	sunflower oil	1 tbsp
1	large onion, finely chopped	1
3	cloves garlic, crushed	3
1 tsp	garam masala	1 tsp
2¾ pts	boiling water	1½ litres
2-3 tbsps	vegan bouillon	2-3 tbsps
	salt and freshly ground pepper	
1 tbsp	chopped fresh parsley	1 tbsp

First rinse the lentils. Cover with plenty of cold water in a large saucepan. Bring this to the boil and simmer for 10 minutes, drain well.

Wash, trim and chop the leek, cut the potato into small cubes. Heat the oil in a large saucepan and fry the onion and garlic for about 4 minutes until soft. Next add the garam masala and drained lentils and stir well.

Pour over the boiling water and cook for a further 15 minutes.

Mix in the potatoes, leeks and bouillon powder and cook this uncovered, stirring occasionally for a further 10 minutes until soft but not mushy.

Season with salt and freshly ground pepper.

Spoon the soup into warmed bowls and sprinkle with chopped parsley. Serves 4-6.

PER SERVING	
Energy Kcals	244
Protein g	13.8
Fat g	3.9
Polyunsaturated fatty acids g	2.22
Saturated fatty acids g	0.44
Carbohydrate g	41.1
Calcium mg	62

This soup can also be made with watercress and produces a wonderful nutritious soup.
 I buy Marigold Bouillon (vegan variety) which is available from most health food shops and makes a delicious vegetable stock.

Cream of Spinach and Nutmeg Soup

This should be a lovely fresh looking green soup. To make it more impressive, pour a swirl of soya cream onto the top before serving. The less you cook the spinach the more the colour and nutrients are retained.

1 tbsp	vegetable oil	1 tbsp
1	large onion, roughly chopped	1
2	sticks of celery, washed and chopped	2
1 lb	weight peeled potato, diced	450 g
1³/₄ pts	fairly strong vegan vegetable stock	1 litre
7 oz	spinach	200 g
¹/₄ tsp	freshly grated nutmeg	¹/₄ tsp
	salt and freshly ground pepper	
	oat drink to serve	

Heat a large saucepan with the oil. Gently cook the onion and celery for about 5 minutes until soft, taking care not to let them brown. Add the diced potato and stir well.

Pour in the stock, bring this up to the boil and simmer about 20 minutes until the potato is beginning to fall apart and the onion is tender. Wash the spinach well, remove any tough stalks but keep the tender ones.

Put the spinach in the pan and push down, cover with lid and allow to cook for about 4 minutes, spinach should all be submerged, it should not be cooked for too long otherwise the soup will become grey; cool slightly.

Purée in a blender or food processor until smooth and creamy. Season with nutmeg, salt and freshly ground pepper.

To serve, heat the soup through gently and if necessary thin down with a splash of oat drink. Serves 4-6.

PER SERVING	
Energy Kcals	130
Protein g	5.1
Fat g	3.5
Polyunsaturated fatty acids g	0.59
Saturated fatty acids g	0.09
Carbohydrate g	26.7
Calcium mg	116

For a different variation, try this recipe with crab, clams or prawns. Or for a vegan chowder, omit fish stock and use vegetable stock. The potato and sweetcorn alone provide a tasty nourishing soup.

Smoked Haddock Chowder

A chowder is a cream based chunky fish soup that originates from North America. We often have this nourishing soup as a meal in itself. The potatoes should just be beginning to break down and slightly thicken the soup. The addition of sweetcorn is not only traditional, it also provides added milkiness to the dish.

1	medium leek	1
1 tbsp	vegetable oil	1 tbsp
1	large onion, finely chopped	1
1 lb	potatoes, cubed (weight peeled)	450 g
1¼ pts	vegetable, fish or chicken stock	725 ml
1 lb	fillet of smoked haddock, skinned, boned and cut into small cubes	450 g
6 oz	frozen, fresh or canned drained sweetcorn kernels	170 g
1	level tablespoon arrowroot	1
14 fl oz	oat drink	400 ml
2 tbsps	chopped fresh coriander to serve	2 tbsps

Wash, trim and thinly slice the leek. In a large pan, heat oil and gently cook the onion and leek for about 5 minutes until soft but not brown.

Add the potatoes and cook for about 3 minutes, stirring regularly. Pour in the stock, mix well and simmer for 20 minutes until the potatoes and leeks are both tender.

Add the cubed haddock, sweetcorn and arrowroot (if using fresh corn off the cob add to the soup after potatoes have been cooking for 5 minutes), simmer for 5 minutes.

Pour in the oat drink and warm through. Serve in warm bowls garnished with fresh coriander. Serves 6.

PER SERVING	
Energy Kcals	197
Protein g	19.4
Fat g	4.0
Polyunsaturated fatty acids g	1.19
Saturated fatty acids g	0.35
Carbohydrate g	26.3
Calcium mg	45

Use parsnips, celeriac, cauliflower, broccoli or celery for a variation.

Creamy Carrot and Coriander Soup

This rich, creamy soup is delicious as a lunch dish with hot crusty bread. It is also delicious with a sprinkling of crispy bacon and parsley on top instead of coriander. This forms the basis of many creamy style vegetable soups.

3/4 oz	vegan margarine	20 g
1	large onion, chopped	1
10 oz	potatoes (peeled and roughly chopped)	275 g
1 lb	carrots (peeled and roughly chopped)	450 g
2 3/4 pts	vegetable stock	1 1/2 litres
5 fl oz	oat drink	150 ml
	small bunch fresh coriander	

Melt margarine in a large saucepan over a medium heat. Add the onion and gently cook for about 4 minutes until soft but not brown.

Stir in the chopped potatoes and carrots and pour over the stock. Bring the soup to the boil and gently simmer for about 30-40 minutes, or until vegetables are soft.

Purée in a blender or food processor until smooth and creamy. Season with salt and freshly ground pepper.

Pour in the oat milk and gently reheat. Serve the soup in hot bowls with freshly chopped coriander sprinkled on top.
Serves 6-8.

PER SERVING	
Energy Kcals	113
Protein g	2.8
Fat g	3.6
Polyunsaturated fatty acids g	1.25
Saturated fatty acids g	0.99
Carbohydrate g	18.4
Calcium mg	36

This could also be made without
noodles for a lighter soup,
I included them to make it a little
more substantial and therefore
also suitable as a light meal.

Miso Soup with Tofu, Noodles and Wakame Seaweed

This soup is very nourishing and high in protein. Miso is readily
available in health food shops. The wakame seaweed is widely
used in Japanese soups and salads, and has no calories. It is very
high in minerals and calcium. Try experimenting with Japanese
foods if you enjoy this soup.

1/2 oz	dried wakame seaweed	10-15 g
1	pack regular tofu, (about 280 g)	1
2 pts	weak vegetable stock (could use secondary bonito stock if available)	1.2 litres
4 oz	medium or thin noodles	110 g
4 tsps	medium-salt Miso	4 tsps
2	spring onions, trimmed and cut into fine rounds, save the green ends for garnish	2

Soak wakame in cold water until it softens (about 10 minutes)
don't over soak. Drain and trim away any tough sections, then
cut into 2 1/2 cm (1 inch) lengths.

Cut the tofu into 1 cm (1/2 inch) cubes. Heat stock over
medium heat until very hot, add noodles and cook for half
required cooking time.

Turn heat down and allow to cool slightly. Add the miso and
stir well. Then stir in the spring onions and tofu, allow the soup
to heat through, but do not boil.

Lastly add the wakame, remove from heat just before soup
boils. Serve in pre-heated bowls garnished with the green ends
of the spring onions. Serves 4.

PER SERVING	
Energy Kcals	174
Protein g	10.1
Fat g	5.0
Polyunsaturated fatty acids g	1.46
Saturated fatty acids g	0.36
Carbohydrate g	23.4
Calcium mg	405

Right:
Smoked Haddock Chowder
(page 26)

Try making this with soaked and cooked yellow split peas for an interesting alternative.

Hummus Dip

Hummus is a popular dip which originates from Lebanon. The texture is often deliciously creamy, yet the ingredients are all extremely nutritious. Hummus will store well for several weeks in the fridge, making it a useful food to have for quick nutritious snacks. Try using it in sandwiches with crisp salad or sprouted alfalfa.

Many supermarkets now stock hummus. However, making it at home is certainly more economical and also you can monitor the salt content, as the bought variety can be deceptively high in salt.

2 cans	chick peas, drained (or equivalent to about 520 g home cooked from dried)	400 g
4 tbsps	tahini (creamed sesame seeds)	4 tbsps
	juice from 2-3 lemons	
3	cloves garlic	3
3 tbsps	olive oil	3 tbsps
2-3 tsps	Maldon salt	2-3 tsps
	paprika powder to garnish	

Blend the chick peas, tahini, lemon juice, and garlic in a food processor until it becomes a creamy and smooth consistency.

Gradually add the olive oil, if mixture is too thick add water spoon by spoon until smooth dropping consistency. Blend in the salt teaspoon at a time, taste for seasoning.

Spoon some into a serving dish and sprinkle the top with paprika if desired. Store the remaining hummus in sealed jars in the fridge. This recipe above makes about 3 jars of hummus. Serves 20.

PER SERVING	
Energy Kcals	62
Protein g	2.5
Fat g	4
Polyunsaturated fatty acids g	1.2
Saturated fatty acids g	0.54
Carbohydrate g	4.4
Calcium mg	32

Left:
Chive Cream Cheese Dip
(page 30)

Try this served on small squares of pumpernickel as a smart canapé topped with smoked salmon, gravlax or mock caviar. Challenge anyone to guess it is dairy free.
  Also delicious as a dip with crudités.

PER SERVING	
Energy Kcals	161.5
Protein g	1.6
Fat g	10.36
Polyunsaturated fatty acids g	7.42
Saturated fatty acids g	2.31
Carbohydrate g	2.1
Calcium mg	1

Chive Cream Cheese Dip

Tofutti cream cheese can be bought from most health food shops and tastes very similar to normal cream cheese, but actually contains less fat. By adding lemon and chives you can make a quick and easy dip, which will store well for up to a week.

4 oz	Tofutti Original (soya cream cheese)	110 g
4 tbsps	soya cream	4 tbsps
2 tsps	lemon juice	2 tsps
10	strands of chives, chopped	10

  Beat the Tofutti and soya cream together in a bowl until smooth.
  Add the lemon juice and chives, mixing well. Store in sealed container in the fridge until required. Makes about 175 g (6 oz). Serves 4.

Add Dijon mustard and use as a coleslaw dressing.

Tahini and Lemon Dip

This makes a smooth and creamy dip suitable for crudités. The tahini and other ingredients form a thick emulsion, so it can be used as a substitute for egg-based mayonnaise. Serve with crisp raw carrot, celery, cauliflower florets and cucumber sticks.

2 tbsps	light tahini	2 tbsps
3 tbsps	water	3 tbsps
2 tbsps	tasteless oil (sunflower or vegetable)	2 tbsps
	juice of 1/2 lemon	
1 tsp	soy sauce	1 tsp
1/2 tsp	runny honey (optional)	1/2 tsp

PER SERVING	
Energy Kcals	380
Protein g	5.8
Fat g	37.7
Polyunsaturated fatty acids g	20.40
Saturated fatty acids g	4.92
Carbohydrate g	4.8
Calcium mg	207

  Mix the tahini with half the water and whisk well until smooth. Continue whisking and gradually drizzle in the oil until the mixture thickens, then stir in the remaining water.
  Season with the lemon juice, soy sauce and honey. Chill in a sealed container until required. Makes about 125 ml (4 fl oz). Serves 4.

Soaking tinned anchovies in milk, helps remove some of the saltiness from them.

Herbed Olive and Anchovy Dip

This is a Mediterranean-style dip that is full of flavour. Delicious served as a dip with crudités or on hot grilled toast.

14	anchovy fillets in oil, drained	14
4 tbsps	oat drink	4 tbsps
3 oz	seeded black olives	75 g
1	slice white bread, crusts removed	1
1	clove garlic, crushed	1
2 tbsps	capers, drained and rinsed	2 tbsps
2 tsps	wine vinegar	2 tsps
1 tbsp	lemon juice	1 tbsp
2 tbsps	olive oil	2 tbsps
2 tbsps	mayonnaise (optional)	2 tbsps
2 tbsps	chopped parsley	2 tbsps
1 tsp	chopped fresh thyme leaves	1 tsp

Combine anchovies and oat drink in bowl, leave to soak for 15 minutes, drain, discarding the oat drink.

Process the anchovies, olives, bread, garlic, capers, vinegar and lemon juice until well combined.

Whilst motor is running drizzle in the olive oil until the mixture becomes smooth.

Finally stir in mayonnaise, if using, and herbs and store in the fridge. Fills 1 large jar. Serves 8.

PER SERVING

Energy Kcals	430
Protein g	1.3
Fat g	46.5
Polyunsaturated fatty acids g	11.72
Saturated fatty acids g	6.90
Carbohydrate g	0.7
Calcium mg	67

For vegetarians try other fillings such as mushroom and aubergines or even spicy aduki or black-eye beans. These could also be deep-fried for a light and crispy texture.

Avocado and Prawn Empanadas

These crisp Mexican-style parcels are perfect to serve as a starter or a light main course with some crisp salad. They are delicious served with either the Tomato and Mint Salsa on page 140 or Roasted Sweetcorn and Lime Salsa on page 138.

	quantity of cornmeal pastry on page 222	
1	beaten egg for glazing	1
1 tbsp	vegetable oil	1 tbsp
1	medium onion, finely chopped	1
2	cloves garlic, crushed	2
1	heaped teaspoon ground cumin	1
2 tbsps	tomato purée	2 tbsps
3	bottled jalapeno peppers, drained, chopped	3
1 tsp	dried oregano	1 tsp
2	good size tomatoes, quartered, seeds removed, chopped	2
12 oz	cooked, peeled tiger prawns (cut into about 3)	350 g
1	large, firm but ripe avocado or 2 smaller ones	1
	salt and freshly ground pepper	
1	egg, beaten	1

Pre-heat the oven to 190C, 375F, gas 5. Grease a large baking tray. Heat the oil in a large saucepan and gently fry the onion and garlic for about 5 minutes until soft.

Stir in the ground cumin and cook for about 2 minutes. Mix in the tomato purée, peppers, oregano and chopped tomatoes.

Remove this mixture from the heat and allow to cool slightly before adding the prawns and the peeled, diced avocado. Season well (the filling should be fairly well seasoned). Divide pastry into 6 portions. Roll each portion into 16 cm (6 in) rounds.

Divide the filling and spoon onto the rounds, brush edges with beaten egg. Fold rounds in half, enclosing filling. Press edges together firmly, trim with knife, and decorate edges with fork. Place the parcels onto the prepared baking tray. Brush the pastry with some beaten egg.

Bake in a hot oven for about 20 minutes until browned and heated through. Serves 6.

PER SERVING	
Energy Kcals	315
Protein g	17.0
Fat g	25.2
Polyunsaturated fatty acids g	1.01
Saturated fatty acids g	1.33
Carbohydrate g	47.1
Calcium mg	113

If using fresh whole crab make sure you discard the small greyish-white stomach sac, just behind the mouth and the long white pointed 'dead man's fingers'. These can be easily distinguished and it is a quick and easy job to remove them.

Crab Rösti Cakes

These crab rösti cakes make an impressive starter or light main course with lemon dressing. The grated half cooked potato holds the cakes together, rather than traditional fish cakes which use mashed potato to bind the fish and are coated in bread crumbs. The result is a much lighter and tastier fish cake.

Try and use fresh crabmeat if possible, otherwise defrosted frozen crabmeat would be a good alternative. Delicious served accompanied with the lemon dressing on page 160.

10 oz	firm waxy potatoes	275 g
10 oz	mixed fresh crabmeat (try and use mainly white crabmeat)	275 g
1 tbsp	fresh dill, chopped	1 tbsp
2	spring onions, finely chopped	2
	zest and juice of one large lemon	
1/2 tsp	cayenne pepper	1/2 tsp
	salt and freshly ground pepper	
	oil for frying	
	sprigs of fresh coriander or parsley to garnish	

First peel the potatoes then steam or boil them in boiling salted water for about 10 minutes. They should be slightly uncooked in the middle. Allow the potatoes to cool.

Shred the potatoes into a large bowl using a cheese grater. In another bowl carefully mix together the crabmeat, dill, spring onion, zest and juice of lemon with the seasonings.

Now carefully combine the grated potato with the crab mixture, mixing well without breaking up the potato too much.

Have a large baking sheet handy, then divide the mixture into eight for starter or four for a light main course. Squeeze each portion into a ball and then slightly flatten each ball into a small round cake. When the cakes are all made, cover with cling film and refrigerate for 1-2 hours to become firmer.

To cook the crab cakes, heat a large frying pan (preferably non-stick) with 1 tablespoon of oil. When the oil is hot but not smoking, pan-fry the crab cakes for about four minutes, then turn the crab cakes carefully with a spatula, repeat on the other side (depending on size) until heated through and golden.

Transfer to a warm serving plate. Garnish with coriander or parsley. Serves 4 or 2 as a light main course.

PER SERVING	
Energy Kcals	147
Protein g	16.1
Fat g	3.9
Polyunsaturated fatty acids g	1.16
Saturated fatty acids g	0.51
Carbohydrate g	12.7
Calcium mg	29

Mussels are at their best in the cold weather, usually from October to March. A sign of freshness is that most of them are tightly closed, if there are too many with open shells don't buy them. Buy extra to account for any that may be discarded. To wash, put in a sink full of cold water. First, throw away any that float on the top, then leave the tap running and scrape off barnacles with a knife, pulling off the hairy beards. Discard any broken mussels, and those that are open and refuse to close tight when given a sharp tap with a knife. Once sorted and cleaned place in a bowl of clean water. Once cooked discard any whose shells haven't opened.

Crispy Garlic and Leek Stuffed Mussels

Mussels go very well cooked with leeks, which, combined with breadcrumbs and garlic make a delicious starter. The dish may be prepared up to a day before, and the final grilling done just before serving. Serve with crusty fresh bread and a squeeze of fresh lemon.

	about 32 good-sized mussels	
½ pt	dry white wine (or stock if preferred)	275 ml
1	small onion, finely chopped	1
1	large leek	1
1 tbsp	olive oil	1 tbsp
4	cloves garlic, peeled and crushed	4
4 oz	crusty white bread	110 g
1 tbsp	chopped fresh French tarragon	1 tbsp
1	bunch of parsley, finely chopped	1
3 oz	vegan margarine	85 g
	more olive oil and wedges of lemon to garnish	

   Begin by washing and scrubbing the mussels. Remove any grit, beards and barnacles. Discard any mussels that are broken or do not shut when given a sharp tap.
   Pour the wine into a large pan with the chopped onion and bring this to the boil. Tip in the prepared mussels, cover with a lid. After about 4 minutes shake pan to ensure the mussels are moved about.
   The mussels are cooked when they have all opened up, this should take about 8 minutes altogether. Remove the pan from the heat and leave to cool. Next, clean and chop the leek finely, discarding any tough outer leaves.
   In a large frying pan, heat the olive oil and gently cook the leek and garlic, stirring occasionally, for about 5 minutes until soft but not brown. Tip into a large bowl and allow to cool slightly. Process the bread into crumbs.
   When leek mixture is slightly cool, add the tarragon, parsley and breadcrumbs mixing thoroughly.
   Stir in the margarine and press the mixture together with a spoon. Season with salt and pepper.
   Open the mussels, leaving one half shell with the mussel inside, discarding the other half shell which will be empty.

PER SERVING	
Energy Kcals	335
Protein g	10.0
Fat g	21.3
Polyunsaturated fatty acids g	5.20
Saturated fatty acids g	5.82
Carbohydrate g	18.0
Calcium mg	124

Using your hands, stuff the mixture into the mussel shell, smoothing down and covering the mussel completely. Lay on a large tray.

Either store stuffed mussels in fridge for use within 2 days or to cook; place under a hot grill for about 5 minutes until golden and crispy.

Drizzle with some more olive oil and serve garnished with lemon wedges. Serves 4 or 2-3 as a light lunch

Fish Fritto Misto

Fritto Misto originates from Italy, where there are many different versions. In some cases a yeast or beer batter is made to coat the fish or shellfish. The version below is much more straight forward and, providing fresh shellfish is used, equally as delicious. Serve hot with mayonnaise mixed with a squeeze of lemon and some salad. Using whole whitebait provides a valuable source of calcium as the entire fish is eaten.

8 oz	peeled king prawns (or ordinary prawns)	225 g
8 oz	small squid (buy ready cleaned from supermarket)	225 g
8 oz	whitebait	225 g
	plenty of plain flour for dusting	
	oil for deep-frying	
	salt and freshly ground pepper	
	lemon wedges and parsley to garnish	

Remove veins from the back of prawns if necessary, cut in half lengthways.

Cut the squid into rings and pat dry using absorbent paper. Wash the whitebait and dry thoroughly. On a large plate, dust all the fish with plenty of flour, shaking off any surplus.

Heat the oil in large saucepan or a deep fat fryer. To determine whether the oil is hot enough for frying, drop a tiny amount of fish into the oil: it should stiffen and instantly come to the surface, this means the oil is ready to cook the fish.

Deep-fry the fish in hot oil, a few pieces at a time until the fish has formed a rich, golden crust on one side; using a slotted spoon turn the fish over to cook the other side.

Remove from the oil, drain on absorbent paper and season with salt and pepper.

Serve hot garnished with wedges of lemon and sprigs of fresh parsley. Serves 6 or 4 as a light meal.

Try and use a fairly good quality vegetable or ground nut oil. The fish is also good if it is fried in a mild flavoured light olive oil.

PER SERVING	
Energy Kcals	329
Protein g	18.5
Fat g	26
Polyunsaturated fatty acids g	2.7
Saturated fatty acids g	0.7
Carbohydrate g	6.5
Calcium mg	399

I have not added extra salt to this recipe as kippers tend to be already quite salty. Try this recipe using crabmeat to make a delicious crab soufflé.

Herb and Kipper Soufflé

Kippers are readily available in most supermarkets or fishmongers and remain an economical fish to buy. This delicious soufflé makes a change to the usual cheese soufflé.

By blitzing the kipper fillets in a blender, most of the smaller bones are broken down and therefore provide a valuable supply of calcium, essential for the lactose-free diet. Serve with a tomato salad or a crisp mixed leaf salad.

1 tsp	vegan margarine, for greasing dish	1 tsp
2	boned kippers, skinned	2
2 oz	vegan margarine	55 g
2 tbsps	plain flour	2 tbsps
5 fl oz	soya milk	150 ml
1 tbsp	chopped fresh chives	1 tbsp
1 tbsp	chopped fresh parsley	1 tbsp
	pinch of mace	
	freshly ground pepper	
4	medium eggs, separated	4

Pre-heat the oven to 200C, 400F, gas 6. You will need a 1 litre soufflé dish, well greased with the margarine (or use 4 small ramekins).

Process the skinned boned kipper until smooth, remove any larger bones which may not have been broken down.

In a small saucepan, gently melt the margarine then stir in the flour. Cook for 1 to 2 minutes then slowly stir in the soya milk until you have a smooth thick glossy paste, keeping the pan over low heat.

Stir in processed kipper, chopped chives, parsley, mace and pepper.

Cool slightly then stir in egg yolks. Next whisk the egg whites in a clean dry bowl until they stand up in peaks when you lift the whisk, be careful not to overdo them or they'll start to flop and go watery.

Stir one tablespoon of the egg white into the kipper mixture, and then carefully fold in remainder. Pour into prepared soufflé dish.

Place in hot oven for 25-30 minutes, until the soufflé has risen and beginning to crack on surface.

Serve immediately before it sinks. Serves 4 or 2-3 as light main or supper dish.

PER SERVING	
Energy Kcals	242
Protein g	14.2
Fat g	24.7
Polyunsaturated fatty acids g	5.06
Saturated fatty acids g	4.89
Carbohydrate g	3.4
Calcium mg	43

You could use small herrings or mackerel if sardines are unavailable. Herrings and mackerel are sometimes slightly cheaper than sardines.

Herb Crumbed Fresh Sardine Fillets

Serve as a starter or light supper. This is a delicious way of jazzing up sardines which are still a fairly inexpensive fish. Don't be alarmed at the prospect of filleting the sardines, just make sure you have a good sharp knife. There will be a few tiny pin bones, which provide a good source of calcium to the diet. Serve with spoonful of warmed roasted tomato sauce on page 139.

8	medium-sized fresh sardines	8
	plain flour	
	salt and freshly ground pepper	
1	egg, beaten	1
2 tbsps	oat drink	2 tbsps
4 oz	stale breadcrumbs	110 g
1 tbsp	finely chopped parsley	1 tbsp
1 tbsp	finely chopped oregano	1 tbsp
	groundnut oil for shallow frying	
	lemon wedges to garnish	

Rinse sardines and using knife scrape off any loose scales. Fillet sardines by using a sharp knife and holding tail, cut down against backbone until you reach the head, cut off at head. Repeat on the other side and tidy the fillets up pulling out larger pin bones.

Alternatively ask the fishmonger to prepare fish for you. To coat the sardine fillets you will need 3 large plates. On the first plate season the flour with salt and freshly ground pepper. On the second plate mix the beaten egg with the oat drink. And on the third, combine the breadcrumbs with the fresh herbs.

Dip each sardine fillet firstly in the seasoned flour then the beaten egg and finally roll them in the breadcrumbs.

Place these on a tray sprinkled with a few of the breadcrumbs to stop them sticking together.

In a large frying pan pour in about 2 tablespoons of groundnut oil. When hot fry several fillets at a time for about 3 minutes each side, until golden brown. Turn over and repeat on the other side. Keep these warm whilst you cook the remaining fillets. You may need to wipe out the pan with kitchen roll to remove any burnt crumbs before adding another 2 tablespoons of groundnut oil. Serve on a warm serving platter garnished with lemon wedges. Serves 4.

PER SERVING	
Energy Kcals	428
Protein g	34.3
Fat g	23.2
Polyunsaturated fatty acids g	8.84
Saturated fatty acids g	4.92
Carbohydrate g	25.3
Calcium mg	168

Change the filling if you are cooking for a vegan. Omit the anchovies and the tuna and use marinated artichoke hearts, peppers or mushrooms.

Niçoise Tartlets

These tartlets have a wonderful Mediterranean theme. I tend to keep most of the ingredients in my store cupboard and often have puff pastry in the freezer. Thus making it a great and impressive dish for an unexpected visitor. For a lunchtime dish you could make one large tart and serve it with a crisp salad. Easy to prepare in advance and keep in the fridge until ready to cook.

1 tbsp	olive oil	1 tbsp
1	small red onion, finely sliced	1
2	cloves garlic, crushed	2
1	370 g pack frozen puff pastry (or see quick flaky pastry recipe, p 223)	1
6 tsps	sun-dried tomato paste	6 tsps
1	200 g tin tuna steak, drained	1
12	cherry tomatoes, cut into quarters	12
18	capers, drained	18
12	marinated anchovy fillets, drained	12
12	black olives	12
	fresh basil leaves to garnish	

Pre-heat the oven to 220C, 425F, gas 6. Heat the olive oil in a small pan and sweat the onion and garlic for about 5 minutes, until soft.

Roll pastry until 2 mm thick and large enough to allow for six 15 x 15 cm (6 x 6 in) squares. Cut 2 cm (³/₄ inch) strips off side of each square.

Cut these strips to the same length as squares, wet one side of each strip and stick this along edge of squares, overlapping at corners. Lay the pastry cases on a baking sheet. Prick the inside of each case with a fork.

Spread the sun-dried tomato paste over the inside of the uncooked pastry cases taking care not to put anything over the side strips.

Spoon one sixth of the tin of tuna, cover with 8 quarters of tomatoes, 3 capers, and some red onion mix.

Top with a cross of anchovy fillet and 2 olives. Repeat for the other five pastry cases.

Bake for about 10-15 minutes, until risen and golden. Serve hot or warm, garnished with basil leaves. Serves 6.

PER SERVING	
Energy Kcals	315
Protein g	8.1
Fat g	20.7
Polyunsaturated fatty acids g	0.39
Saturated fatty acids g	0.48
Carbohydrate g	26.0
Calcium mg	97

The filling could be made with other fish such as fresh cooked salmon, cooked smoked haddock, smoked mackerel, smoked salmon etc.

Smoked Salmon Roulade with Smoked Trout Mousse

This recipe uses mayonnaise and smoked fish to give a deliciously creamy mousse rolled up in smoked salmon. The end result is extremely impressive and suitable for any occasion, whether it be a summer lunch with salad and French bread or an extremely eye catching starter. The roulade can be made well in advance and will last for several days in the fridge .

6 oz	smoked salmon, in thin slices	175 g
2	leaves gelatine (or equivalent alternative)	2
4 fl oz	oat drink	125 ml
4 fl oz	mayonnaise	125 ml
6 oz	hot-smoked trout, weight when skinned and boned	175 g
3 tbsps	lemon juice	3 tbsps
	freshly ground mace	
	sprig fresh dill	
	freshly ground pepper	
	lemon wedges and watercress to garnish	

You will need a rectangular tray about 12½ cm x 22½ cm (5 in x 9 in) covered with cling film, overlapping the edges. Lay out thin layers of the smoked salmon evenly over the cling film.

Next soak the gelatine leaves in a bowl of cold water until they soften (about 5 minutes). Place the oat drink, mayonnaise and smoked trout in the liquidizer, whiz quickly until almost smooth.

Heat the lemon juice in a small pan and when hot, remove the pan from the heat and add the gelatine leaves, stirring well until melted. Pour the melted gelatine into the liquidizer with the smoked trout mixture. Whiz again fairly briefly until thoroughly dispersed.

Mix in ground mace, dill and pepper (you should not need salt because of saltiness of smoked fish). Spread evenly over smoked salmon, chill until set. When the mousse is set, using the cling film, lift the salmon on the long edge of the tray and roll it over and over like a Swiss roll, pulling away the cling film as it rolls. Secure firmly in place by wrapping the roll up in cling film (it should resemble a fat sausage) and chill. To serve unwrap roulade and slice with a sharp knife.

Garnish with lemon wedges and watercress. Serve with hot bread or toast. Serves 4-6.

PER SERVING	
Energy Kcals	302
Protein g	13.4
Fat g	29.6
Polyunsaturated fatty acids g	3.55
Saturated fatty acids g	4.06
Carbohydrate g	0.5
Calcium mg	21

This dish could also be made with prawns (freshly shelled prawns even better).

The smaller the squid the more tender it should be. Take care not to overcook squid as it becomes tough and rubbery.

Squid with Chillies and Tomatoes

There was a time when squid was generally only available in an unprepared way, this meant lots of inky mess and strange things to be pulled out of the squid. Not a job for the squeamish cook ! Nowadays, it is usually available ready prepared from most fishmongers and supermarkets. Squid is quite economical and the combination of tomatoes and chilli makes for an exceptional dish. Serve this with hot Italian bread.

2 tbsps	olive oil (or use the oil from the drained sun-dried tomatoes)	2 tbsps
2	spring onions, finely chopped	2
1	large red chilli, de-seeded and finely chopped	1
2	tomatoes, finely chopped	2
1 tbsp	tomato purée	1 tbsp
8	marinaded sun-dried tomatoes, finely chopped	8
1 tbsp	chopped parsley	1 tbsp
1 tbsp	fresh oregano chopped (could use 1 teaspoon dried)	1 tbsp
1 lb	fresh prepared squid, cut into rings	450 g
	salt and freshly ground pepper	

Heat 1 tablespoon of the oil in a large wok or frying pan until medium hot. Add the spring onions, chillies, tomatoes, tomato purée and sun-dried tomatoes and stir quickly for 4 minutes.

Stir the parsley and oregano into the sauce and pour out into a separate dish.

Wash out the wok or pan and add remaining oil, when very hot add the squid. Toss the squid in the pan quickly for 30 seconds.

Pour in the tomato sauce and mix well with the squid. Season with salt and freshly ground pepper.

Serve whilst hot. Serves 4 or 2/3 as a light meal with pasta.

PER SERVING	
Energy Kcals	181
Protein g	18.1
Fat g	10.3
Polyunsaturated fatty acids g	2.89
Saturated fatty acids g	1.63
Carbohydrate g	4.5
Calcium mg	34

Chinese-Style Crispy Pork Strips

Pork belly should be available from most butchers. It is a very economical cut of pork and these are very easy and very tasty, and may also appeal to children. Try barbecuing instead of grilling for a fabulous barbecue dish.

For the Pork Strips

1¹/₂ lb	sheet belly pork	675 g
2 tsps	Chinese five spice	2 tsps
1	red chilli, deseeded and chopped	1
2	cloves garlic, peeled and crushed	2
1 inch	piece ginger, finely chopped	2¹/₂ cm
	pinch salt	
¹/₂ pt	water	275 ml

For the sauce

2 tbsps	soy sauce	2 tbsps
1 tbsp	dry sherry	1 tbsp
1 tbsp	dark brown sugar	1 tbsp
1	level teaspoon cornflour	1

Pre-heat the oven to 180C, 350F, gas 4. Trim the skin off the pork. Then using a sharp knife cut the meat into about 8 strips.

Lay the pork strips in a large baking dish and cover with the Chinese five spice, chilli, crushed garlic and chopped ginger and salt.

Pour the water into the dish, cover with tin foil and bake for about 1 hour.

Pour off the remaining juice into a small saucepan, skim off any excess pork fat which may be floating at the top, and discard. Lay the pork strips on a suitable tray for grilling.

To this pork juice stir in the soy sauce, sherry and dark brown sugar. Bring to boil and cook for about 1 minute.

Mix cornflour with 1 tbsp water until smooth, add to the sauce, stirring well.

Bring the sauce to boil and stir until the sauce begins to thicken (if it is too thick add dash of water).

Heat the grill. Spoon over a little of the sauce over the pork strips.

When the grill is hot, grill for about 3 minutes either side until they become crisp.

Heat the sauce and serve with pork strips. Serves 4 or 2-3 as main course with noodles or rice.

PER SERVING	
Energy Kcals	458
Protein g	32.7
Fat g	34.1
Polyunsaturated fatty acids g	5.25
Saturated fatty acids g	12.33
Carbohydrate g	4.9
Calcium mg	14

The longer you marinade the kebabs the more flavour the chicken will have.

If you are using wooden skewers soak them in water first to stop them charring.

Marinated Lime and Sesame Chicken Sticks

These chicken sticks are quick and easy to prepare and have a delicate Thai flavour. Served simply with a wedge of lime they provide a nutritious low-fat starter, however, if you want more of a special dish serve with my hot Peanut and Coconut Chilli Sauce.

2	chicken breasts	2
2	limes	2
1 tsp	sweet paprika	1 tsp
1 tbsp	sesame oil	1 tbsp
2	cloves garlic, crushed	2
4	wooden skewers	4
1	red pepper, de-seeded and cut into cubes	1
1 tbsp	sesame seeds	1 tbsp
	rocket leaves or salad to garnish	

Remove the skin of the chicken breasts and cut each breast into about 10 cubes.

In a bowl mix the cubed chicken with the zest and juice of one lime, paprika, sesame oil and garlic. Leave for several hours to marinade. Pre-heat grill.

Spike the cubed chicken onto the skewers alternating with the red pepper.

Lay the chicken sticks under the hot grill for about 15 minutes, turning from time to time to ensure even cooking. Half way through the cooking drizzle over any of the sesame and lime marinade.

Sprinkle the chicken sticks all over with the sesame seeds. Serve each chicken stick on a small warm plate and drizzle over any cooking juices.

Garnish with some rocket leaves and a wedge of lime. Serves 4 or 2 as a light main served with rice.

PER SERVING	
Energy Kcals	147
Protein g	18.2
Fat g	6.7
Polyunsaturated fatty acids g	2.32
Saturated fatty acids g	1.40
Carbohydrate g	3.8
Calcium mg	33

This salad may also be made with smoked chicken breast.

Smoked Duck Salad with Spiced Walnuts

This starter is a real treat and easy to prepare in advance, without spooning over the dressing. The smoked duck tastes wonderful with the sweet and sour flavour of the onion marmalade and the spiciness of the walnuts.

Smoked duck is quite a luxury ingredient and fairly expensive, but cut thinly it goes quite a long way. They have started selling it at our local farm shop, but you should find it in your local delicatessen or buy it mail order from a smokery.

1	crisp cos lettuce or 2 little gem lettuces	1
4 oz	Spiced Walnuts (see page 146)	110 g
1	smoked duck breast, skin and fat removed	1
1/4 pt	Tarragon French Dressing (see page 159)	150 ml
4 tbsps	Onion Marmalade (see page 144)	4 tbsps

Wash and dry the lettuce, break it into pieces. Pile the lettuce into the centre of four individual plates. Sprinkle the spiced walnuts over the lettuce.

Next slice the smoked duck into thin strips. Lay thin slices of the smoked duck over the top of the salad.

Drizzle a couple of spoonfuls of dressing over each plate.

Finally dollop a tablespoon of the onion marmalade onto the sliced duck.

Serve with crisp warm French bread. Serves 4 or 2 as light main course.

PER SERVING	
Energy Kcals	541
Protein g	7.0
Fat g	53.4
Polyunsaturated fatty acids g	32.3
Saturated fatty acids g	6.0
Carbohydrate g	7.47
Calcium mg	38.8

Vary the nuts according to what you have in your store cupboard. For a much creamier texture increase the quantity of peanut butter. Also almond butter is a nice substitute for peanut butter.

Mushroom and Nut Pâté

This tasty vegetarian pâté is made with a mixture of lentils and nuts. The addition of peanut butter enables the pâté to become rich and creamy in texture. It will keep well up to about 8 days in the fridge and makes a quick and nutritious snack. Try spreading it on hot toast or with grated carrot in a crispy bread sandwich.

4 oz	uncooked red lentils	110 g
1½ pts	water for cooking lentils	860 ml
1 tbsp	olive oil	1 tbsp
1	large or 2 medium onions, finely chopped	1
2	cloves garlic, crushed	2
7 oz	button mushrooms, wiped and very finely chopped	200 g
1 tsp	vegan bouillon powder	1 tsp
1 tsp	ground cumin	1 tsp
½ tsp	ground turmeric	½ tsp
1 tsp	ground coriander	1 tsp
½ tsp	chilli powder	½ tsp
1 tsp	Dijon mustard	1 tsp
3 tbsps	crunchy peanut butter	3 tbsps
	juice of ½ lemon	
5 oz	ground roasted hazelnuts or peanuts	140 g
1 tbsp	chopped fresh coriander, save a few leaves for garnish	1 tbsp
	salt and freshly ground pepper	

Rinse the lentils in a sieve under the cold tap. Put the lentils in a large saucepan with the water and bring to the boil. Skim off any scum that forms.

Boil gently for about 10-15 minutes until soft, but not completely mushy. Strain through a sieve and leave to dry.

Next heat a large frying pan with the oil, add the onion and garlic and cook for about 5 minutes until beginning to soften.

Mix in the mushrooms and stir well and cook for several minutes. Add bouillon powder and spices and fry for about 4 minutes until mixture dries out. Transfer to a large bowl. Add the cooked lentils, mustard, peanut butter, lemon juice, roasted nuts, coriander and seasonings. Refrigerate for at least 1 hour. Serve, smoothed into individual ramekins each garnished with a coriander leaf. Serves 10.

PER SERVING	
Energy Kcals	158
Protein g	7.8
Fat g	10.0
Polyunsaturated fatty acids g	2.90
Saturated fatty acids g	1.72
Carbohydrate g	10.2
Calcium mg	23

Omit anchovies for a vegan alternative. Try using different toppings, such as griddled aubergine, peppers or asparagus or marinated artichoke hearts. For the meat eater, thin slices of ham or bacon would be delicious with the tomatoes.

Important note – try and use fresh young garlic as some older garlic becomes bitter and unpleasant in taste.

Roasted Cherry Tomato Bruschetta

Brushetta are little Italian toasts, an excellent way of using up any left over stale French bread or Italian Ciabatta.

The combination of flavours and the olive oil on crisp bread toasts make a delicious Mediterranean-style dish also suitable for a light summer lunch, especially when you have a glut of small tomatoes.

Do not be alarmed by the amount of garlic used, as the cooking process takes away the strong taste associated with raw garlic. Boiling the garlic beforehand allows for easy peeling and begins to cook it slightly.

8	cloves garlic, unpeeled	8
1	medium red onion, cut in half and then sliced	1
4 tbsps	olive oil	4 tbsps
2 tbsps	salted capers, rinsed	2 tbsps
1	50 g can anchovies, drained	1
24	cherry tomatoes	24
	freshly ground pepper	
1 tbsp	balsamic vinegar	1 tbsp
1	ciabatta loaf	1
2 tbsps	vegan pesto (found in health food shops alternatively you can use sun-dried tomato paste)	2 tbsps
	garnish with fresh basil leaves	

Pre-heat the oven to 220C, 400F, gas 6. Put garlic cloves in small pan of cold water, bring to boil and cook for 2-3 minutes, drain and peel.

In a large oven dish, roast the red onion and garlic cloves mixed with 2 tablespoons of the olive oil in the oven for about 10 minutes. Remove from the oven and stir in the capers, halved anchovy fillets, cherry tomatoes and freshly ground pepper. Return to the oven and roast for a further 15 minutes. Stir in the balsamic vinegar.

Meanwhile, slice the Ciabatta into about 12 slices and place them on a baking tray. Drizzle with the remaining olive oil and some more pepper. Bake for about 5 minutes, turn the Ciabatta slices over and repeat for several minutes until golden and crisp.

Spread pesto onto the crisp bruchettas and spoon over the hot tomato mix and any remaining roasting juices and garnish with fresh basil leaves. Serves 4.

PER SERVING	
Energy Kcals	102
Protein g	1.5
Fat g	8.0
Polyunsaturated fatty acids g	0.82
Saturated fatty acids g	1.15
Carbohydrate g	6.5
Calcium mg	21

If it is easier use about 175 g (6 oz) frozen, defrosted spinach. Squeeze out excess water and add to onions whilst still frying. Also delicious with chopped sun-dried tomatoes added to the filling or if you are unable to buy pine nuts, which are quite expensive, you could use flaked almonds for an interesting texture and flavour.

Crispy Spinach and Pine Nut Filo Parcels

These are a great way of starting a meal. You could serve them with sun-dried tomato, basil and garlic dressing on page 163, otherwise serve as light meal with tomato and pepper coulis on page 141.

If made slightly smaller by cutting the sheets into 3 they are a great idea for canapes. The addition of mustard gives them more of a savoury flavour.

10 oz	fresh spinach leaves	285 g
1	medium onion, finely chopped	1
2	cloves garlic, crushed	2
1 tbsp	olive oil	1 tbsp
6 oz	Tofutti Original (soya cream cheese)	170 g
1 tbsp	Dijon mustard	1 tbsp
2 oz	pine nuts	50 g
	good pinch of grated nutmeg	
	salt and freshly ground pepper	
4	sheets of filo pastry, thawed if frozen	4
1½ oz	vegan margarine, melted	45 g

Pre-heat the oven to 200C, 400F, gas 6. Wash and trim stalks from the spinach. Put the spinach leaves into a large saucepan, covered, over a medium heat and cook for approximately 5 minutes.

Drain, rinse under cold water and press down in a sieve to drain off any excess water. Chop the spinach once it is drained of excess water.

In a frying pan gently cook the onion and garlic in the olive oil for about 8 minutes or until soft and beginning to caramelise. Mix the softened onions with chopped spinach, Tofutti Original, mustard, pine nuts and seasonings.

Take the filo pastry out of wrapping and keep under a damp tea cloth until required.

Taking one sheet at a time, cut in half lengthways and brush with melted margarine.

Spoon an eighth of the filling at one end of the pastry strip.

Fold diagonally and again until you reach the end, having made a triangular parcel.

Place on an oiled baking sheet. Bake for about 15-20 minutes until crisp and golden brown. Serve hot. Serves 4.

PER SERVING	
Energy Kcals	427
Protein g	12.2
Fat g	23.5
Polyunsaturated fatty acids g	2.3
Saturated fatty acids g	3.2
Carbohydrate g	47.0
Calcium mg	169

You could use warm pitta bread instead of tortillas.

Hummus, Chilli and Crisp Vegetable Wrap

This is an ideal vegan snack that can be taken to work, eaten cold or warmed up slightly in the oven or microwave.

4	flour tortillas, about 20 cm (8 inch) diameter	4
4 tbsps	hummus (shop bought or home made)	4 tbsps
4 tsps	sweet chilli sauce (or hot chilli sauce for a less sweet taste)	4 tsps
4 oz	finely shredded red or green cabbage	110 g
2	medium carrots, peeled and grated	2
	freshly ground pepper	

Warm the tortillas according to manufacturers instructions. Spread 1 tablespoon hummus, followed by 1 teaspoon of chilli sauce on each tortilla.

Sprinkle over cabbage, carrot and pepper.

Roll up each tortilla into a sausage and serve. Serves 2.

VEGAN

PER SERVING	
Energy Kcals	254
Protein g	7.3
Fat g	1.3
Polyunsaturated fatty acids g	0.27
Saturated fatty acids g	0.11
Carbohydrate g	56.7
Calcium mg	133

Bacon, Tomato and Watercress Wrap

This wrap has a hot filling and is best assembled just before serving. The roasted tomatoes prevent the filling from becoming dry and make a mouth-watering combination with the bacon and watercress.

6	rashers smoked or unsmoked streaky bacon, rind removed	6
4	medium tomatoes, quartered	4
2	spring onions, chopped	2
	drizzle of olive oil	
2 tsps	balsamic vinegar	2 tsps
4	flour tortillas, about 20 cm (8 inch) diameter	4
1 tbsp	sun-dried tomato paste	1 tbsp
1	small bunch of watercress	1
	freshly ground pepper	

Pre-heat the oven to 200C, 400F, gas 6. In a large baking dish, lay the bacon at one end. At other end lay the quartered tomatoes, sprinkled with spring onions.

Drizzle over a little olive oil and the balsamic vinegar. Grind on some black pepper.

Roast in the oven for 10 minutes, until the tomatoes are soft and the bacon is cooked.

Warm tortillas slightly according to instructions. Spread a little sun-dried tomato paste over each tortilla.

Spoon tomato and onion mixture onto each tortilla and spread around.

Lay the roughly chopped bacon and watercress over the tomatoes.

Roll up each tortilla and serve immediately. Serves 2.

PER SERVING	
Energy Kcals	420
Protein g	23.8
Fat g	17.1
Polyunsaturated fatty acids g	2.5
Saturated fatty acids g	5.1
Carbohydrate g	57.0
Calcium mg	178

Light Meals and Lunches

Caribbean-Style Spare Ribs

Moroccan Lamb Burgers

Smoked Ham and Lentil Pie

Baked Eggs in Pancetta and Mushroom Tartlets

*Risotto of Artichoke Hearts and
Mushrooms Topped with Parma Ham*

Caramelised Onion, Bacon and Red Lentil Flan

Spaghetti Carbonara-style

*Sautéed Chicken Livers in a Creamy Wine and
Sage Sauce on Garlic Bread Croûtons*

Spicy Chicken Quesadillas

Griddled Fresh Tuna on Potato Niçoise

Smoked Salmon and Spinach Quiche

Potato Pancakes

Aubergine and Red Lentil Loaf

Baked Stuffed Field Mushrooms

Chick Peas with Tomatoes and Coriander

Curried Spinach and Eggs

Potato, Bean and Corn Frittata

Sweet Potato and Chick Pea Cakes

Caribbean-Style Spare Ribs

Pork ribs are an affordable cut of meat. These deliciously messy ribs make an ideal meal for summer barbecues and should be popular with all the family.

1	onion, peeled and roughly chopped	1
2	small or 1 large red chilli, de-seeded and quartered	2
3	garlic cloves	3
1 tsp	ground allspice	1 tsp
1/2 tsp	ground cinnamon	1/2 tsp
1 inch	piece of fresh root ginger, peeled and roughly chopped	2.5 cm
	handful fresh thyme sprigs, leaves removed or 1 teaspoon dried	
1/4 tsp	ground black pepper	1/4 tsp
	juice and grated zest of 1 lime	
5 tbsps	cider or white wine vinegar	5 tbsps
3 1/2 fl oz	dark soy sauce	100 ml
2 tbsps	dark muscovado sugar	2 tbsps
3 tbsps	groundnut or sunflower oil	3 tbsps
4 lb	pork ribs	1.8 kg

Place the onion, chillies, garlic, allspice, cinnamon, ginger, thyme and black pepper in food processor and whiz for about 30 seconds until well blended.

Add the lime juice and zest, vinegar, soy sauce, sugar and oil and whiz again until it becomes a purée consistency.

Lay the pork ribs in a large ceramic (non metallic) baking dish. Pour the marinade over the ribs.

Marinade in the fridge for 4-24 hours, basting occasionally.

Cook, on a barbecue, basting occasionally with marinade, cook the remaining sauce in a pan and serve with the ribs.

Alternatively grill under a low to medium preheated grill for about 25-30 minutes turning occasionally and brushing with marinade, until tender inside but beginning to char on the edges. Serves 6.

PER SERVING	
Energy Kcals	366
Protein g	28.3
Fat g	24.3
Polyunsaturated fatty acids g	4.87
Saturated fatty acids g	8.04
Carbohydrate g	8.2
Calcium mg	37

Add fresh chilli for a hot and fiery touch. I try and use unsulphured apricots for this recipe, they are darker than the bright orange sulphured variety, and perfect for this dish.

Moroccan dishes sometimes use prunes, why not try them instead of the apricots for a different taste?

Moroccan Lamb Burgers

Moroccan dishes are becoming increasingly popular. The balance of fruit and spices make these burgers an interesting addition to a barbecue or a light lunch.

The stickiness of the chopped apricots holds the burger together surprisingly well and they also add a sweetness which may appeal to children. Serve with Harissa Dressing (see page 161) and Spiced Rice (see page 129).

1	small onion, peeled and quartered	1
1 inch	piece fresh root ginger, peeled and chopped	2.5 cm
2	cloves garlic	2
1	small bunch coriander, washed	1
1 tsp	ground cinnamon	1 tsp
1½ tsps	ground coriander	1½ tsps
1½ tsps	ground cumin	1½ tsps
2 oz	dried apricots, finely chopped	55 g
1 lb	lean minced lamb	450 g
	salt and freshly ground pepper	

Place the onion, ginger, garlic and coriander in a food processor, finely chop.

Add the spices, apricots, lamb and salt and pepper, pulse briefly keeping the mixture chunky.

Shape into four burgers, refrigerate until required.

Heat a large non-stick frying pan. Fry the burgers for about 5 minutes on either side, using a fish slice, press down occasionally to cook through.

Alternatively cook on a barbecue or under a hot grill on an oiled baking sheet.

They should be dark golden brown and just cooked through. Serves 6.

PER SERVING	
Energy Kcals	265
Protein g	22.9
Fat g	15.2
Polyunsaturated fatty acids g	0.73
Saturated fatty acids g	6.99
Carbohydrate g	9.8
Calcium mg	42

For a vegan dish, substitute ham with chopped mushrooms and leeks, fried with the onion.

Smoked Ham and Lentil Pie

This is a cheap and hearty pie. The nutty lentils mixed with the ham, are particularly tasty with the wholegrain mustard mashed potato topping. Try serving this with lightly steamed green vegetables or a crisp salad.

4 oz	brown or puy lentils	110 g
1 tbsp	olive or sunflower oil	1 tbsp
1	medium onion, finely chopped	1
2	cloves garlic, crushed	2
12 oz	ham hock, weight of meat off the bone and cut into small dice (smoked or un-smoked)	350 g
1	400 g tin chopped tomatoes	1
1 tbsp	tomato purée	1 tbsp
	sprig of fresh thyme	
	freshly ground pepper	
	quantity of wholegrain mashed potato for four people, (see page 123)	

Pre-heat the oven to 200C, 400F, gas 6. Rinse the lentils. Cover with plenty of cold water in a large saucepan, bring to the boil, cover and simmer gently for about 20-25 minutes until the lentils are soft. Drain well.

In a large saucepan heat the oil and cook the onions and garlic for about 5 minutes until soft.

Stir in the diced ham and cook for a further 5 minutes.

Tip in the chopped tomatoes and purée, mix well. Cover the pan and simmer for about 15 minutes. Season with thyme and ground pepper.

You will probably not need salt as the ham will make the dish salty enough.

Pour into large baking dish. Cover with wholegrain mashed potato and smooth down with a fork.

Put into the hot oven and cook for about 25 minutes until golden, if necessary grill the top to make a crisp golden topping before serving. Serves 4.

PER SERVING	
Energy Kcals	230
Protein g	25.4
Fat g	6.7
Polyunsaturated fatty acids g	1.16
Saturated fatty acids g	1.60
Carbohydrate g	18.1
Calcium mg	39

Avoid giving the elderly or pregnant women undercooked eggs.

For a vegetarian alternative, substitute the pancetta with freshly steamed, drained and chopped spinach well seasoned with freshly ground nutmeg.

Baked Eggs in Pancetta and Mushroom Tartlets

These make a wonderful light meal. The tartlets can be prepared in advance and up to the stage before the egg is added. The baked egg in the middle gives the tartlet a lovely richness especially if the yolk remains slightly runny. Serve with a dressed salad.

12 oz	shortcrust pastry (see recipe on page 223 or use a suitable bought pastry)	350 g
1	large onion, finely chopped	1
2	cloves garlic, crushed	2
1 tbsp	vegetable oil	1 tbsp
6 oz	closed cap mushrooms, finely chopped	175 g
4 oz	pancetta (or smoked back bacon), chopped	110 g
1 tbsp	chopped parsley (or French tarragon if available)	1 tbsp
	salt and freshly ground pepper	
6	free-range eggs	6

You will also need 6 quiche tins with 10 cm (4 inch) base diameter, 1 cm ($1/2$ inch) deep and a 14 cm ($51/2$ inch) plain cutter

Pre-heat the oven to 180C, 350F, gas 4. Roll out the pastry on a floured surface to a thickness of about 3 mm ($1/8$ inch), and large enough to cut out six 14 cm ($51/2$ inch) rounds.

Grease the tins and line each with the pastry, prick the base with a fork. Allow pastry cases to relax in the fridge for about 30 minutes.

Then place the tins on a solid baking sheet in the hot oven for about 10-15 minutes until golden. Remove from oven. Sauté the chopped onion and garlic in the oil for about 5 minutes until soft.

Add the mushrooms, cook for several minutes, if the mixture becomes wet, increase temperature and cook out the liquid, remove from heat and add pancetta, parsley, and seasonings.

Spoon this mushroom mixture in the tartlet cases making a well in the centre. Then break an egg into a small cup, tip this into centre of tartlet. Repeat with remaining tartlets.

Return to oven for 12-15 minutes or until just set and yolks are still soft and creamy. Remove from the tins and serve straight away as the eggs will continue cooking. Serves 6.

PER SERVING	
Energy Kcals	329
Protein g	7.4
Fat g	26.3
Polyunsaturated fatty acids g	4.23
Saturated fatty acids g	7.06
Carbohydrate g	30.2
Calcium mg	62

Omit ham for vegans and use a good vegetable stock. Alternatively try using smoked salmon instead of ham.

If you have fresh artichokes you may wish to cook these and remove the heart, this is quite a time consuming job, but well worth it.

Risotto of Artichoke Hearts and Mushrooms Topped with Parma Ham

Many people are now realising that risottos are actually quite simple to make and can be tackled at home. The combination of artichokes, mushrooms and Parma ham make this creamy risotto extremely appetizing and moreish. Serve with a crisp salad.

2 tbsps	olive oil	2 tbsps
8 oz	button mushrooms, wiped and sliced	225 g
8	marinated artichoke hearts, drained and quartered	8
1	red onion, finely chopped	1
2	cloves garlic, crushed	2
7 oz	Arborio rice	200 g
5 tbsps	dry white wine	5 tbsps
22½ fl oz	chicken stock, heated	650 ml
1 tbsp	soya cream	1 tbsp
	salt and freshly ground pepper	
4 oz	thinly sliced Parma ham, cut in thin strips	110 g
	whole chives cut in half to garnish	

Heat frying pan with 1 tablespoon olive oil and fry the sliced mushrooms, after about 4 minutes add the artichoke hearts, cook briefly then tip into a bowl and set aside.

Meanwhile heat remaining oil in a large saucepan, sauté the red onion and garlic for about 5 minutes until soft.

Add the rice and stir off the heat until rice is coated. Return the pan to the heat, add all the wine and then 2 ladlefuls of stock, simmer, stirring constantly until the rice has absorbed nearly all the liquid, add more stock and repeat.

After about 20-25 minutes, nearly all the stock will have been absorbed by the rice, each grain with have a creamy coating but remain al dente.

Add the artichokes and mushrooms to the rice, and heat through. Just before serving add the soya cream and seasonings.

Spoon onto 4 warm plates garnished with strips of Parma ham and chives. Serves 4.

PER SERVING	
Energy Kcals	378.3
Protein g	19.2
Fat g	11.3
Polyunsaturated fatty acids g	1.64
Saturated fatty acids g	2.36
Carbohydrate g	47.4
Calcium mg	109.5

Omit bacon for a vegetarian version. The wholemeal pastry in this recipe does not require much pre-cooking.

If using white shortcrust pastry, you will need to 'bake it blind' see recipe for spinach and smoked salmon quiche page 61.

Caramelised Onion, Bacon and Red Lentil Flan

This is not your typical creamy quiche filling, however the red lentils break down enough to give it a smooth, wholesome texture, which is very nutritious, and the mustard gives added flavour. Serve warm or cold with a crisp salad.

8 oz	wholemeal pastry (see page 224)	225 g
3 oz	dried red lentils	75 g
2	medium to large onions, peeled and sliced in half rings	2
1 tbsp	olive oil	1 tbsp
4 oz	unsmoked or smoked back, rind removed, diced	110 g
1 tsp	vegan bouillon powder	1 tsp
7 fl oz	soya milk	200 ml
1 tbsp	Dijon mustard	1 tbsp
	2 eggs plus 1 egg yolk, beaten together	
	salt and freshly ground pepper	
1 tbsp	chopped parsley	1 tbsp
1	sprig of fresh thyme	1

Pre-heat the oven to 180C, 350F, gas 4. Lightly grease a 22½ cm (9 inch) flan or quiche dish (a deeper dish is preferable as this has quite a substantial amount of filling).

Roll out the pastry and line the tin, easing any overlapping pastry back into the sides, prick the base with a fork, bake in the oven for 5 minutes to set the pastry.

Meanwhile, rinse the lentils and place in a small pan covered with plenty of water. Bring to the boil then simmer for about 8-10 minutes until almost cooked but not mushy, drain well.

In a large frying pan, sauté the onions with the olive oil over medium heat for about 10 minutes, stirring well, remove from heat when soft and beginning to caramelise.

Add the bacon to the onions and cook over a medium heat for a further 4 minutes until just cooked. Stir in the lentils. Set aside. In a large bowl blend the bouillon powder with 2 tablespoons of boiling water, add the soya milk, mustard, eggs and season with salt and freshly ground pepper. Mix well then finally stir in the chopped parsley and thyme leaves.

Spoon the onion and lentil mixture into the half cooked pastry case. Carefully pour the egg mixture into the pastry case, so that all the filling is well covered.

Return to oven and cook for about 35 minutes until risen, firm and golden. Serves 6.

PER SERVING	
Energy Kcals	317
Protein g	10.7
Fat g	19.6
Polyunsaturated fatty acids g	3.19
Saturated fatty acids g	5.62
Carbohydrate g	30.5
Calcium mg	63

For vegetarian dish omit bacon; you could add walnuts for a more nutritious meal.

For a vegan dish omit bacon and egg.

Warning for pregnant or elderly people: omit the egg yolks.

Spaghetti Carbonara-style

The idea of adding hummus to hot spaghetti may seem a bit strange. The result is however surprisingly delicious and creamy, with a slightly grainy texture not too dissimilar to Parmesan. Serve a rocket or lettuce salad with this pasta dish.

1 tbsp	olive oil	1 tbsp
1	medium onion, peeled and finely chopped	1
2	cloves garlic, crushed	2
4 oz	smoked streaky bacon, rind removed, diced	110 g
4 oz	button mushrooms, wiped and sliced	110 g
12 oz	dried spaghetti or tagliatelle	340 g
4 oz	hummus (the bought variety is excellent for this dish)	110 g
1 tbsp	mild Dijon mustard	1 tbsp
2	egg yolks	2
2 tbsps	finely chopped parsley	2 tbsps
	salt and freshly ground pepper	

Heat the oil in a saucepan, add onions and garlic and fry gently for 5 minutes, stirring continuously.

Next add the diced bacon and, stirring well cook for 2 minutes, then add the mushrooms and cook for a further 4 minutes on a slightly higher heat.

Set aside whilst you cook pasta. Don't worry if the mushrooms become slightly wet, the pasta will absorb any liquid.

Cook the pasta in boiling salted water for 8-10 minutes or until al dente (tender but still firm to the bite). Drain well.

Immediately toss the pasta with the mushroom and bacon mixture, return to low heat, add hummus, mustard, egg yolks, half the parsley and season well. Stir the pasta well over a low heat, for several minutes to cook the yolks, although not too hot or you will curdle the yolks.

To serve; tip on to hot plates and sprinkle over the remaining parsley. Serves 4 as light main or 6 as a starter.

PER SERVING	
Energy Kcals	482
Protein g	19.6
Fat g	143
Polyunsaturated fatty acids g	1.04
Saturated fatty acids g	2.2
Carbohydrate g	70
Calcium mg	58

Try this dish with mushrooms for a delicious vegan alternative. It can also be served as a starter for 8 with one croûton each.

Sautéed Chicken Livers in a Creamy Wine and Sage Sauce on Garlic Bread Croûtons

Chicken livers are extremely economical and nutritious. They can usually be bought in tubs frozen from the butcher. This recipe incorporates them in a fairly sophisticated dish. The croûtons add to the texture and appearance of the dish.

For the croûtons

8	slices thick cut white bread (alternatively use granary bread for a nuttier texture)	8
4	cloves garlic, crushed to a smooth paste	4
4 tbsps	olive oil	4 tbsps

For the chicken livers

1 lb	chicken livers, defrosted if frozen	450 g
1 tbsp	olive oil	1 tbsp
2	small shallots, finely chopped	2
1	dozen fresh sage leaves	1
4 tbsps	dry white wine	4 tbsps
4 tbsps	strong chicken stock or vegetable	4 tbsps
4 tbsps	soya cream	4 tbsps
	salt and freshly ground black pepper	
	chopped parsley to garnish	

Pre-heat the oven to 190C, 375F, gas 5. Using large round cutter, or a cup, cut out 8 discs from the slices of bread. You can use the remainder for breadcrumbs.

Lay the bread on a large baking sheet and spread each bread disc all over with garlic, coating them well.

Drizzle the olive oil over the garlic bread discs and bake them in the oven for about 10-15 minutes, until golden and crisp. Keep warm when cooked.

Meanwhile, prepare the chicken livers. Examine livers carefully for green spots and cut these away and remove any bits of fat.

Rinse the livers in cold water then gently pat dry with kitchen paper.

Next heat the oil in a large frying pan and sauté the shallots for about 4 minutes.

PER SERVING	
Energy Kcals	443
Protein g	6.9
Fat g	32
Polyunsaturated fatty acids g	1.84
Saturated fatty acids g	0.77
Carbohydrate g	37.5
Calcium mg	79

Turn the heat up high and add in the chicken livers and the sage leaves.

Cook for about 2 minutes, turning frequently, until they lose their raw, red colour.

Transfer the chicken livers and sage to a warm plate using a slotted spoon.

Pour the wine and stock into the hot pan, simmer for about 1 minute scraping the pan well to remove cooking residues.

Return the livers to the pan and heat thoroughly.

Lower the heat, stir in the soya cream and season well.

Lay a croûton on each of the four plates, spoon the livers and sauce over each croûton.

Top with another croûton placed at an angle. Sprinkle with chopped parsley and serve immediately. Serves 4.

Spicy Chicken Quesadillas

Use bought tortillas or follow recipe on page 148 for homemade flour tortillas.

If you are unable to get soya mozzarella and want a touch of something resembling sour cream, try spooning onto the tortillas a dollop of tofu and almond sour cream on page 192.

Serve with Chilli Bean Salsa (see page 134) or Roasted Sweetcorn and Lime Salsa (see page 138).

Mexican food has become extremely popular recently. It is a fun way of cooking, with lots of diverse and interesting flavours. These Quesadillas can be kept in the fridge, rolled and ready to fry, so that when your friends arrive there is very little work left to do. What's so good with this dish is that if you are cooking for lots of people, some of whom may eat dairy, you can vary the cheese accordingly.

1 lb	skinned chicken breast	450 g
2 tsps	ground cumin	2 tsps
2	cloves garlic, crushed	2
2 tsps	ground coriander	2 tsps
1/2 tsp	chilli powder	1/2 tsp
2 tbsps	groundnut oil	2 tbsps
8	flour (or corn) tortillas	8
4	spring onions, sliced	4
1	red pepper, de-seeded and thinly sliced	1
2	jalapeno green chillies, thinly sliced	2
8	slices of soya mozzarella	8

Cut the chicken into thin strips and place in bowl with cumin, garlic, coriander and chilli powder. Mix the chicken well then leave to marinate in the fridge for 2 hours.

Heat half a tablespoon of the oil and fry the chicken strips in batches, until golden and just cooked through.

Soften the tortillas in a microwave or follow manufacturers instructions.

Mix the spring onions, red peppers, chillies and chicken in a bowl.

Divide chicken mixture among tortillas, fold and roll to enclose filling.

To re-heat, cook in batches seam-side down, in a large hot frying pan with the remaining oil, turn occasionally until golden.

Cover each Quesadilla with a slice of soya mozzarella and place under a hot grill until the soya mozzarella just starts to melt. Serve immediately. Serves 4.

PER SERVING	
Energy Kcals	473
Protein g	32.9
Fat g	11.5
Polyunsaturated fatty acids g	3.6
Saturated fatty acids g	2.3
Carbohydrate g	62.6
Calcium mg	131

If fresh tuna is unavailable, or for a picnic, use tinned tuna steak, drained and mixed with the potato salad. Try using fresh marinated anchovies rather than the tinned variety, these are much tastier and less salty.
They can now be found in some supermarkets on the delicatessan counter.
  Refreshing cooked vegetables in cold water helps retain a good green colour and prevents further cooking.

Griddled Fresh Tuna on Potato Niçoise

This well-balanced light meal is great for barbecues if you make salad and dressing in advance, then barbecue the fish to order.
  Fresh tuna is now readily available in most supermarkets and fishmongers and being an oily fish it contains the essential fatty acids.

8 oz	small new potatoes	225 g
4 oz	French beans	110 g
2 tbsp	capers, drained	2 tbsp
10	marinated anchovies, finely sliced	10
8	sun-dried tomatoes marinated in oil, drained and chopped	8
2 oz	pitted black olives	55 g
14	cherry tomatoes, washed and halved	14
4	175 g/6 oz tuna loin steaks cut about 2 cm (3/4 inch) thick	4
	double quantity of the Sun-dried Tomato, Garlic and Basil Dressing (see page 163)	
	fresh basil to garnish	

  Boil or steam the new potatoes until cooked but not too soft.
  Steam the French beans, when cooked but still crisp, refresh by running cold water over them.
  Mix potatoes, beans, capers, anchovies, sun-dried tomatoes, olives and tomatoes in bowl, refrigerate.
  To cook the tuna, lightly oil a griddle pan, place over a high heat and when hot put in tuna steaks for about 1 minute.
  When the tuna steaks have changed to a white colour two thirds of the way through and have good brown griddle marks underneath, carefully turn the steaks and cook for a few more seconds.
  Spoon the potato salad mixture on 4 plates.
  Lay the tuna on top of the potato salad and drizzle about 2 tablespoons of dressing over the top of each plate, garnish with fresh basil leaves. Serves 4.

PER SERVING	
Energy Kcals	363
Protein g	43.8
Fat g	15.8
Polyunsaturated fatty acids g	5.15
Saturated fatty acids g	3.26
Carbohydrate g	12.1
Calcium mg	58

Right:
Creamy Chilli Chicken with Basil and Coconut (page 76)

Try making this quiche with smoked haddock for another delicious combination.

Smoked Salmon and Spinach Quiche

Most savoury quiches contain cheese, however the combination of spinach and smoked salmon are so delicious that you forget about missing cheese completely. Quite often in fish mongers they will have cheap bags of salmon offcuts.
These are ideal for this quiche as the salmon is chopped up.
This quiche may be served hot, warm or cold with a mixed leaf or tomato salad.

5 oz	fresh spinach	140 g
8 oz	shortcrust pastry (see recipe on page 223 or use a suitable bought pastry)	225 g
4 oz	Tofutti Original (soya cream cheese)	110 g
5 fl oz	soya milk	150 ml
1	large egg plus 1 egg yolk, beaten	1
1 tbsp	Dijon mustard	1 tbsp
	freshly grated nutmeg	
	salt and freshly ground pepper	
4 oz	chopped smoked salmon (offcuts are fine)	110 g

Pre-heat the oven to 180C, 350F, gas 4. To prepare the spinach, wash well and either steam for 2 minutes or place in a large covered pan and heat until wilted, refresh by running it under cold water, squeeze dry, and chop.

Roll out the pastry on a floured surface and line a greased 20 cm (8 inch) flan dish or tin, easing any overlapping pastry back into the sides, prick base with a fork. Bake the pastry case blind using greaseproof paper and dried beans for 15 minutes on the centre shelf.

Remove from the oven, take out the paper and beans. Return to the oven for a few more minutes to dry.

Beat the Tofutti with the soya milk until smooth. Add the eggs, mustard, nutmeg and seasonings, stirring well.

Lay chopped spinach and the smoked salmon evenly on the pastry base.

Pour the egg mixture over the spinach and salmon.

Bake at the same temperature for about 25-30 minutes until the centre is set and the filling golden and puffy. Serves 4.

PER SERVING	
Energy Kcals	375.5
Protein g	15.5
Fat g	37.8
Polyunsaturated fatty acids g	9.18
Saturated fatty acids g	7.16
Carbohydrate g	24.4
Calcium mg	124.1

Left:
Smoked Salmon and Spinach Quiche (page 61)

You can make these and freeze them, but allow them to cool first. When thawed just heat through, covered with foil, in a warm oven.

Potato Pancakes

For these pancakes it is important to use an older more floury variety of potato rather than the yellow waxy type.

Here are some of the different toppings you could try:
– slices of smoked salmon topped with chive soya cream cheese decorated with whole chives
– warm crispy bacon and sun-dried tomato sprinkled on a dollop of chive soya cream cheese
– quick fried diced smoked salmon, capers and parsley
– for the vegan try roasting garlic, peppers and aubergines
– mushrooms tossed in garlic, parsley and olive oil.

10 oz	potatoes quartered (weight peeled)	275 g
6 fl oz	soya cream	175 ml
2 oz	vegan margarine	50 g
1 oz	plain flour	25 g
4	eggs, beaten	4
	oil for frying	
	salt, pepper and nutmeg	

Steam or boil potatoes until tender but not wet and mushy. Drain well.

In a large bowl, mash the hot potatoes with the soya cream and margarine until smooth.

Beat in the sifted flour and eggs, this should result in a thick pouring consistency. Season well with salt, pepper and nutmeg.

Heat a large lightly oiled non-stick frying pan.

Drop about half a ladle full of the mixture into the frying pan, it should spread slightly, make as many pancakes as you can fit in the pan.

Cook for about 1 minute, turn and heat the other side, they should be golden and spongy to touch when cooked.

Serve warm with different toppings. Makes about 12.

PER PANCAKE	
Energy Kcals	98
Protein g	1.67
Fat g	9.53
Polyunsaturated fatty acids g	3.21
Saturated fatty acids g	1.67
Carbohydrate g	6.85
Calcium mg	5

Many of the ingredients may be changed for a different variation. Mushrooms could be used instead of aubergines. Cashew nuts or brazil nuts instead of the hazelnuts. Yellow split peas instead of the lentils.

Aubergine and Red Lentil Loaf

Savoury loaves made out of nuts and pulses were one of the first dishes introduced when vegetarianism became popular. They are not really so popular now as many other more sophisticated vegetarian dishes are the fashion. However, this type of loaf is very nutritious and often very tasty.

This loaf has the interesting addition of spices and aubergine as well as the nuts and pulses. I find the aubergine prevents the loaf from being too dry. Made in advance, it reheats very well or I actually enjoy eating it cold the next day with a tomato salad and mixed leaves and perhaps some warm brown rice. If serving this loaf hot try serving it with the Tomato and Red Pepper Coulis on page 141 and maybe the Cucumber Salad on page 154.

4 oz	dried red lentils	110 g
2	medium onions, finely chopped	2
2 tbsps	olive oil	2 tbsps
1	small aubergine, cut into small cubes	1
2	cloves garlic, crushed	2
1 tbsp	mild curry powder	1 tbsp
1 tsp	cumin powder	1 tsp
1 tsp	turmeric	1 tsp
1/2 tsp	coriander powder	1/2 tsp
1 tsp	vegan bouillon powder	1 tsp
3 oz	breadcrumbs	85 g
2 oz	hazelnuts, finely chopped	55 g
1	egg, beaten	1
2 tbsps	chopped fresh coriander	2 tbsps
	salt and freshly ground pepper	

VEGETARIAN

PER SERVING

Energy Kcals	337
Protein g	13.8
Fat g	16.4
Polyunsaturated fatty acids g	2.23
Saturated fatty acids g	1.46
Carbohydrate g	41.9
Calcium mg	105

Pre-heat the oven to 180C, 350F, gas 4. Grease and line the base of a 1.2 litre (2 pint) loaf tin.

Rinse the lentils and tip into a small pan, cover with plenty of water, bring to boil then simmer for about 8-10 minutes until tender, drain and leave to dry out.

In a large saucepan sweat the onion in the olive oil for about 3 minutes.

Add the aubergine and garlic, continue cooking, stirring well for about 6 minutes until soft.

Stir in the curry powder, cumin, turmeric, coriander powder and bouillon and fry for several minutes to cook the spices.

Mix in the lentils, breadcrumbs and hazelnuts, until well blended.

Add the beaten egg, fresh coriander and season well.

Pour into the prepared loaf tin and smooth down.

Bake for about 40 minutes until the top is crisp and golden and the loaf feels firm to the touch in the centre. Skewer the centre of the roast and if the skewer comes out very wet, cook for longer.

Leave for a few minutes then turn out onto a warm plate to serve. Serves 4-6.

Larger field mushrooms have a more intense flavour than the small cup variety.

Baked Stuffed Field Mushrooms

These are one of my favourite vegetarian dishes, especially as they are so incredibly easy to prepare with the mushrooms requiring no pre-cooking. They can be made in advance and cooked when required.

They would also be suitable as part of a buffet lunch or as a starter made using smaller mushrooms.

Delicious served with the roasted tomato sauce on page 139 and a green salad or as a hot main meal with the red pepper and tomato coulis on page 141.

4	very large field mushrooms (if you cannot get field mushrooms use the ordinary cup variety allowing for extra per person)	4
1	large onion, finely chopped	1
1 tbsp	olive oil	1 tbsp
3	cloves garlic, crushed	3
2	sticks celery, finely chopped	2
3 oz	breadcrumbs (granary bread is tastiest)	75 g
1	bunch parsley (the more greener the tastier the stuffing)	1
2	sprigs fresh thyme	2
2 oz	flaked almonds	50 g
	salt and freshly ground pepper	
4 oz	soya cheese (homemade variety works well, see page 145)	110 g
	a little extra olive oil to drizzle	

VEGAN

PER SERVING

Energy Kcals	265
Protein g	12.6
Fat g	9.0
Polyunsaturated fatty acids g	4.08
Saturated fatty acids g	0.89
Carbohydrate g	36.1
Calcium mg	104

Pre-heat the grill and also the oven to 190C, 375F, gas 5. Wipe the mushrooms and remove the stalks and lay the mushrooms in a suitable baking dish.

In a large frying pan, sweat the onions in the olive oil over a medium heat, for about 5 minutes until fairly soft.

Stir in the garlic and celery and fry gently for a further 4 minutes, stirring regularly.

If making breadcrumbs in a processor, add the herbs whilst processing the bread. If you already have breadcrumbs, chop the herbs finely and mix them together.

Grill the flaked almonds until golden turning regularly to prevent them blackening.

In a large bowl combine the breadcrumbs, onion mixture and almonds. Then crumble or grate in the soya cheese, mix well and season.

If the mixture seems very dry add an extra tablespoon of olive oil to moisten it (this will hold it together better for stuffing).

Fill the mushrooms, packing the mixture in well, return them to the baking dish and drizzle with extra olive oil.

Bake in the oven for about 20-25 minutes until the mushrooms are soft and the top is golden brown. Transfer to warm plates to serve. Serves 4.

Some washed finely sliced spinach could be stirred into the hot mixture just before serving.

Chick Peas with Tomatoes and Coriander

This is a nutritious and satisfying dish using chick peas which have a distinctive nutty flavour and are one of the most versatile beans. I sometimes like to cook them myself so they are slightly more crunchy than the tinned variety, although having a tin available in the store cupboard is extremely handy. Serve this with brown rice and a crisp salad or as an accompaniment to a selection of Indian dishes.

1 tbsp	vegetable oil	1 tbsp
1	medium onion, finely chopped	1
3	cloves garlic, crushed	3
2	small green chillies, de-seeded and finely chopped	2
1/2 tsp	ground paprika	1/2 tsp
1 tsp	ground cumin	1 tsp
1 tsp	ground coriander	1 tsp
1/2 tsp	garam masala	1/2 tsp
4	large ripe tomatoes, roughly chopped (or 1 x 400 g tin of chopped tomatoes)	4
1 tsp	brown sugar	1 tsp
1	400 g tin of chick peas drained (net drained weight about 240 g) or equivalent cooked from dried	1
2 tbsps	chopped fresh coriander	2 tbsps
	salt and pepper	

Heat the oil in a medium saucepan, add the onion and fry gently for about 4 minutes.

Stir in the garlic, chillies and spices and continue frying for several minutes.

Next add the tomatoes and sugar, simmer gently for about 10 minutes until tomatoes turn to a purée.

Stir in the chick peas and the fresh coriander and heat for about 3 minutes until chick peas are heated through.

Season well and serve in a warm dish. Serves 2-3.

VEGAN

PER SERVING

Energy Kcals	265
Protein g	12.6
Fat g	9.0
Polyunsaturated fatty acids g	4.08
Saturated fatty acids g	0.89
Carbohydrate g	36.1
Calcium mg	104

Try and use free-range eggs
whenever possible.

Curried Spinach and Eggs

This is a very tasty, quick and nutritious supper. Serve hot with
either brown rice or hot naan bread.

1 lb	fresh spinach or 170 g (6 oz) frozen leaf spinach	450 g
1 tbsp	groundnut oil	1 tbsp
1	medium onion, finely chopped	1
2	cloves garlic, crushed	2
1 tsp	black mustard seeds	1 tsp
2 tsps	medium curry powder	2 tsps
1 tsp	turmeric	1 tsp
1/2 tsp	chilli powder	1/2 tsp
8 1/2 fl oz	vegetable stock	250 ml
3 1/2 fl oz	coconut cream	100 ml
	salt and freshly ground pepper	
	pinch of nutmeg	
1 tbsp	chopped fresh coriander	1 tbsp
6	fresh eggs	6

Wash and prepare spinach. Put into a pan without water,
cover and cook gently (or you could steam it above some rice).
After about 5 minutes the spinach will have reduced by two-
thirds (it should be just under-cooked).

Drain, rinse with cold water to retain colour, squeeze all
water out, roughly chop.

In a large frying pan, heat the oil and sweat onions and garlic
for about 5 minutes until soft, add the mustard seeds and
powdered spices and fry, stirring well for a further 5 minutes.

Next mix in the stock and coconut cream and bring to boil.

Stir in the spinach, season, and heat through and keep warm.
Put the eggs in a small saucepan immersed in cold water, bring
up to the boil then gently simmer for about 6-7 minutes until
just hard boiled. Remove shell, and cut in half, whilst still hot.

Serve spinach in a large warm dish and lay the halved eggs
over the top. Sprinkle with coriander to serve. Serves 4.

VEGETARIAN

PER SERVING

Energy Kcals	164
Protein g	4.9
Fat g	21.5
Polyunsaturated fatty acids g	2.58
Saturated fatty acids g	8.50
Carbohydrate g	6.8
Calcium mg	206

I quite often cook this with any combination of fillings, such as peppers, mushrooms, ham, bacon, broccoli, asparagus etc.

Potato, Bean and Corn Frittata

A frittata is an open Italian omelette. Unlike many omelettes which may be creamy or runny a frittata is set firm, but not stiff and dry. It is not folded as is a conventional omelette, but consists of a single thin layer at the bottom of the pan in which it is made. Also the filling ingredients are added to the eggs while they are uncooked, and the frittata is then cooked slowly over a low heat.

1 tbsp	olive oil	1 tbsp
4	spring onions, washed and sliced	4
1	clove garlic, crushed	1
8 oz	cooked new potatoes, diced	225 g
4 oz	cooked fresh sweetcorn (scraped off the cob)	110 g
4 oz	french beans, blanched and refreshed, cut into 1 1/2 cm (1/2 inch) lengths	110 g
6	eggs, beaten and seasoned with salt and pepper	6
1 tbsp	chopped fresh parsley	1 tbsp
1 oz	vegan margarine	25 g

Using a large heavy-based omelette pan, heat the oil and gently fry the spring onions, garlic and new potatoes or about 8 minutes until the potato begins to turn golden. Then add in the sweetcorn and the beans and mix well.

Break the eggs into a large bowl and whisk until well blended, stir in the parsley.

Tip the vegetables from the pan into the eggs, add the parsley and mix thoroughly until all the ingredients are well combined. Pre-heat the grill.

Wipe out the omelette pan, then gently heat the margarine until it is beginning to foam but not burning.

Tip in the egg and vegetable mixture and smooth down. Cook over a low to medium heat for about 8 minutes until the eggs have set and only the surface is runny.

Place the pan under the hot grill and cook the top for about 3 minutes until golden and slightly risen.

Cut out into 4 large wedges, slide each onto a serving dish to serve. Serves 4.

VEGETARIAN

PER SERVING	
Energy Kcals	108
Protein g	2.7
Fat g	11.8
Polyunsaturated fatty acids g	0.59
Saturated fatty acids g	0.52
Carbohydrate g	17.8
Calcium mg	39

There are two readily available varieties of sweet potato, one being bright orange inside when cooked, the other yellow with a chestnut flavour. Either sort would be suitable.

Sweet Potato and Chick Pea Cakes

These crispy cakes are packed with flavour and goodness. They are ideal as a meal on their own or as a side dish. Serve hot with Tomato and Sweet Chilli Relish (see page 142) and perhaps the Cucumber Mint and Soya 'Yogurt' Salad (see page 154)

1	large or 2 smaller sweet potatoes (weight about 500 g)	1
1	medium onion, finely chopped	1
1	small leek, washed, finely chopped	1
3	cloves garlic, crushed	3
3 tbsps	vegetable oil	3 tbsps
1 tsp	vegan bouillon powder	1 tsp
1	green chilli chopped finely, seeds discarded (optional)	1
1½ tsps	ground cumin	1½ tsps
½ tsp	ground coriander	½ tsp
½ tsp	ground turmeric	½ tsp
1	400 g tin chick peas drained (net drained weight about 240 g) or equivalent cooked from dried	1
	salt and freshly ground pepper	
1 tbsp	plain flour	1 tbsp
1 tbsp	sesame seeds	1 tbsp

Pre-heat the oven to 180C, 350F, gas 4. Peel, cube and steam or boil sweet potato for about 10-15 minutes until soft.

Drain well and using a potato masher, mash until smooth.

Sweat the onion, leek and garlic in a frying pan in 1 tablespoon oil for about 15 minutes over medium heat, until soft.

Add the bouillon powder, chilli and spices into the pan, stir well and continue cooking for 2 minutes.

In a large bowl, mash the chick peas, leaving them slightly chunky.

Add the onion and sweet potato to the chick peas, combine well.

Season with salt and pepper, leave to cool slightly.

On a large plate mix the flour with the sesame seeds.

VEGAN

PER SERVING	
Energy Kcals	339
Protein g	8.1
Fat g	15.8
Polyunsaturated fatty acids g	7.44
Saturated fatty acids g	1.82
Carbohydrate g	44.0
Calcium mg	104

Divide the potato mixture into 8 and shape into round cakes about 2 cm (1 in) thick. Roll each cake in the flour and sesame seeds.

In a large clean frying pan, heat the oil and fry the cakes for 4 minutes on each side, over a medium heat until golden.

Place on a baking tray and finish off in oven for 10 minutes until heated right through. Serves 4.

Main Dishes – Fish, Meat and Vegetarian

Spicy Fillet of Beef Stroganoff

Rich Daube of Beef

Seared Calves' Liver with Bacon, Sage and Sherry Vinegar Sauce

Creamy Chilli Chicken with Basil and Coconut

Creole Chicken

Chicken Casseroled in Cider with Mushrooms and Dijon Mustard

Chicken and Mushroom Pie

Chicken Breasts with Mushroom, Bacon and Green Peppercorn 'Cream' Sauce

Duck Breast with an Orange and Juniper Red Wine Sauce

Roasted Leg of Duck with Ginger and Honey

Lamb Hot Pot with Pearl Barley

Marinated Lamb Kebabs

Lamb Tagine

Pork Steak with a Hazelnut and Sage Crust

Fillet of Trout Tandoori Style

Grilled Fillet of Sea Trout with Creamy Watercress Sauce

Flaky Fish, Prawn and Leek Pie

Cajun Blackened Fish

Griddled Tuna Loin with Salsa Verde

Grilled Fillet of Grey Mullet with Soy, Honey and Horseradish Dressing

Grilled Skate Wing with a Warm Vierge Dressing

Roasted Fillet of Cod with a Herb and 'Cheese' Style Crust

Monkfish and King Prawn Brochettes

Crunchy Oat-Coated Mackerel Fillets

Potato-Crusted Haddock and Curried Tomato Bake

Smoked Haddock, Tomato and Leek in Dill Pancakes

Smoked Fish Cakes

Smoked Cod Rarebit

Spinach, Almond and Mushroom Gougère

Puy Lentil and Mushroom Moussaka

Mediterranean Vegetable and Chick Pea Lasagne

Split Pea and Vegetable Cobbler

Thai Green Vegetable and Cashew Nut Curry

Individual Wild Mushroom and Walnut Strudels

This dish is also delicious made with pork fillet and more economical. If using pork fillet cut in strips. They will need to be cooked slightly longer to ensure the pork is thoroughly cooked through, whereas beef fillet can be served slightly pink.

Spicy Fillet of Beef Stroganoff

This classic stroganoff is made with thin strips of beef fillet which are cooked very quickly. Fillet of beef is quite expensive so this is a special occasion dish, but well worth it. I added cayenne to give it bit of a kick!

Serve this stroganoff with rice and some green vegetables.

1 lb	beef fillet	450 g
8 oz	small button mushrooms, wiped	225 g
1½ oz	vegan margarine	40 g
1	medium onion, halved and thinly sliced	1
1¼ tsp	cayenne pepper	1¼ tsp
7 fl oz	dry white wine or dry cider	200 ml
7 fl oz	good beef stock (chicken stock will also do)	200 ml
½ tbsp	vegetable oil	½ tbsp
3 tbsps	brandy	3 tbsps
3 tbsps	soya cream	3 tbsps
	salt and freshly ground black pepper	
	freshly ground nutmeg	
1 tbsp	chopped parsley	1 tbsp

Cut the beef fillet into thin strips of 0.5 cm (¼ inch) wide and 6 cm (2½ inch) long. Trim the stalks and slice the mushrooms. Melt the margarine in a frying pan over a medium heat, and cook the onion for about 5 minutes until soft.

Stir in the mushrooms and 1 teaspoon cayenne, increase the heat and cook for about 2 minutes.

Pour the wine over the mushrooms and allow to boil for a few seconds then add the stock. Continue simmering until the liquid is about half the initial amount. Pour out into a bowl.

Heat the oil in a large, clean, heavy frying pan as hot as possible without burning. Drop in the beef strips.

Shake and toss over a fast heat to brown and seal the edges without overcooking in the middle. Take pan off the heat. Remove beef strips from pan.

Pour the brandy into the fairly hot pan. Set light to the brandy and when flames die down pour in mushroom and stock mixture. Return the meat and allow to heat through for several minutes. Gently stir in 2 tablespoons of the soya cream, add salt and pepper and a good grating of fresh nutmeg. Serve in a warm serving dish.

Drizzle top with remaining soya cream and sprinkle the remaining ¼ teaspoon of cayenne over the soya cream, finely sprinkle the chopped parsley over the beef. Serves 4.

PER SERVING	
Energy Kcals	346
Protein g	25.3
Fat g	22.2
Polyunsaturated fatty acids g	3.92
Saturated fatty acids g	7.34
Carbohydrate g	6.6
Calcium mg	24

Rich Daube of Beef

This is a wonderful way of cooking tougher cuts of meat and fairly easy to make. I quite often cook this for friends coming to supper, as it can be prepared well in advance, and improves after a day or two. I have used shin of beef which is easy to prepare and has little wastage. Ask your local butcher for beef shin. Then simply slice across in steak-like pieces, which looks much nicer than a casserole with small cubes of meat. Serve with baked or new potatoes and the sauce from the daube will be enough to make them delicious without the need to add a butter substitute. The daube may be served with rice or potatoes and vegetables.

2 lb	shin of beef	900 g
12 oz	piece of lightly smoked streaky bacon (buy whole from butchers)	350 g
2-3 tbsps	oil	2-3 tbsps
2	medium onions, sliced	2
3	cloves garlic, crushed	3
2	sticks celery, chopped	2
	seasoned flour (plain flour with salt and pepper)	
1	bottle of red wine	1
1 pt	good brown stock	570 ml
	a few sprigs of fresh thyme, stalks removed	
2	bay leaves	2
	salt and pepper	

Pre-heat the oven to 150C, 300F, gas 2. Trim the meat and cut it into steak-like pieces (or ask butcher to do so) about 2.5 cm (1 inch) thick.

Next trim off the rind and excess fat from the bacon, cut it into 5 mm (1/4 inch) chunks.

Heat 1/2 tablespoon oil in a large frying pan. Fry the onions, garlic and celery for a few minutes, then tip them into a large deep casserole dish.

Stir the bacon into the hot pan and fry for 1 minute, tip into the casserole dish with the onions.

Toss the meat in the seasoned flour. Heat a drizzle of oil in the pan and brown the beef pieces very well a few at a time. Place into the casserole dish when browned.

If the bottom of the pan becomes dark or too dry, remove the beef, then pour in a little wine and scrape any sediment stuck

PER SERVING	
Energy Kcals	498
Protein g	44
Fat g	23
Polyunsaturated fatty acids g	2.7
Saturated fatty acids g	7.3
Carbohydrate g	9.9
Calcium mg	47

on the bottom of the pan (this is called deglazing). Pour this liquid into the casserole dish. When all the meat is browned, deglaze the pan once more. Any remaining wine pour over the beef in casserole dish, followed by the stock, thyme and bay leaves.

Cover the casserole dish with tin foil. Bake slowly for 3 hours or until meat is tender.

After this time, adjust the sauce by pouring all the liquid into a saucepan, leaving the meat in the casserole dish. Bring the liquid to the boil and simmer until it has reduced by half and becomes slightly thicker and stronger tasting, season well with salt and pepper (I sometimes add a dash of dark soya sauce instead of salt, this gives a good dark colour to the sauce), pour sauce over the meat.

Return to the oven, uncovered for about 10 minutes. Serve hot from the oven. Serves 6.

When buying calves' liver, it should be milky brown in colour with a fine even texture. Whereas lambs' liver is darker, being reddish-brown in colour.

Avoid Pigs' liver, except for making pâtés and terrines.

Seared Calves' Liver with Bacon, Sage and Sherry Vinegar Sauce

Calves' liver is considered quite a luxury, so if you are on a budget it would be equally as delicious with lambs' liver, which is considerably cheaper. The liver is best served slightly pink in the middle, if overcooked it becomes tougher and darker. Serve with potatoes and green vegetables.

1 tbsp	sunflower oil	1 tbsp
4	shallots, peeled and finely chopped	4
6	rashers rindless smoked back bacon, finely chopped	6
2 tsps	plain flour	2 tsps
1½ tbsps	sherry vinegar	1½ tbsps
5 fl oz	red wine	150 ml
8½ fl oz	good dark stock	250 ml
1 tsp	chopped fresh sage	1 tsp
1 tsp	sugar	1 tsp
	salt and freshly ground pepper	

PER SERVING	
Energy Kcals	300
Protein g	30.6
Fat g	14.0
Polyunsaturated fatty acids g	4.42
Saturated fatty acids g	3.87
Carbohydrate g	6.8
Calcium mg	21

1 lb	calves' liver, ask butcher to slice into 4 slices about 1 cm ($\frac{1}{2}$ inch) thick	450 g
	flour for dusting	
	dash of oil for frying	
8	extra sage leaves for garnishing	8

Heat the oil in a small saucepan, add the shallots and bacon. Cook slowly for 10 to 15 minutes until the shallots are soft and beginning to caramelise.

Sprinkle the flour over the shallots and stir well over a medium heat for about half a minute, remove pan from the heat.

Pour in the vinegar and red wine and, stirring well, return to the heat.

Add the stock, sage and sugar and bring to a boil then simmer for 5 minutes, until the sauce thickens slightly. Season well.

To cook the calves' liver, heat a large griddle or heavy frying pan, brushed with oil, to a high temperature.

Lightly dust the liver with some extra flour and season with pepper.

Place the liver on the hot griddle, leave for about 2 minutes until the heat has cooked the liver through almost to the top.

Quickly flip over the liver, cook briefly on the other side, before serving browned underside up on warmed plates.

Reheat the sauce and carefully pour over the liver.

Garnish each portion with 2 fresh sage leaves and serve immediately. Serves 4.

Thai 7 Spice Seasoning is a World Cuisine spice powder found in most supermarkets; it contains chilli powder, garlic, coriander powder, ground lemon peel, cinnamon, cumin, star anise, onion powder, jalapeno powder and cloves. If you cannot find it use a combination of these spices found in your store cupboard.

For a vegan dish, omit the chicken and try using sautéed mushrooms, aubergines and chick peas. Add the flour and spices to the sautéed vegetables before adding the stock etc.

Creamy Chilli Chicken with Basil and Coconut

This Thai-style chicken stir-fry is very quick and easy to prepare and makes a delicious meal served with Thai fragrant rice and salad.

Coconut milk, although fairly sweet, is a great addition to the lactose-free diet, as it not only contains some calcium, it also gives dishes a lovely creamy taste. It is particularly good in Thai-style dishes, which have a hot and sweet taste.

4	chicken breast fillets	4
2 tbsps	groundnut oil	2 tbsps
1	onion finely chopped	1
1	red bird's-eye chilli, de-seeded and finely sliced	1
1	red pepper, de-seeded and finely diced	1
2 tsps	Thai 7 Spice Seasoning	2 tsps
2 tsps	chilli sauce	2 tsps
2 tbsps	fish or soy sauce	2 tbsps
1	large bunch fresh basil, shredded, save a few leaves for garnishing	1
1	400 g tin coconut milk	1

Skin the chicken breasts and cut into 1 cm (½ inch) strips.

Heat a wok with the oil and quickly stir-fry the onion, chilli and peppers for about 2 minutes, stirring constantly.

Stir in the chicken strips and Thai seasoning and fry for about 3 minutes until chicken is tender.

Pour the chilli sauce and fish sauce over the chicken and cook for a further minute.

Stir in the shredded basil leaves and the coconut milk, simmer gently until well heated through.

Serve in a warmed dish. Serves 4.

PER SERVING	
Energy Kcals	274
Protein g	39.4
Fat g	7.8
Polyunsaturated fatty acids g	0.87
Saturated fatty acids g	1.43
Carbohydrate g	12.3
Calcium mg	67

Also delicious made with fillet of fish, prawns or fillet of pork.

Creole Chicken

This Cajun-style dish has a rich and spicy flavour. The fiery heat of the dish is mellowed down by the addition of soya cream. Serve with the Spicy Potato Wedges on page 125 or with plain rice.

2 tbsps	plain flour	2 tbsps
2 tbsps	sweet paprika	2 tbsps
2 tbsps	Cajun spice	2 tbsps
4	chicken breasts	4
2 tbsps	olive oil	2 tbsps
1	large onion, chopped	1
2	cloves garlic, crushed	2
1	large red pepper (or 2 small), de-seeded, halved and sliced	1
14 fl oz	vegetable or chicken stock	400 ml
7 fl oz	soya cream	200 ml
1/2 tsp	dried basil	1/2 tsp

Mix the flour, paprika and Cajun spice on a large plate. Skin the chicken breasts and cut them into large chunks, roll them in the spiced flour mixture.

Heat a medium saucepan with one tbsp oil. Sweat the onion, garlic and peppers for about 5 minutes over a medium heat.

As soon as the onions are beginning to soften, tip the remaining spiced flour mixture into the pan. Cook gently for about a minute, stirring well.

Remove the pan from the heat and gradually add the stock. Return the sauce to the heat, bring to the boil, stirring constantly, and cook for about 1 minute until the sauce thickens. Heat a large frying pan with the remaining oil. Sear the chicken pieces for several minutes on either side until golden.

Pour the sauce over the chicken and simmer for about 4 minutes.

Stir in the soya cream and basil and gently heat through. Serve the chicken on warm plates and pour over the sauce. Serve immediately. Serves 4.

PER SERVING	
Energy Kcals	314
Protein g	32.2
Fat g	15.9
Polyunsaturated fatty acids g	6.5
Saturated fatty acids g	2.5
Carbohydrate g	14.6
Calcium mg	39

Rather than jointing a whole chicken, you may find it cheaper and easier to use chicken thighs and drum sticks ready jointed. This also allows you to choose better quality chicken – the thighs and legs of organic or free-range chicken are often much cheaper than the breast. Allow for one whole thigh per person.

Chicken Casseroled in Cider with Mushrooms and Dijon Mustard

This delicious rich casserole could be served with a crisp jacket potato, steamed potatoes or brown rice. The addition of a mild variety of mustard blends with the stock and cider to give a rich, creamy sauce without the addition of a cream substitute. This casserole may be prepared a day or two in advance. It is also suitable for freezing so long as the chicken has not been previously frozen.

4 lb	chicken	1.8 kg
1 oz	plain flour seasoned with salt and pepper	25 g
2 tbsps	vegetable oil	2 tbsps
1	onion finely chopped	1
7 oz	button mushrooms, halved	200 g
10 fl oz	dry cider (white wine could also be used)	275 ml
3	generous tablespoons Dijon mustard (mild variety)	3
10 fl oz	chicken stock (preferably made earlier using chicken carcass)	275 ml
2	stalks fresh thyme	2
1 tbsp	chopped parsley	1 tbsp

Pre-heat the oven to 190C, 375F, gas 5. Joint the chicken into 8 pieces, roll the chicken pieces in the seasoned flour.

Heat a large frying pan with 1 tablespoon oil, brown the pieces for approximately 4 minutes on either side.

Remove the chicken pieces from the pan and place in suitable oven dish. Heat the remaining oil and sauté the onion and mushrooms for about 4 minutes. Sprinkle over the remaining plain flour and stir well. Gradually pour in the cider and mustard, stirring well and bring to boil. Stir in the stock mixing well, bring to the boil and allow to simmer for several minutes. Season with extra salt and freshly ground pepper if necessary and add the thyme leaves pulled off their stalks. Pour this sauce over the browned chicken pieces. Cover with foil and bake in the oven for about 1 hour until tender. Remove from the oven, the sauce should be the consistency of single cream. Garnish with chopped parsley before serving. Serves 3-4.

PER SERVING	
Energy Kcals	695
Protein g	59.0
Fat g	46.6
Polyunsaturated fatty acids g	8.05
Saturated fatty acids g	11.37
Carbohydrate g	17.0
Calcium mg	62

The same dish can be done with rabbit or pheasant instead of chicken.

Also you could just roast legs and thighs for this dish and save the breast, this would make it more economical.

Wait until the filling is cold before topping with pastry.

Chicken and Mushroom Pie

This traditional pie is perfect for a cold winter's day. It can be prepared in advance and kept chilled with the uncooked pastry top. Serve with some steamed sprouts or spring greens.

2 tbsps	sunflower oil	2 tbsps
1	onion, finely chopped	1
2 oz	plain flour	50 g
10 fl oz	good strong chicken stock	275 ml
5 fl oz	soya milk	150 ml
1 tsp	chopped fresh french tarragon or 1/2 teaspoon dried tarragon	1 tsp
1 tsp	Dijon mustard	1 tsp
	salt and freshly ground pepper	
4 tbsps	soya cream	4 tbsps
3 lb	whole chicken, poached, boned and cut into large chunks	1.35 kg
8 oz	button mushrooms, wiped and sliced	225 g
8 oz	flour-quantity wholemeal or shortcrust pastry (see pages 223-4)	225 g

1 beaten egg mixed with
1 pinch of salt and 1 teaspoon water (egg wash)

Pre-heat the oven to 190C, 375F, gas 5. Heat 1 tablespoon of oil in a large saucepan and sweat the onion for about 8 minutes until soft but not brown.

Remove the pan from heat, stir in the flour. Return to a low heat and cook for 2 minutes until the flour is a pale golden brown.

Remove the pan from the heat and gradually blend in the chicken stock.

Return once more to a medium heat and stir until you have a thick shiny sauce.

Pour in the soya milk, stirring well and gently bring the sauce to the boil.

Stir in the tarragon, mustard, seasoning and soya cream, simmer for 2 minutes. Taste, add more seasoning if necessary. Allow to cool.

In a clean frying pan, heat up the remaining oil. When hot, quickly fry the mushrooms for about 4 minutes until just cooked. Leave to cool slightly.

PER SERVING	
Energy Kcals	703.7
Protein g	30.8
Fat g	22.9
Polyunsaturated fatty acids g	2.99
Saturated fatty acids g	4.43
Carbohydrate g	86.7
Calcium mg	97

Roll the pastry on a floured board into a large oval 5 cm (¹/₄ inch) thick. Using an upturned 1 litre oval pie dish, in which you will be baking the pie, cut around the pastry rim, making a lid for the pie.

Tip the mushrooms and the chicken into the sauce, mix well then pour into the pie dish.

Wet the edge of the pastry and lift wet side down onto the pie.

Use any left over pastry to decorate the top of the pie if you wish to.

Prick the top with a skewer several times. Brush with beaten egg.

Bake for about 30 minutes, until the pastry top is golden and risen and the pie is well heated through. Serves 4.

This dish could be made with pheasant or guinea fowl breast.

Chicken Breasts with Mushroom, Bacon and Green Peppercorn 'Cream' Sauce

This sauce makes a plain chicken breast into something rich and exotic. The peppercorns give an interesting spicy addition. Ideal served with rice or potatoes.

2 tbsps	olive oil	2 tbsps
4	chicken breasts, excess fat and skin removed	4
1	large onion, peeled, halved and sliced	1
7 oz	unsmoked streaky bacon, rind removed and finely chopped	200 g
8 oz	mushrooms, thinly sliced	225 g
3.5 fl oz	dry white wine	100 ml
1 tsp	green peppercorns (marinated in brine)	1 tsp
7 fl oz	vegetable or chicken stock	200 ml
7 fl oz	soya cream	200 ml
	salt and freshly ground pepper	

PER SERVING	
Energy Kcals	476
Protein g	45
Fat g	28.5
Polyunsaturated fatty acids g	8.6
Saturated fatty acids g	7.4
Carbohydrate g	6.15
Calcium mg	40

Pre-heat the oven to 180C, 350F, gas 4. Heat a large non-stick frying pan with 1 tablespoon of the olive oil. When hot add chicken breasts and sear for about 1 minute on each side until golden brown.

Place in an oven dish and bake for about 15-20 minutes. Meanwhile, add the remaining olive oil to the frying pan and sweat the onion for about 5 minutes until just soft.

Add the bacon and mushrooms and, stirring well, continue cooking for a further 5 minutes.

Pour in the wine, green peppercorns and stock and bring to boil, cook for about 4 minutes.

Lastly add the soya cream, stir well and season, and warm over a low heat.

Remove chicken from the oven and slice each breast in half at a diagonal, the meat should be white throughout, if any pinkness remains cook the chicken for longer.

When the chicken is cooked arrange on warm plates and spoon over the sauce. Serves 4.

Slashing the duck breast helps to cook it evenly and also releases more of the fat. Leaving the duck breast to rest for 5 minutes before carving will make the meat more tender. This recipe could be made using pigeon breasts.

Duck Breast with an Orange and Juniper Red Wine Sauce

Duck breasts are increasingly easy to find nowadays and extremely popular with most people. They are best cooked at a higher temperature for a short time and served slightly pink in the middle.

This is a great dish when you want to serve something special. Make the sauce in advance and reheat to serve. Delicious served with the Potato and Celeriac Boulangère (see page 122) or try with the Stir-fried Cabbage and Carrot (see page 118).

1 tbsp	vegetable oil	1 tbsp
1	large onion, sliced	1
3	sticks of celery, chopped	3
4 oz	mushroom stalks or old mushrooms, chopped	110 g
1	carrot, sliced	1
10 fl oz	red wine	275 ml
1¼ pts	chicken stock	725 ml
	sprig of thyme	
2	bay leaves	2
12	juniper berries	12
5 fl oz	orange juice	150 ml
	zest of one orange	
4	duck breasts, trim excess fat	4
	salt and freshly ground pepper	

Pre-heat the oven to 220C, 425F, gas 7. In a large saucepan, heat the oil and cook the onion, celery, mushroom stalks and carrot for about 10 minutes until they begin to brown but not burn.

Pour in the red wine to deglaze the pan, allow to boil for a few seconds.

Next add the stock, herbs and juniper berries and simmer uncovered for about 30 minutes, until it has reduced by about two-thirds.

Pass everything through a fine sieve, pick out the juniper berries from the sieve and put back in the gravy along with the orange juice and zest, set aside until you begin to cook the duck.

PER SERVING	
Energy Kcals	633
Protein g	16.1
Fat g	56.3
Polyunsaturated fatty acids g	6.59
Saturated fatty acids g	14.54
Carbohydrate g	9.7
Calcium mg	64

Slash the skin of the duck diagonally about 4 times on each breast, season with salt and pepper.

Heat a large pan (preferably one with oven-proof handle) until hot, add duck breasts skin side up.

Cook for 2 minutes, then turn skin side down and cook for a further 2 minutes.

Pour off excess duck fat and put duck breasts in the oven for a further 10 minutes, remove from oven and leave to rest for 5 minutes.

Meanwhile, return the sauce to the stove, bring to the boil and simmer for about 5 minutes until it begins to thicken slightly.

Pour any excess juices (not the fat) from the duck breasts into sauce.

Slice each duck breast into about 4 diagonal slices and place slices on a warm plate. Pour over the hot sauce before serving. Serves 4.

Chicken legs could be used instead of duck.

Roasted Leg of Duck with Ginger and Honey

Duck legs are often the most affordable way of buying duck. As with chicken legs, duck legs benefit from a longer slower roasting time, and as a result, they will be tender and well cooked. For this recipe I have slashed the duck legs prior to marinading, which allows the spices to infuse into the duck, and this, along with the ginger and honey gives the duck a delicious oriental taste. The longer you can marinade the duck legs the more the flavour will develop. Serve with Sesame Noodles on page 127 and some stir-fry vegetables.

4	duck legs	4
4 tsps	Chinese five spice	4 tsps
1 inch	fresh ginger, peeled and very finely chopped	2$^1/_2$ cm
4 tbsps	runny honey	4 tbsps
4 tsps	dark soy sauce	4 tsps
4 tsps	light soy sauce	4 tsps

Slash the duck legs with a sharp knife and rub them over with the Chinese five spice.

Lay the duck legs in an oven-proof dish and leave to marinade in the fridge for 3 hours or overnight.

Pre-heat the oven to 180C, 350F, gas 4. Place the duck legs in the oven for 40 minutes until the duck is well cooked through, and the skin is sizzling and crispy.

Remove from the oven, drain off most of the surrounding fat. In a small bowl mix together the ginger, honey and the light and dark soy sauce.

Drizzle all this sauce over and around the duck legs and return to oven for further 10 minutes.

Remove from the oven and leave the duck legs to relax for 5 minutes before serving. Serves 4.

PER SERVING	
Energy Kcals	665
Protein g	21.7
Fat g	60.6
Polyunsaturated fatty acids g	9.1
Saturated fatty acids g	17.4
Carbohydrate g	8.8
Calcium mg	15.8

For a dish similar to Lancashire Hot Pot, place a layer of thinly sliced peeled potato on the top 40 minutes before the end of the cooking time.

Lamb Hot Pot with Pearl Barley

This rustic dish contains almost all the ingredients for a complete meal. Although perhaps a crisp baked potato served alongside to mop up all the juice, would make it more complete! I have used pearl barley which provides a good source of calcium as well as an interesting nutty flavour to the dish. Neck or scrag end of lamb is a fairly economical cut. By cooking the meat on the bone, the meat remains more succulent and tender.

2¹/₂ lb	lean middle neck or scrag end of lamb (also could be done with shoulder cut up on bone)	1.125 kg
1¹/₄ pt	good stock (beef, lamb or chicken)	725 ml
1	large onion, sliced	1
3	sticks celery, cut into 1 cm (¹/₂ inch) chunks	3
3	carrots, cut into 2.5 cm (1 inch) chunks	3
3	bay leaves	3
1	sprig of fresh rosemary	1
1¹/₂ tbsps	pearl barley	1¹/₂ tbsps
	salt and freshly ground pepper	

Pre-heat the oven to 180C, 350F, gas 4. Cut the meat into chops, trimming away excess fat.

Heat a heavy pan without oil (as the lamb is naturally quite fatty) and fry the lamb to brown all sides of it.

Place the browned lamb chops into a large casserole dish.

Deglaze the pan with a splash of the stock scraping the bottom of the pan to remove all the sediment.

Place the onions, celery, carrot and herbs in the casserole dish with the lamb.

Pour over the stock and pearl barley. Season and cover with tin foil.

Place in oven and cook for 2 hours (remove foil after 1 hour, continue cooking uncovered). The lamb should be tender and beginning to fall away from the bone. Check the sauce for seasoning.

Serve hot from the casserole dish. Serves 4.

PER SERVING	
Energy Kcals	698
Protein g	34.9
Fat g	57.7
Polyunsaturated fatty acids g	2.98
Saturated fatty acids g	27.87
Carbohydrate g	10.5
Calcium mg	66

Made into smaller kebabs, it could also be a little starter served with tomato chilli relish (see page 142).

Don't forget to soak the wooden skewers before threading on the meat, to prevent charring.

Marinated Lamb Kebabs

These Middle Eastern-style kebabs remind me of summer barbecues. It is one of my husband Ian's favourite dishes, which I often cook served with Spiced Rice see page 129, a Tomato and Mint Salsa see page 140 and a Cucumber, Mint and Soya 'Yogurt' Salad see page 154, a perfect combination. In this recipe I have grilled the kebabs, however they are also perfect for barbecuing.

1¹/₂ lb	cubed lean leg of lamb	700 g
3 tbsps	olive oil	3 tbsps
2 tbsps	soy sauce	2 tbsps
1	large sprig of rosemary, leaves pulled of the stalk	1
4	cloves garlic, crushed	4
1	red or green pepper	1
1	onion	1
8	bay leaves	8
4 or 8	wooden or metal skewers	4 or 8
1	lemon to garnish	1

In a large bowl mix the lamb pieces with the olive oil, soy sauce, rosemary, and garlic.

Leave in the fridge to marinade for 4 hours or more.

Cut pepper and onion into 2 cm (³/₄ inch) squares.

Thread the lamb pieces onto the skewers alternating each piece of lamb with a square of onion then pepper with 2 bay leaves on each skewer.

Place on high shelf under hot grill for about 4-6 minutes each side, until the outside is well browned and the inside is still slightly pink and juicy.

Serve with wedges of lemon. Serves 4.

PER SERVING	
Energy Kcals	412
Protein g	33.4
Fat g	28.5
Polyunsaturated fatty acids g	1.78
Saturated fatty acids g	11.08
Carbohydrate g	5.8
Calcium mg	28

Follow the recipe using chicken legs and thighs to make Chicken Tagine.

This dish is equally as delicious made with dried apricots.

Lamb Tagine

This Moroccan meat stew derives its name from the traditional round dish with a conical lid resembling a pointed hat. The pieces of meat are slow cooked with spices and either prunes or apricots. The generous quantities of black pepper and spices provide a delicate balance with the sweetness of the fruit. I have used boned shoulder of lamb although leg of lamb would be equally as good. You could serve this dish with the traditional accompaniment of couscous and a crisp salad.

8 oz	stoned dried prunes	225 g
2 lb	boned shoulder of lamb	900 g
1 oz	plain flour	30 g
2 tsps	ground cumin	2 tsps
1 tsp	ground cinnamon	1 tsp
2 tsps	ground coriander	2 tsps
1 tsp	ground black pepper	1 tsp
2 tbsps	vegetable oil	2 tbsps
1	large onion, fine chopped	1
2	cloves garlic, crushed	2
1½ pt	good stock (beef, lamb or chicken)	875 ml
	salt	
1 tbsp	chopped fresh coriander	1 tbsp

Put the prunes in a small bowl and pour over enough water to cover completely. Leave to soak overnight.

Pre-heat the oven to 170C, 325F, gas 3.

Cut the lamb into large chunks about 5 x 5 cm (2 x 2 inch) and remove excess fat, skin and gristle.

On a large plate mix the flour, cumin, cinnamon, coriander and pepper. Roll the lamb pieces in the flour mixture, coating well.

Heat a large frying pan with half a tablespoon oil and brown the lamb pieces half at a time.

Place lamb pieces in a large casserole dish or a tagine. Brown the rest of the lamb in another half a tablespoon oil and place in the dish.

Add remaining 1 tablespoon oil to the pan with the onions and garlic, cook for about 2 minutes then tip in the remaining flour and spice mixture.

Stir for 1 minute, then gradually pour in half of the stock and mix well.

PER SERVING	
Energy Kcals	657
Protein g	43.1
Fat g	46.7
Polyunsaturated fatty acids g	2.36
Saturated fatty acids g	19.14
Carbohydrate g	29.2
Calcium mg	79

Pour this sauce and the remaining stock over the lamb, cover with foil and bake for 1½ hours until the meat is tender and beginning to fall apart.

Remove from oven and pour off the liquid into a medium saucepan. Stir the prunes and their soaking liquid into the saucepan. Bring to the boil over medium heat, reduce until slightly thick, you should have about 425 ml (¾ pint) of liquid.

Season well with salt. Pour over lamb and either leave to cool until required or reheat in the oven until piping hot, approximately 20 minutes. Sprinkle with fresh coriander to serve. Serves 4.

Pork Steak with a Hazelnut and Sage Crust

In this recipe a simple pork steak is coated in a crisp hazelnut and sage coating, transforming it into something far more exotic. I recommend you make the Creamy Cider and Wholegrain Mustard Sauce (see page 135) to compliment the pork steak perfectly.

5 oz	hazelnuts	150 g
10	fresh sage leaves	10
4	lean leg of pork steaks, off the bone	4
1	level tablespoon plain flour, seasoned with salt and pepper	1
1	large egg, beaten	1
1 tbsp	oat drink	1 tbsp
1 oz	vegan margarine	25 g
1 tsp	vegetable oil	1 tsp
	salt and pepper	

In a food processor grind the hazelnuts with the sage leaves until quite fine but not completely powdery. Tip onto a large plate. Trim any excess fat off the pork and roll in the seasoned flour. Next coat the floured pork steaks evenly in the beaten egg mixed with the oat drink.

Lastly roll the pork steaks in the hazelnut and sage mixture. Refrigerate until needed. Pre-heat the oven to 200C, 400F, gas 6.

In large frying pan melt the margarine with the oil over a medium heat.

Lay the pork in the hot fat and cook for several minutes until golden brown. Turn over and repeat on other side.

Put the pork steaks in an oven-proof dish and bake in oven for about 8 minutes. Serves 4.

This could be made with fillet of pork, cut into medallions or for a more economical dish use pork chops.

PER SERVING	
Energy Kcals	622
Protein g	34.4
Fat g	55.9
Polyunsaturated fatty acids g	7.68
Saturated fatty acids g	12.20
Carbohydrate g	4.1
Calcium mg	68

This could also be done with whole trout. Slash the skin with 3 diagonal slashes either side and marinate. Cook under a hot grill for about 4 minutes on either side so that the skin turns crispy brown.

Try this dish using other fish fillets such as salmon, cod or haddock.

Fillet of Trout Tandoori Style

Trout is still a fairly inexpensive fish. In some supermarkets you can also find organic trout that has not been commercially farmed, and even this is quite affordable. For anyone who may find plain fish bland, this dish is both interesting in colour and flavour. Serve with Minted Yoghurt Sauce on page 136, some brown rice and a salad.

For Marinade

2 tsps	grated fresh ginger	2 tsps
2	cloves garlic, crushed	2
1 tsp	salt	1 tsp
1 tsp	ground cumin	1 tsp
1/2 tsp	chilli powder	1/2 tsp
1 tsp	ground turmeric	1 tsp
2 tsps	paprika	2 tsps
1 tbsp	sunflower oil	1 tbsp
2 tbsps	lemon juice	2 tbsps
2 tbsps	garam masala	2 tbsps
2	big or 4 small rainbow trout, filleted and pin bones removed	2
1 tbsp	groundnut oil	1 tbsp
1	lemon cut in wedges	1
	watercress to garnish	

Mix all the marinade ingredients together in a bowl.

Spread the marinade over the trout fillets, putting most of the marinade on the skinless side.

Leave in the fridge to marinate for up to six hours.

Heat large non-stick pan with the groundnut oil.

Fry the fillets about 2-4 minutes on each side until golden and crisp (the time depends on thickness of fillet).

Serve on a warm plate garnished with lemon wedges and watercress. Serves 4.

PER SERVING	
Energy Kcals	280
Protein g	37.1
Fat g	15.9
Polyunsaturated fatty acids g	5.6
Saturated fatty acids g	2.89
Carbohydrate g	0.3
Calcium mg	48.6

Try this sauce with salmon, cod, trout fillet or smoked fish.

If watercress is unavailable, baby spinach leaves make a good alternative.

For a delicious vegetarian dish serve the sauce with warm new potatoes and hard-boiled eggs.

Grilled Fillet of Sea Trout with Creamy Watercress Sauce

This sauce has a lovely creaminess and colour which compliments grilled fillets of sea trout perfectly. Serve with new potatoes and steamed vegetables. Watercress is a valuable source of vitamins and minerals. It is rich in potassium, calcium and phosphorus, as well as having good quantities of iron, iodine, sodium and magnesium. For this sauce the watercress is hardly cooked at all, this helps retain the nutrients and the colour.

1/2 tbsp	mild olive or sunflower oil	1/2 tbsp
4	sea trout fillets (about 200 g per person)	4
10 fl oz	good fish stock (could use chicken or vegetable bouillon)	275 ml
3 oz	watercress, washed	75 g
7 oz	mayonnaise	200 g
1 tbsp	freshly squeezed lemon juice	1 tbsp
	salt and freshly ground pepper	

Lightly oil the fish and lay the fillets on a baking sheet. Pre-heat the grill.

In a small pan bring the stock to the boil.

Remove the stock from the heat and stir in the watercress. Pour into a liquidiser and blend thoroughly until you have a smooth green liquid.

Pour the sauce back into the pan and gradually whisk in the mayonnaise, it should slightly thicken and have the consistency of single cream. Season well.

Place the fish fillets under hot grill.

Cook for 4-5 minutes, turn, and repeat for 2 minutes until the fish is just cooked through (the cooking time will slightly depend on the thickness of the fish fillets).

Lay the fish fillets on warm serving plates.

Gently warm the sauce, whisking continuously and gradually add the lemon juice.

Spoon the sauce over the fish fillets and serve. Serves 4.

PER SERVING	
Energy Kcals	591
Protein g	40.4
Fat g	47.5
Polyunsaturated fatty acids g	4.34
Saturated fatty acids g	5.86
Carbohydrate g	0.2
Calcium mg	63

Use cheaper cuts of fish such as coley or red fish. Also for an alternative omit the prawns and use 2 hard-boiled eggs instead.

Flaky Fish, Prawn and Leek Pie

This dish can be prepared in advance and then chilled prior to the final cooking. It is an impressive and tasty supper for your friends. Serve with new or boiled potatoes and green vegetables.

12 oz	fish fillet (haddock, cod, salmon etc)	350 g
	salt and freshly ground pepper	
2 oz	vegan margarine	50 g
1 oz	plain flour	25 g
2	small leeks, finely sliced	2
5 fl oz	vegetable stock (or a stock made with prawn shells)	150 ml
5 fl oz	oat drink	150 ml
2 tbsps	chopped parsley	2 tbsps
1 tsp	chopped dill or tarragon	1 tsp
1 tbsp	capers drained (optional)	1 tbsp
1/2 tbsp	lemon juice	1/2 tbsp
6 oz	freshly peeled prawns or thawed frozen prawns	175 g
1 lb	puff pastry	450 g
1	egg beaten for the glaze	1

Pre-heat the oven to 220C, 425F, gas 7. Lay the fish in a greased baking dish, season well with salt and pepper, dot with 10 g (1/2 oz) of the margarine.

Cover with tin foil and bake for 15-20 minutes until the fish is just cooked, remove from the oven and allow the fish to cool. Remove the skin and any bones from the fish, and flake into large pieces.

Melt remaining margarine in a saucepan, add the leeks and gently sauté for 10-15 minutes, stirring regularly, until the leeks are tender.

Stir the flour into the leeks and cook for about 2 minutes over a medium heat until the flour is cooked but not browned.

Gradually stir the stock and oat drink into the flour, stirring continuously; simmer for about 5 minutes, the sauce should become thick.

Season with herbs, capers, lemon juice, salt and pepper.

Carefully stir the fish into the sauce then leave to cool completely. When cool stir in the prawns.

On a floured surface, roll the pastry into a 35 cm (14 inch) square.

PER SERVING	
Energy Kcals	499
Protein g	20.3
Fat g	33.6
Polyunsaturated fatty acids g	7.2
Saturated fatty acids g	11.1
Carbohydrate g	30.9
Calcium mg	95.6

Lift onto a large oiled baking sheet, lightly glaze the edge of the pastry with the beaten egg.

Spoon the cold fish and prawn filling in the centre of the pastry.

Pull the opposite corners of the pastry to the centre and pinch all the edges together firmly, so you have a square with the pinched edges in the shape of a cross.

Glaze pastry all over with beaten egg.

Bake for about 25-30 minutes, until pastry is golden and risen.

Serve immediately. Serves 6.

Choose fish fillets of an even thickness and preferably no more than 2 cm (¾ inch) thick for best results. This allows the spices to be well absorbed into the fish.

Cajun Blackened Fish

This is a really interesting way of cooking any fish fillet such as haddock, cod or red fish. It is also delicious made with salmon fillet and served with a tangy salsa. Serve with plain basmati rice.

3 tbsps	Cajun spice mix (if you are unable to buy Cajun spice mix, follow the recipe on page 147)	3 tbsps
2 tsps	sweet paprika powder	2 tsps
4	fish fillets (about 200 g per portion), skinned	4
1 tbsp	sunflower oil	1 tbsp
2 oz	vegan margarine	50 g

Mix 2 tablespoons of the Cajun spices with the paprika (remember to save 1 tablespoon of Cajun spice mix for later).

Coat the fish liberally in the spice mix and refrigerate for 6-8 hours. The longer the fish is left coated in the spice mix the more flavour it will have.

Heat large non-stick shallow pan over high heat with the oil. Place fillets in hot pan to cook 2 minutes on high heat.

Turn and cook further few minutes until just cooked though.

Each side of the fish should be well charred. Remove the fish from the pan and keep warm.

In the same pan melt the margarine, gently so it does not split, mix in the remaining tablespoon of Cajun spice mix.

Serve fish on hot plate and pour melted spiced margarine over each fillet. Serves 4.

PER SERVING	
Energy Kcals	253
Protein g	30
Fat g	14.7
Polyunsaturated fatty acids g	4.5
Saturated fatty acids g	3.7
Carbohydrate g	0.12
Calcium mg	18.6

Right:
Mediterranean Vegetable and Chick Pea Lasagne (page 107)

Tuna is readily available from most supermarkets and fishmongers. Keep an eye out for it when it is on special offer. If it is fresh, it is good for freezing, provided it hasn't been previously frozen.

Griddled Tuna Loin with Salsa Verde

This sauce is unusually tangy. It goes extremely well with griddled fresh tuna or swordfish. You can store the salsa in the fridge for several days. Serve this dish with rice or new potatoes.

Salsa

3½ fl oz	olive oil	100 ml
2 oz	drained cornichons (you could use gherkins)	50 g
2 oz	drained capers	50 g
	juice from 1 lemon	
	bunch fresh parsley	
	bunch fresh dill	
	bunch fresh coriander	
4	(175-200 g/6-7 oz) tuna loin steaks, about 2 cm (¾ inch) thick	4
	oil for brushing	
	salt and freshly ground pepper	

Place all the salsa ingredients in a food processor or liquidiser and blend until just smooth.

Lightly oil a griddle pan, brush tuna with oil and sprinkle with salt and pepper.

When pan is very hot, griddle the tuna steaks for about 1 minute.

Turn the fish when it has changed to white colour two thirds of the way through, and has brown griddle marks on the underneath.

Turn the steaks quickly and cook on the other side for about 30 seconds.

Cook according to personal preference, I personally like it to be slightly pink in the middle, this also keeps the tuna tender.

Transfer to warm plates and spoon a dollop of salsa on the top. Serves 4.

PER SERVING	
Energy Kcals	504
Protein g	44.6
Fat g	36.1
Polyunsaturated fatty acids g	5.25
Saturated fatty acids g	6.18
Carbohydrate g	0.2
Calcium mg	38

Left:
Celeriac, Walnut and Apple Salad with a Mint Tofu Mayonnaise (page 153)

This dressing would also be suitable served with mackerel.

Grated horseradish can be bought in a jar from some health food shops, farm shops and supermarkets. It lasts well in the fridge and can be mixed to make a creamed horseradish. If preferred substitute grated fresh ginger for the horseradish.

Grilled Fillet of Grey Mullet with Soy, Honey and Horseradish Dressing

Grey mullet is quite an inexpensive fish, which is slightly oily, although not as oily as mackerel or herrings. The warm dressing adds an oriental touch to the dish, which compliments the fish well by cutting the oiliness. Delicious served with noodles or rice and stir-fry vegetables. Ask your fishmonger to fillet the mullet.

4	fillets grey mullet, each weighing about 200 g (7 oz)	4
1 tbsp	olive oil	1 tbsp
Dressing		
4	spring onions	4
2 tbsps	light soy sauce	2 tbsps
2 tbsps	groundnut oil	2 tbsps
1 tsp	balsamic vinegar	1 tsp
2 tsps	fresh grated horseradish	2 tsps
2 tsps	runny honey	2 tsps

Cut 2 of the spring onions into thin julienne strips for garnish. Finely chop the remaining 2 spring onions.

In a small saucepan, combine the chopped spring onions, soy sauce, groundnut oil, balsamic, horseradish and honey and mix well.

Heat the grill, lay the grey mullet on a lightly oiled baking sheet, brush the fish with olive oil and season with salt and pepper.

Grill for about 4 minutes either side until the fish is cooked through and golden.

Lay the fish on a warm plate.

Warm the dressing up slightly and spoon over the mullet.

Garnish each fillet with the strips of spring onions to serve. Serves 4.

PER SERVING	
Energy Kcals	293
Protein g	37.6
Fat g	15.1
Polyunsaturated fatty acids g	1.75
Saturated fatty acids g	1.36
Carbohydrate g	1.8
Calcium mg	141

I also occasionally do this recipe using fillets of salmon, which is a delicious alternative for those who are not keen on skate. Pan-fry the salmon without oil in a very hot non-stick pan to achieve a crisp coating.

Grilled Skate Wing with a Warm Vierge Dressing

This dish looks colourful and delicious, and is very easy to prepare. The dressing can be made in advance. Serve with rice or potatoes and a few leaves of watercress or baby spinach for a highly nutritious meal.

Dressing

1	red pepper	1
1	red onion, peeled	1
2 tbsps	capers, drained	2 tbsps
2 tbsps	sliced black olives	2 tbsps
6 tbsps	olive oil	6 tbsps
2 tbsps	balsamic vinegar	2 tbsps
1 tbsp	lemon juice	1 tbsp
1 tbsp	chopped parsley	1 tbsp
	salt and freshly ground pepper	
4	skate wings weighing about 225-250 g (8-9 oz) each or 2 bigger wings each cut in half	4
	olive oil for brushing	
	salt and freshly ground pepper	

Halve the pepper and remove seeds, slice thinly lengthways. Halve the onion and also slice thinly lengthways.

Mix the remaining dressing ingredients in a bowl with the pepper and onion and season with salt and pepper.

Pre-heat the grill. Lay the skate wings on a large greased tray, brush with olive oil and season with salt and pepper.

Grill for about 8-10 minutes either side, until the flesh begins to part from the bone easily and loses its transparent look.

Serve each skate on a warm plate. Warm the dressing in a small pan.

Spoon dressing over each skate. The peppers and onions will sit on top of the skate, whilst the juices from the dressing will surround the skate. Serves 4.

PER SERVING	
Energy Kcals	328
Protein g	16.2
Fat g	26.5
Polyunsaturated fatty acids g	2.48
Saturated fatty acids g	3.75
Carbohydrate g	6.3
Calcium mg	60

Use any white fish fillets.
The uncooked fish fillets topped with the crust may be prepared the day before and stored in the fridge.

Roasted Fillet of Cod with a Herb and 'Cheese' Style Crust

This is a great way to cook plain white fish. We have made this dish at our family restaurants, with a herb and fresh Parmesan crust, so I was surprised at how tasty it was made with the soya cheese and mustard powder instead of Parmesan.
Serve with the Aioli Sauce (see page 132), new potatoes and green vegetables.

4	chunks of cod fillet (about 200-240 g/7-8 oz per person)	2
6 oz	white bread	175 g
4 oz	homemade soya cheese (see page 145) or use bought soya cheddar	110 g
1 tsp	mustard powder	1 tsp
1	bunch of parsley	1
	good sprig of fresh dill	
	good sprig of fresh basil	
2 tbsps	olive oil	2 tbsps
	salt and freshly ground pepper	

Pre-heat the oven to 190C, 375F, gas 5. Lay the fish portions skin side down on large greased baking sheet.

In a food processor, process the bread, soya cheese, mustard powder and herbs until well crumbed.

Stir in the olive oil and season well. Press the mixture on the top of the fish fillets, so it lies evenly about 1/2 cm (1/4 inch) thick.

Lay the fish on the baking sheet and roast in the oven for about 15-20 minutes until the crust is golden and the fish is cooked through.

Serve on warm plates. Serves 4.

PER SERVING	
Energy Kcals	327
Protein g	19.4
Fat g	13.9
Polyunsaturated fatty acids g	0.59
Saturated fatty acids g	0.77
Carbohydrate g	33.2
Calcium mg	196

If using wooden skewers, soak them in hot water for several minutes before threading the food on to them. This helps prevent them charring during cooking.

They would be equally as delicious made using salmon or swordfish and may be less expensive.

Monkfish and King Prawn Brochettes

Monkfish is an ideal fish for brochettes as it has a slightly meaty texture and holds its shape well. These would be perfect for a barbecue or a smart dinner party dish. They could be served with plain basmati rice which looks quite stylish put into a ramekin or tea cup and turned out onto each plate as a timbale shape.

1lb 4oz	fresh monkfish tail	560 g
16	king prawns – uncooked if possible, either in or out of shell	16
4	wooden or metal skewers	4
	lime and coriander dressing on page 162	

Prepare monkfish; skin, fillet and cut into $2^{1}/_{2}$ cm (1 inch) square cubes (try and aim for about 16-20 cubes in total).

Push alternate cubes of monkfish then king prawn onto the 4 skewers.

Cover and leave in the fridge until required. Pre-heat the grill. Lay the kebabs on a suitable baking dish for grilling.

Brush the kebabs with the dressing. Cook under hot grill 5-8 minutes.

Turn and repeat until the fish becomes slightly golden in colour. Baste occasionally with the dressing. Serve on hot plates.

Pour any juices from oven dish over the brochettes.

Warm the remaining dressing in a small saucepan and spoon some of it over each brochette ensuring each person gets plenty of chilli, ginger and coriander mixture.

Garnish with chopped coriander leaves. Serve any remaining dressing in a jug. Serves 4.

PER SERVING	
Energy Kcals	240
Protein g	36.8
Fat g	8.8
Polyunsaturated fatty acids g	2.58
Saturated fatty acids g	1.73
Carbohydrate g	3.6
Calcium mg	87

Mackerel should be bought very fresh, make sure the fish you choose is bright, rigid and shiny not dull and tired looking.

Crunchy Oat-Coated Mackerel Fillets

For this dish the mackerel fillets have been cooked in crunchy golden porridge oats, making this dish more appealing to those who may not be fish lovers, but who know the benefits of eating fresh oily fish. A tangy sauce such as the Gooseberry and Ginger Sauce on page 139 is the perfect accompaniment as the sharpness of the gooseberries cuts the oiliness of the fish.

4	mackerel fillets, about 200 g (7 oz) each	4
4 tbsps	oat drink	4 tbsps
4 tbsps	fine porridge oats	4 tbsps
2 tbsps	olive oil	2 tbsps
1	large lemon cut into wedges	1

Remove any small bones from the mackerel fillets.
Dip each fillet first in the oat drink then roll them liberally in the oats.
Heat a large frying pan with the oil.
When hot, fry the fillets for about 2-3 minutes on either side until crisp and golden and just cooked through.
Serve on a hot plate with wedges of lemon. Serves 4.

PER SERVING	
Energy Kcals	573
Protein g	40.1
Fat g	41.6
Polyunsaturated fatty acids g	7.60
Saturated fatty acids g	7.69
Carbohydrate g	10.1
Calcium mg	58

For a delicious vegan dish try using parsnips instead of haddock and potato.

Potato-Crusted Haddock and Curried Tomato Bake

Serve as a complete meal, maybe with a few salad leaves or baby spinach. The bake can be made a day in advance and kept in the fridge before cooking. The addition of coconut milk gives the dish a delicious buttery flavour.

1½ lbs	waxy potatoes	675 g
2 tbsps	olive oil	2 tbsps
1	medium onion, finely chopped	1
1 tbsp	chopped fresh ginger	1 tbsp
2	cloves garlic, crushed	2
1 tsp	garam masala	1 tsp
1 tsp	ground turmeric	1 tsp
2 tsps	ground cumin	2 tsps
1 tsp	ground coriander	1 tsp
6	tomatoes (about 480 g/1 lb), chopped coarsely (or use 1 tin of chopped tomatoes)	6
1 tsp	vegan bouillon powder	1 tsp
2 tbsps	chopped fresh coriander leaves	2 tbsps
4	small fillets or 2 large fillets fresh haddock, skinned, about 175-200 g (6-7 oz) per person	4
5 fl oz	coconut milk	150 ml
	salt and freshly ground pepper	

Pre-heat the oven to 190C, 375F, gas 5. Peel and slice the potatoes into slices about 5 mm (¼ inch) thick.

Boil or steam the potatoes for about 8-10 minutes until half cooked, allow to cool.

Heat 1 tablespoon of the olive oil in a medium pan, sweat the onion, ginger and garlic for about 5 minutes until soft.

Stir in the ground spices and cook, stirring well, for about 2 minutes.

Add the tomatoes and bouillon powder and stir over the heat for about 5-10 minutes or until tomato is tender, stir in the fresh coriander and season well.

Layer half the potatoes on the base of a large greased baking dish.

PER SERVING	
Energy Kcals	381
Protein g	43.5
Fat g	7.6
Polyunsaturated fatty acids g	1.37
Saturated fatty acids g	1.15
Carbohydrate g	38.4
Calcium mg	88

Cut the fish fillets into quarters and lay them over the potatoes.

Spoon the tomato sauce over the fish, covering well.

Top with the remaining potatoes, pour over the coconut milk and drizzle with 1 tablespoon olive oil. Season with salt and freshly ground pepper.

Bake for about 25 minutes until cooked through.

Grill the top if necessary for a golden potato crust. Serves 4.

Smoked Haddock, Tomato and Leek in Dill Pancakes

These pancakes were a great success, and enjoyed by all the family. Serve with new potatoes and salad.

For the filling

1 lb	smoked haddock fillet	450 g
1 pt	oat drink	570 ml
2	medium leeks, cleaned, sliced	2
2 oz	vegan margarine	50 g
1½ oz	plain flour	40 g
1 tsp	Dijon or wholegrain mustard	1 tsp
	salt and pepper	
	large pinch of ground nutmeg and mace	
1 tsp	vegan bouillon powder	1 tsp
5 tbsps	soya cream	5 tbsps
3	tomatoes, diced finely, seeds discarded	3

For the pancakes

4 oz	plain flour	110 g
½ tsp	salt	½ tsp
2	large eggs	2
½ pt	oat drink	275 ml
2 tbsps	sunflower oil	2 tbsps
1 tbsp	chopped fresh dill (or ½ tablespoon dried)	1 tbsp
	vegetable oil for frying the pancakes	

Try using blanched chopped spinach instead of tomatoes for a delicious variation.

For a vegetarian dish, fill with chopped egg, leek and spinach. Or how about using prawns in the filling?

Make them in advance and refrigerate or freeze (as long as the haddock has not been previously frozen). Defrost thoroughly before cooking.

PER SERVING	
Energy Kcals	342
Protein g	27.7
Fat g	23.0
Polyunsaturated fatty acids g	8.25
Saturated fatty acids g	4.70
Carbohydrate g	13.2
Calcium mg	78

To make the filling:

Pre-heat the oven to 200C, 400F, gas 6. Arrange the haddock skin-side down in a greased baking dish.

Pour over 275 ml ($^1/_2$ pint) of the oat drink.

Cover with tin foil and bake in the oven for 15-20 minutes until the fish is just cooked.

Pour the cooking liquid into a jug with the remaining 275 ml ($^1/_2$ pint) of oat drink and set aside for filling.

Flake haddock, remove bones and skin and set aside.

Bring a small pan of water to the boil and cook the leeks for about 4 minutes until just tender. Drain and run under cold water to refresh.

In a medium saucepan, melt the margarine then add the flour, mixing well, heat through, then gradually stir in the oat drink mixture.

When you have a smooth liquid, bring to the boil, stirring thoroughly for several minutes, until the sauce thickens.

Add the mustard, seasonings, bouillon and soya cream and stir well.

Divide the sauce into two. In one bowl, mix 275 ml ($^1/_2$ pint) of the sauce with the leeks, flaked smoked haddock and tomatoes. The other quantity of sauce should be set aside for the pancake topping.

To make pancakes:

Sift flour in a bowl with the salt.

Make a well in the centre and break the eggs into it.

Whisk the eggs, gradually incorporating the flour then slowly beat in the oat drink. The mixture should be the consistency of single cream. Then beat in the sunflower oil and the dill.

Heat a small frying pan with some vegetable oil, then tip the oil out onto a saucer to reuse for the next pancake.

Spoon about 2 tablespoons of batter into the pan, swirl around until the base of pan is evenly covered. Cook for about half a minute, lift the edge with palette knife and see if it is tinged gold as it should be.

Flip over the pancake and cook for about 15 seconds.

Slide the pancake onto a plate whilst you use up the remaining batter.

Make as many as 12 pancakes.

To assemble pancakes:

Pre-heat the oven to 200C, 400F, gas 6. Oil a large baking dish.

Divide the filling equally among the pancakes, spoon onto the centre and roll to form a cigar shape. Lay flap side down evenly spaced in the baking dish.

Cover with the remaining sauce, leaving the top of the pancakes slightly uncovered.

Bake for about 20-25 minutes until golden. The tops of the pancakes should be slightly crispy. Serves 4.

You could also use smoked kipper fillets in this recipe. As they have many small pin bones I would suggest you process the kipper in a food processor first. The dish would contain plenty of calcium as the bones will have been ground up.

Smoked Fish Cakes

These fish cakes make a pleasant change from the cod and salmon variety you can buy from supermarkets. I recommend that you serve them with the Tangy Mayonnaise on page 140 and a crisp salad.

1 lb	mashing potatoes	450 g
1 lb	mixed fish (1 small fillet of smoked haddock, 1 fillet of smoked mackerel, 1 small fillet of white fish [cod, haddock])	450 g
3	spring onions, washed, outer leaves removed, cut into thin rings	3
1	large egg, beaten	1
2 tsps	capers	2 tsps
2 tbsps	chopped parsley	2 tbsps
1 tbsp	lemon juice	1 tbsp
1 tsp	anchovy essence	1 tsp
	freshly ground pepper	

Coating

1½ oz	plain seasoned flour	40 g
1	egg, beaten	1
1 tbsp	oat drink	1 tbsp
5 oz	breadcrumbs	150 g
	vegetable oil for pan-frying the fish cakes	
	lemon wedges to serve	

Pre-heat the oven to 180C, 350F, gas 4. Peel and chop the potatoes. Boil until soft then mash well.

Place the fish (except smoked mackerel, which has already been cooked) on a greased baking tray, cover with tin foil and bake for about 20 minutes, until the fish is just cooked. Leave to cool slightly.

Flake the haddock, cod and mackerel into a large bowl, discarding any skin and bones.

In a large bowl, mix together the mashed potato, the flaked fish and all the remaining fish cake ingredients and seasonings, mix thoroughly.

Divide the mixture into 8 equal balls, flatten out and pat into a neat shape.

PER SERVING	
Energy Kcals	348
Protein g	28.4
Fat g	4.6
Polyunsaturated fatty acids g	0.47
Saturated fatty acids g	0.14
Carbohydrate g	58.1
Calcium mg	132

Dip each fish cake into the flour, then the beaten egg mixed with oat drink, then the breadcrumbs.

Pan-fry the fish cakes in a small amount of vegetable oil, for about 3 minutes either side on medium heat until golden brown.

Then transfer the fish cakes to the oven and cook for about 10-15 minutes, they should then be well heated throughout and crisp on the outside.

Serve with lemon wedges. Serves 4.

Smoked Cod Rarebit

Smoked fish goes very well with the tomatoes and the cheese-style topping. For anyone missing the flavour of real cheese this tastes quite convincingly cheesy! Delicious served with rice or potatoes.

4	smoked cod fillets, skinned (175-200 g /6-7 oz) or bigger fillets cut in half	4
4	large tomatoes	4
1	egg	1
1	egg yolk	1
2 tbsps	Dijon mustard	2 tbsps
3 oz	homemade soya cheese on page 145 or hard soya cheddar, grated	75 g
1 tsp	Worcestershire sauce	1 tsp
	salt, freshly ground pepper and a pinch of cayenne	
1 tbsp	freshly chopped parsley	1 tbsp
	watercress to garnish	

Pre-heat the oven to 180C, 350F, gas 4. Lay the fillets on a large greased baking dish, keeping them separate.

Cut each tomato into six discs. Cover the fillets with a layer of sliced tomatoes.

Beat together all the remaining ingredients. Spread over the tomatoes to form an even layer.

Bake for 20-25 minutes or until golden and slightly risen.

Lay each fillet onto a warm plate garnished with sprigs of watercress. Serves 4.

If you prefer use smoked haddock fillet.

Ensure you remove all the pin bones before covering with rarebit topping.

PER SERVING	
Energy Kcals	264
Protein g	42.2
Fat g	10.6
Polyunsaturated fatty acids g	0.81
Saturated fatty acids g	0.74
Carbohydrate g	3.0
Calcium mg	131

Experiment with the fillings, it is great filled with ratatouille.

Also try blanched asparagus, when in season, instead of the spinach.

The dish will keep well if covered in the fridge for several days before cooking, however, the raw choux mix may discolour slightly but don't worry as once cooked it will look as good.

Spinach, Almond and Mushroom Gougère

A gougère is a cheese choux pastry ring with a savoury filling. The dish can be stored or even frozen prior to baking, then cooked just before serving, making a great instant meal without getting hot and bothered.

Savoury choux pastry

3½ fl oz	soya milk	100 ml
1½ fl oz	water	50 ml
2 oz	vegan margarine	50 g
2½ oz	strong white flour	60 g
½ tsp	salt	½ tsp
2	eggs, beaten	2
1 tbsp	Dijon mustard	1 tbsp
½ tsp	bouillon powder	½ tsp
	pinch cayenne pepper	

Filling

8 oz	spinach	225 g
1	large onion, finely chopped	1
2	cloves garlic, crushed	2
1 tbsp	olive oil	1 tbsp
7 oz	button mushrooms, wiped and sliced	200 g
6 oz	Tofutti Original (soya cream cheese)	175 g
3 oz	whole blanched or flaked almonds	75 g
½ tbsp	chopped fresh tarragon	½ tbsp
	grated nutmeg	
	salt and freshly ground pepper	

Pre-heat the oven to 200C, 400F, gas 6. Rinse the spinach and discard larger stalks. Place the spinach in a large saucepan with a lid over a medium heat, for about 4 minutes until the spinach is wilted.

Drain and rinse with cold water, squeeze out all the liquid and chop.

To make the pastry; heat the soya milk and water over medium heat, add the margarine until melted.

PER SERVING	
Energy Kcals	509
Protein g	11
Fat g	44.9
Polyunsaturated fatty acids g	18.58
Saturated fatty acids g	8.58
Carbohydrate g	23.1
Calcium mg	193

Tip in the flour and salt and stir vigorously over the heat until the mixture forms a ball.

Set aside to cool slightly, then gradually add the eggs, mustard and seasonings and beat until you have a shiny smooth pastry.

For the filling; sweat the onion and garlic in olive oil for about 5 minutes.

Add the sliced mushrooms and fry them for a further 4 minutes, allow to cool, pour off any excess liquid.

Combine the soya cream cheese, almonds, spinach, tarragon and seasonings with the mushrooms and stir well.

Grease a large oven dish (or 4 individual dishes).

Spoon the raw choux pastry around the edge and then the spinach filling in centre.

Bake for 20-25 minutes until crisp and golden around the edges, and well risen.

Serve immediately before the pastry sinks. Serves 4.

Puy Lentil and Mushroom Moussaka

This is one of my favourite vegetarian dishes. As with traditional moussaka I put egg yolks in the topping which sets slightly, this increases the protein value of the meal. There is no need to use a cheese substitute in the white sauce. Serve with green vegetables or a salad.

Obviously for a vegan omit the egg yolks, it is still delicious. Substitute different pulses or beans for the puy lentils such as green lentils or split peas, aduki or black-eye beans, or you could use TVP to replicate the real thing.

If you eat meat then lamb mince could be used.

Kallo organic liquid seasoning is found in most supermarkets and health food shops, it contains soya and other natural flavourings and is a good ingredient to add flavour to many dishes.

6 oz	puy lentils	175 g
1	large or 2 small aubergines, sliced into 1 cm (1/2 inch) discs	1
1 tbsp	olive oil, and more to drizzle	1 tbsp
1	medium onion, finely chopped	1
3	cloves garlic, crushed	3
1	red pepper, chopped	1
1	400 g tin chopped tomatoes	1
1 tbsp	tomato purée	1 tbsp
1 tbsp	tomato ketchup (optional but gives good flavour)	1 tbsp
1 tbsp	chopped fresh basil or 1 teaspoon dried basil	1 tbsp

1 tsp	vegan bouillon	1 tsp
2 tsps	kallo organic liquid seasoning	2 tsps
8 oz	button mushrooms chopped	225 g

White sauce

2 oz	vegan margarine	50 g
1½ oz	plain flour	35 g
1 pt	oat drink	570 ml
1 tsp	vegan bouillon	1 tsp
2 tsps	Dijon mustard	2 tsps
	grated nutmeg	
	salt and cayenne pepper	
2	egg yolks (omit for vegan)	2

Pre-heat the oven to 200C, 400F, gas 6. Wash and drain lentils, cover with plenty of water in a saucepan. Bring to the boil then simmer for about 30 minutes until tender. Drain and put to one side.

Place the aubergine on an oiled baking tray, drizzle with olive oil, and put in oven to roast for 20 minutes.

In a large saucepan, fry onion and garlic in the tablespoon of olive oil for 3 minutes, add the red pepper and fry for a further 5 minutes. Stir in the tinned tomatoes, tomato purée, ketchup, lentils, herbs and seasonings, cook for 5 minutes.

Heat a small frying pan with a drizzle of oil and quickly fry the mushrooms for several minutes and add to the lentil mixture and season thoroughly. Pour the lentil mixture into a large oven dish. Turn off oven, place the lentil mixture into the oven to dry out slightly whilst you are making the white sauce.

In a clean saucepan, melt the margarine, remove from the heat and add the flour, stir well and return to the heat and cook for 1 minute.

Remove from heat and add the oat drink gradually until the sauce is smooth and glossy, return to heat and cook, stirring continuously until it thickens, allow the sauce to boil briefly, then set the pan aside.

Season with bouillon and mustard, nutmeg, salt and pepper and allow to cool for about 10 minutes.

In a small bowl mix 2 tablespoons of sauce with the egg yolks, mixing well, then pour back into the remaining sauce.

Remove baking dish from the oven and reheat oven to 180C, 350F, gas 4.

Place aubergines in a layer over the lentil mixture. Then cover the aubergines with the white sauce.

Bake for about 30 minutes until the sauce is golden brown and bubbling. Serves 4-6.

VEGETARIAN OR VEGAN

PER SERVING

Energy Kcals	463
Protein g	20.4
Fat g	23.8
Polyunsaturated fatty acids g	6.15
Saturated fatty acids g	44.8
Carbohydrate g	120
Calcium mg	193

This dish could also be made using soya beans, black-eye beans, TVP or cashew nuts instead of the chick peas. By adding soya beans or TVP you would increase the protein value of the dish.

Mediterranean Vegetable and Chick Pea Lasagne

This delicious lasagne can be made in advance and frozen before the final cooking stage. I have added chick peas as they have a lovely nutty texture; they also increase the protein content of the dish.

2 tbsps	olive oil	2 tbsps
2	small onions (preferably red), finely chopped	2
3	cloves garlic, crushed	3
1	red or yellow pepper, deseeded and diced	1
1	medium aubergine, cut onto 1 cm (1/2 inch) cubes	1
1	400 g tin chopped tomatoes	1
2	courgettes, diced	2
7 fl oz	vegetable stock	200 ml
1 tbsp	tomato purée	1 tbsp
2 tbsps	sun-dried tomato paste	2 tbsps
2 tsps	chopped fresh oregano (or 1 teaspoon dried)	2 tsps
2 tbsps	chopped fresh parsley	2 tbsps
1	400 g tin of chick peas drained (net drained weight about 240 g) or equivalent cooked from dried	1
	salt and freshly ground pepper	
1	box dried lasagne (no-pre-cooking-required-type) (about 250 g, probably don't need it all)	1
2 oz	soya cheese, finely grated	50 g
1 oz	fine breadcrumbs	25 g

White sauce

1 1/2 oz	vegan margarine	40 g
1 oz	plain flour	25 g
17 1/2 fl oz	oat drink	500 ml
2 tsps	Dijon mustard (or 1/2 teaspoon mustard powder)	2 tsps

VEGAN

PER SERVING

Energy Kcals	316
Protein g	13.1
Fat g	14.6
Polyunsaturated fatty acids g	3.96
Saturated fatty acids g	3.15
Carbohydrate g	36.7
Calcium mg	76

1	level teaspoon vegan bouillon powder	1

salt and freshly ground pepper

Pre-heat the oven to 200C, 400F, gas 6. For the vegetable sauce; heat the oil in a large saucepan and sauté the onions and garlic for about 5 minutes.

Add the pepper and aubergine, fry over a medium heat for 10 minutes stirring occasionally.

Stir in the tomatoes, courgettes, stock, tomato purée and paste, cover and simmer for 10 minutes or until all vegetables are just tender but not overcooked. Mix in the herbs and chick peas and season well. Remove from heat and set to one side.

For the white sauce; melt the margarine in a small pan, add the flour and cook over a medium heat, stirring constantly for about 2 minutes.

Gradually add the oat drink, mustard and bouillon powder and bring to the boil, stirring constantly until the sauce thickens, season well.

In large, greased, rectangular ovenproof dish, spread half the vegetable sauce. Then drizzle about 2 tablespoons white sauce over this, then place one layer of lasagne evenly on top, breaking some lasagne sheets up in order to cover completely.

Pour over the remaining vegetable sauce, then a drizzle of the white sauce followed by a second layer of lasagne sheets.

Cover with the remaining white sauce.

Mix the grated soya cheese with the breadcrumbs and sprinkle this mixture evenly over the top of the dish.

Bake for about 35 minutes until well heated through and the top is bubbling and golden brown.

If necessary grill the top to get it golden brown before serving. Serves 6.

This dish is equally as nice with other types of beans or lentils. Instead of the split peas, aduki beans are particularly good.

The scones could be baked separately as savoury 'cheese-style' scones.

Split Pea and Vegetable Cobbler

A cobbler is a vegetable bake with a savoury scone topping. It is a hearty, filling meal, and extremely economical. This version uses yellow split peas, giving an interesting texture. The addition of soya flour makes the scones more nutritious, and along with the yeast extract and mustard powder gives the scones a savoury cheese taste. Serve with some leafy vegetables. Any left over is great re-heated.

Split pea and vegetable base

4 oz	dry yellow split peas, soaked in cold water for 10 minutes	110 g
1	large onion, finely chopped	1
1 tbsp	olive oil	1 tbsp
1	leek, finely chopped	1
2	sticks celery, finely chopped	2
3	cloves garlic, crushed	3
2	medium carrots, peeled and diced	2
1	400 g tin chopped tomatoes	1
2 tbsps	tomato purée	2 tbsps
6 fl oz	vegetable stock (using vegan bouillon powder)	175 ml
4 oz	french beans, top and tailed and cut into 1/4 lengthways	110 g
1	large sprig fresh thyme	1
1 tbsp	freshly chopped parsley	1 tbsp
	salt and freshly ground pepper	

Scone topping

6 oz	self-raising flour	175 g
2 oz	soya flour (use wholemeal flour if preferred)	50 g
1 tsp	mustard powder	1 tsp
2 oz	vegan margarine	50 g
1 tsp	yeast extract	1 tsp
4 fl oz	cold water	125 ml
	soya milk for brushing	

VEGAN

PER SERVING	
Energy Kcals	329
Protein g	12.9
Fat g	12.7
Polyunsaturated fatty acids g	3.65
Saturated fatty acids g	2.94
Carbohydrate g	43.4
Calcium mg	168

Pre-heat the oven to 200C, 400F, gas 6. Drain the yellow split peas, then tip in to a small saucepan covered with cold water, bring to the boil and simmer for about 20-25 minutes until just tender (not over-cooked as they will be cooked further).

In a separate large saucepan, over a medium heat sweat the onion in the olive oil.

After a couple of minutes add the leek, celery, garlic and carrots, continue cooking for about 8 minutes.

Add the chopped tomatoes, purée and stock and French beans. Continue cooking until the vegetables are just tender, but still slightly crisp (about 5-10 minutes).

Mix in the split peas, herbs and season well.

Pour into large ovenproof dish (preferably a large shallow dish, if the dish is too deep the mixture will not heat through in time). Smooth down and set to one side whilst you make the scone topping.

Mix the flours and mustard powder, rub in the margarine until it resembles breadcrumbs.

Stir the yeast extract into water until dissolved.

Using knife, pour the water into the flour mixture and blend until it forms dough.

Knead lightly in extra flour.

Roll out to about 1 cm (1/2 inch) thick and, using a 4 or 5 cm (1 1/2 or 2 inch) fluted or plain pastry cutter, cut out about 12 scones (allowing for 2 scones per serving).

Place the scones on top of the vegetable mixture, brush with a little soya milk.

Bake in pre-heated oven for 15-20 minutes, until scones are golden and risen.

To serve, spoon onto individual plates with 2 scones sitting on the mixture. Serves 6.

Quorn could be added for extra protein.

Roasted peanuts are also good substituted for the cashew nuts. Instead of soy sauce you could use the traditional Thai fish sauce (nam pla).

Thai Green Vegetable and Cashew Nut Curry

This may seem a long recipe, but once you make the Thai paste it will store well in an airtight jar. The combination of sweet potato, cashew nuts and vegetables in this curry makes it a delicious substantial dish. Serve with Thai jasmine rice.

Paste

1 tsp	coriander seeds	1 tsp
1 tsp	cumin seeds	1 tsp
2 oz	fresh coriander, strip leaves off and save stalks	50 g
4	small green chillies (deseeded and roughly chopped)	4
2	stalks lemon grass, tender inner parts, roughly chopped	2
2	shallots, roughly chopped	2
4	cloves garlic, roughly chopped	4
1 inch	piece fresh ginger, peeled and roughly chopped	2½ cm
2 tbsps	chopped fresh basil	2 tbsps
2 tbsps	chopped fresh mint or lemon mint	2 tbsps
4	kaffir lime leaves	4
2	strips of lime zest	2
2 tbsps	groundnut oil	2 tbsps
	salt and freshly ground pepper	

Curry

	groundnut oil for frying	
6	shallots, halved or quartered	6
3	cloves garlic, finely chopped	3
1 tsp	fennel seeds	1 tsp
1	large aubergine, cut into cubes	1
2	small sweet potatoes (weight about 500 g) peeled and cubed	2
1	large red pepper, cubed	1
½ pt	vegan vegetable stock	275 ml

VEGAN

PER SERVING	
Energy Kcals	342
Protein g	8.7
Fat g	21.2
Polyunsaturated fatty acids g	5.06
Saturated fatty acids g	4.26
Carbohydrate g	32.8
Calcium mg	111

3 oz	French beans, trimmed and cut into 10 mm (1/2 inch pieces)	75 g
3	kaffir lime leaves, fresh or dried	3
1 tsp	light brown sugar	1 tsp
	juice of 1 lime	
3 tbsps	light soy sauce	3 tbsps
1/2 pt	coconut milk	275 ml
	few sprigs of basil and coriander including leftover stalks to garnish	
4 oz	cashew nuts roasted	110 g

To make the paste:

Fry the coriander and cumin seeds in a dry frying pan until darkening slightly to release flavour. Leave to cool, grind in a pestle and mortar or a coffee grinder, until ground and put to one side.

Next process all the remaining ingredients in a food processor to form a paste.

Tip the paste into a bowl and mix in the ground spices.

This paste can be made in advance – it will keep in sealed jar, refrigerated for about one week.

To make the curry:

Heat about 2 tablespoons of groundnut oil in a deep frying pan or wok over a medium heat. Cook shallots until brown.

Add the garlic, fennel seeds and aubergine. Fry for about 4 minutes, set aside on a plate.

Fry sweet potato and peppers in a little more groundnut oil for about 4 minutes.

Add 2 tablespoons of the Thai paste, cook for a further 2 minutes.

Stir in the vegetable stock, aubergine mixture and French beans and cook for 10 minutes.

Add the kaffir leaves, sugar, lime juice, soy sauce and coconut milk and 1 tablespoon remaining Thai paste.

Check seasoning adding salt and pepper.

Simmer for 5 minutes until all vegetables are tender but still slightly firm.

Just before serving, scatter basil, coriander and cashew nuts into the pan. Serves 4.

If you are unable to find all these mushrooms, don't worry just using ordinary mushrooms would be fine, although not as exotic.

Individual Wild Mushroom and Walnut Strudels

These tasty strudels can be made in advance and cooked when required. Serve with a crisp dressed salad and perhaps the Roasted Tomato Sauce (see page 139).

4 oz	stale bread	110 g
3	cloves garlic, peeled	3
	bunch of fresh parsley	
2 tbsps	olive oil	2 tbsps
1	onion, chopped	1
1	small leek, chopped	1
8 oz	mixed mushrooms, such as oyster, shiitake, morel, flat and field	225 g
2 tbsps	soya flour	2 tbsps
1 tbsp	soy sauce	1 tbsp
1 tsp	vegan vegetable bouillon powder	1 tsp
1 tsp	chopped fresh tarragon	1 tsp
2 oz	walnut pieces, roughly chopped	50 g
	freshly ground pepper	
2 oz	vegan margarine	50 g
4	sheets of filo pastry, each measuring about 45.5 x 30.5 cm (18 x 12 inches)	4
	sesame seeds to sprinkle	

Pre-heat the oven to 200C, 400F, gas 6. Place the bread, garlic and parsley in a food processor and process for about 30 seconds or until finely crumbed, tip this breadcrumb mixture into a bowl.

Heat the olive oil in a large pan and sauté the onion and leek over medium heat for about 5 minutes.

If using shiitake and morel mushrooms chop finely and roughly chop flat, oyster or field mushrooms.

Add the chopped mushrooms to the onions and cook for a further 5 minutes.

Mix in the soya flour, soy sauce, bouillon, tarragon and walnuts, fry gently for a further minute. Season with pepper, you may not need to add salt. Leave to cool.

Melt the margarine in a small saucepan.

Lay out a single sheet of filo pastry on floured surface,

VEGAN

PER SERVING	
Energy Kcals	418
Protein g	11.8
Fat g	26.6
Polyunsaturated fatty acids g	10.3
Saturated fatty acids g	5.25
Carbohydrate g	36.4
Calcium mg	106

shortest side at the front, long sides at side, brush the sheet with the margarine.

Sprinkle with a handful of the breadcrumb mixture, covering the entire sheet.

Spoon one quarter of the mushroom mixture at the front of the rectangle, leaving about 3 inches at either end.

Begin to roll up. After one rotation, brush the ends and fold them in 3 inches either side, brush dry sides and roll up into sausage. The mixture should be completely contained in the filo pastry.

Repeat for the remaining strudels, lay them on a greased baking sheet.

Brush with margarine and sprinkle with sesame seeds.

Bake for about 15-20 minutes or until pastry is crisp and golden. Serves 4.

Vegetables

Cumin Spiced Cauliflower

French Beans à la Greque

Crunchy Stir-fried Cabbage and Carrots with Caraway

Piquant Vegetables

Broad Beans with Smoked Bacon

Roasted Parsnips with Sesame and Honey

Potato and Celeriac Boulangère

Creamy Wholegrain Mustard Mashed Potato

Roasted Garlic and Olive Oil Mashed Potato

Spicy Potato Wedges

Pan-fried 'Cheese' Polenta

Sesame Noodles

Sicilian Caponata

Spiced Rice

Yorkshire Puddings

Try this dish with broccoli instead.

Cumin Spiced Cauliflower

This is a interesting way of cooking cauliflower; delicious with rice and other Indian dishes or as a quick light supper with naan bread.

1	large cauliflower	1
1 tbsp	groundnut oil	1 tbsp
1 tsp	cumin seeds	1 tsp
1 tsp	black mustard seeds	1 tsp
1 tsp	ground cumin	1 tsp
1 tsp	ground coriander	1 tsp
1/2 tsp	ground turmeric	1/2 tsp
5 fl oz	vegetable stock	150 ml

Break cauliflower into florets, keeping on as much stalk as possible. Cut the bigger florets if necessary.

Heat oil in a large wok or frying pan. When hot add cumin seeds and mustard seeds.

Cook for one minute stirring continuously, without burning.

Add ground cumin, coriander and turmeric, cook for further minute.

Add cauliflower and toss the florets in the spices. Pour in the vegetable stock and mix thoroughly.

Cover and simmer for about 5 minutes on medium heat until the cauliflower is cooked but still firm.

Serve immediately. Serves 6.

PER SERVING	
Energy Kcals	65
Protein g	5.0
Fat g	4.2
Polyunsaturated fatty acids g	1.47
Saturated fatty acids g	0.6
Carbohydrate g	3.8
Calcium mg	45

You can also use okra for this dish as they contain large amounts of calcium.

This dish is good to freeze, it is also a great way of using up courgettes or runner beans.

French Beans à la Greque

This has to be one of the nicest ways of cooking French beans. In the summer my parents are always giving me buckets full of home grown beans. I usually cook a large batch of this recipe and eat them either hot with a baked potato or cold as part of a salad. This dish seems to improve when reheated the following day.

2 tbsps	olive oil	2 tbsps
2	cloves garlic, crushed	2
12 oz	French beans, top and tailed	350 g
1/2 pt	vegetable stock	275 ml
4 oz	tomato purée	110 g
1 tsp	sugar	1 tsp
	salt and freshly ground pepper	

Heat olive oil in a medium saucepan. Add garlic and French beans and stir over medium heat for 2 minutes.

Add stock, tomato purée and stir well.

Simmer over a low heat, stirring occasionally, for about 15-20 minutes until sauce has reduced slightly and thickened and the beans are just cooked.

Season with sugar, salt and pepper, before serving. Serves 4-6.

PER SERVING	
Energy Kcals	37
Protein g	2.4
Fat g	0.4
Polyunsaturated fatty acids g	0.23
Saturated fatty acids g	0.07
Carbohydrate g	6.4
Calcium mg	35

Crunchy Stir-fried Cabbage and Carrots with Caraway

Use other vegetable combinations, courgettes, red cabbage, Chinese leaves etc.
   You may omit the caraway seeds for children. If you don't like caraway, black mustard seeds are also a good combination with cabbage.

This is an ideal way of cooking vegetables to retain the maximum amount of water soluble vitamins, and the addition of stock gives the stir-fry more flavour. To make more of a meal add chopped bacon with the vegetables and serve with the Spicy Potato Wedges (see page 125).

1 lb	white cabbage	450 g
8 oz	carrots	225 g
2 tbsps	olive oil, or walnut oil	2 tbsps
5 fl oz	vegetable or chicken stock	150 ml
1 tsp	caraway seeds	1 tsp
	salt and freshly ground pepper	

Shred the cabbage finely. Peel the carrots and either cut into thin julienne strips or use a vegetable peeler and make ribbons. Heat a large wok or frying pan, heat the oil until hot, throw in the cabbage and carrots.

Stir-fry for several minutes then add the stock, caraway seeds and seasonings.

Continue frying for a further 3 or 4 minutes until the cabbage is cooked but still slightly crisp.

Serve in a warm dish. Serves 4.

PER SERVING	
Energy Kcals	117
Protein g	2.2
Fat g	8.1
Polyunsaturated fatty acids g	1.11
Saturated fatty acids g	1.11
Carbohydrate g	10.1
Calcium mg	81

Suitable for freezing. Otherwise it lasts well for several days in the fridge.

Piquant Vegetables

I discovered this dish whilst experimenting with Cajun cooking. It makes a delicious accompaniment to Cajun-style fish or chicken.

1 tsp	vegetable oil	1 tsp
1	medium onion	1
1	medium green pepper	1
1	small red pepper	1
3	sticks celery	3
2	cloves garlic, crushed	2
1 tsp	paprika	1 tsp
1 tsp	Cajun spice mix (either bought or the homemade recipe on page 147)	1 tsp
1	400 g can chopped tomatoes	1
1/4 tsp	tabasco	1/4 tsp
1/2 pt	water	275 ml
1/2 tsp	dried oregano	1/2 tsp
1 tsp	sugar	1 tsp
	salt and freshly ground pepper	

Finely chop onion, peppers and celery.

Heat a large frying pan with the oil and sweat the vegetables and garlic for about 5 minutes.

Stir in the spices and fry for one minute then mix in the tomatoes, tabasco, water, oregano and sugar and simmer uncovered for about 12 minutes.

Season with salt and pepper before serving. Serves 4.

PER SERVING	
Energy Kcals	73
Protein g	3.1
Fat g	1.9
Polyunsaturated fatty acids g	0.94
Saturated fatty acids g	0.21
Carbohydrate g	11.7
Calcium mg	44

The season for broad beans is fairly short, although you could use beans defrosted from frozen, which are available throughout the year. Also try with other beans such as cooked haricot, cannellini or butter beans.

Broad Beans with Smoked Bacon

Delicious as a vegetable accompaniment or as a quick supper dish with rice, pasta or potatoes.

2 lb	broad beans	900 g
2 tbsps	olive oil	2 tbsps
1	large red onion, cut in half and thinly sliced	1
6 oz	smoked back or streaky bacon	175 g
2	cloves garlic, crushed	2
½ tbsp	sherry vinegar	½ tbsp
1 tbsp	chopped parsley	1 tbsp
	salt and freshly ground pepper	

Remove the beans from the pods. Steam or boil for about 5-8 minutes until just tender.

Remove the rind from the bacon and cut rashers into strips.

Meanwhile, in large frying pan, heat up 1 tablespoon olive oil, and sauté the onion for about 5 minutes.

Add the bacon and garlic and cook for a further 8-10 minutes over medium heat, until beginning to caramelise and turn golden at the edges, throw in the sherry vinegar and cook for a further minute.

Tip the beans into the mixture and heat through for several minutes.

Remove from heat, add remaining olive oil, parsley, salt and pepper. Serves 4.

PER SERVING	
Energy Kcals	343
Protein g	20.5
Fat g	19.9
Polyunsaturated fatty acids g	3.30
Saturated fatty acids g	4.78
Carbohydrate g	21.6
Calcium mg	73

Use a combination of root vegetables such as carrots, beetroot, sweet potato etc.

Roasted Parsnips with Sesame and Honey

This jazzes up your Sunday roast, and might make parsnips more appealing to children.

1 lb	parsnips	450 g
1 tbsp	vegetable oil	1 tbsp
	salt and freshly ground pepper	
1 tbsp	sesame oil	1 tbsp
1½ tsps	runny honey	1½ tsps
2 tsps	sesame seeds	2 tsps

Pre-heat the oven to 200C, 400F, gas 6. Peel and cut parsnips into about 7.5 cm (3 inch) long and 2.5 cm (1 inch) thick batons.

On a large baking dish, mix the parsnips with the vegetable oil, salt and pepper.

Roast for about 30 minutes, turning once or twice.

When the parsnips are cooked through, golden and slightly crisp, remove from oven.

Mix sesame oil and honey together.

Toss the parsnips with the oil and honey mixture until completely covered.

Sprinkle over sesame seeds. Return to oven and cook for a further 10 minutes.

Serve immediately. Serves 4.

PER SERVING	
Energy Kcals	172
Protein g	2.5
Fat g	10.2
Polyunsaturated fatty acids g	4.32
Saturated fatty acids g	1.35
Carbohydrate g	18.9
Calcium mg	64

Try with parsnip instead of the celeriac.

Potato and Celeriac Boulangère

This combination is a winner; it is a great low fat vegetable accompaniment, with the stock preventing the dish from becoming dry.

14 oz	old potatoes	400 g
10 oz	celeriac	275 g
1	onion, sliced	1
12 fl oz	chicken or vegetable stock	330 ml
1 tbsp	olive oil	1 tbsp
	salt and freshly ground pepper	

Pre-heat the oven to 180C, 350F, gas 4. Peel potatoes and celeriac.

Cut into thin slices. Lay alternating slices of celeriac and potato with the onion in a shallow greased roasting tin, making sure the onion is not on the top.

Season the stock with salt and pepper.

Pour the stock over the potato and celeriac, brush the top with the olive oil, drizzling the remainder over.

Bake uncovered for about one hour until lightly browned on top. To test if the vegetables are cooked, push a metal skewer or sharp knife into the dish and it should feel soft.

If after about 40 minutes, the top is burning but it is not cooked, cover with foil and continue cooking.

Serve immediately. Serves 4.

PER SERVING	
Energy Kcals	137
Protein g	3.5
Fat g	4.3
Polyunsaturated fatty acids g	0.45
Saturated fatty acids g	0.54
Carbohydrate g	22.3
Calcium mg	44

Creamy Wholegrain Mustard Mashed Potato

Delicious with pork or liver, or as a topping for pies such as the Smoked Ham and Lentil pie (see page 52).

1½ lb	old potatoes	700 g
1 tbsp	vegan margarine	1 tbsp
2 tbsps	soya cream	2 tbsps
1 tbsp	wholegrain mustard	1 tbsp
	salt and freshly ground pepper	

Peel and cut potatoes into half or quarter depending on size.

Steam or boil the potatoes until they are cooked through and fairly soft, drain.

In large pan gently melt margarine with soya cream, then remove from the heat.

Tip in the potatoes, mash well, until completely smooth.

Stir in mustard and seasonings. Serve hot. Serves 4.

PER SERVING	
Energy Kcals	213
Protein g	4.8
Fat g	9.1
Polyunsaturated fatty acids g	4.3
Saturated fatty acids g	1.77
Carbohydrate g	29.7
Calcium mg	13

Try using some sweet potato or parsnips for a more exotic touch.

Roasted Garlic and Olive Oil Mashed Potato

This is a great way of making mash without butter and cream, it is also a lot more nutritious. Don't worry, once the garlic is roasted it is not as potent as a whole bulb of raw garlic, and think how healthy it is. Delicious served with meats, fish or just about anything.

1½ lb	old potatoes	700 g
1	head of garlic, whole	1
3 tbsps	olive oil	3 tbsps
1 tsp	maldon salt	1 tsp
	freshly ground pepper to taste	

Pre-heat the oven to 200C, 400F, gas 6. Slice approx 1 cm (½ inch) off the top stalk-end of the garlic so as to just reveal each clove.

Roast in the oven for approx 20-25 minutes until soft and golden not dark brown.

Meanwhile peel the potatoes and either steam or boil until cooked. Don't worry if they are slightly overcooked as this makes for a wetter mashed potato.

When garlic is cool enough to handle, peel off skin and pop out the whole garlic cloves, they should be soft.

In a bowl mash the garlic, olive oil and salt to form a paste.

Add the garlic paste to the mash and more olive oil if it seems dry, then season with freshly ground pepper.

Heat through gently before serving. Serves 4-6.

PER SERVING	
Energy Kcals	192
Protein g	3.6
Fat g	9.3
Polyunsaturated fatty acids g	1.17
Saturated fatty acids g	1.27
Carbohydrate g	24.9
Calcium mg	9

Right:
Banana and Cashew Nut Ice Cream (page 171)

A great way to use up any left over new potatoes.

Spicy Potato Wedges

Perfect as an accompaniment to pork and lamb dishes.
The addition of Cajun spices makes the potatoes rather special.
Even my children love these, despite the slightly spicy kick.

1 lb	new potatoes, washed but unpeeled	450 g
2 tsps	Cajun spice mix, bought (or see page 147)	2 tsps
1 tsp	paprika	1 tsp
1 tsp	maldon salt	1 tsp
1	clove garlic, crushed	1
1 tbsp	olive oil	1 tbsp

Pre-heat the oven to 200C, 400F, gas 6. Boil the potatoes until nearly cooked.

Leaving skins on the potatoes, cut them into quarters lengthways.

Place potatoes in a roasting dish and cover them evenly in the spices, salt, crushed garlic and olive oil, until well coated.

Bake in the oven for about 20 minutes until cooked through, crisp and golden brown.

Serve hot. Serves 4.

PER SERVING	
Energy Kcals	119
Protein g	1.8
Fat g	4.1
Polyunsaturated fatty acids g	0.54
Saturated fatty acids g	0.64
Carbohydrate g	20.2
Calcium mg	6

Left:
Tangy Citrus Cheesecake (page 185)

Suitable for a gluten-free diet.
Make ahead and store for up to
2 days in the fridge.

Pan-Fried 'Cheese' Polenta

Delicious served with Italian dishes such as Sicilian Caponata
(see page 128). Usually this is made with strong cheddar,
however with the addition of mustard, soya flour and yeast
extract, a cheese-flavour is achieved.

1¼ pts	water	725 ml
4 oz	easy cook, fine polenta	110 g
2 oz	soya flour	50 g
2 tsps	French mustard	2 tsps
1 tsp	yeast extract	1 tsp
	salt and freshly ground pepper	
1-2 tbsps	olive oil	1-2 tbsps

Bring the water to the boil in a medium size pan. When the
water is at a rolling boil add the polenta beating the mixture
vigorously to stop lumps forming.

Simmer for about 10 minutes, stirring occasionally.

Continue beating and add the soya flour, mustard, yeast
extract and seasonings.

Continue cooking over a medium heat for several minutes.

Pour into 20 cm (8 inch) greased ceramic flan dish and
smooth down flat.

Refrigerate for about 2 hours until set. When cool, cut into 4
quarters.

Heat the olive oil in a large non-stick frying pan. Place the
polenta slices in the frying pan.

Cook over medium heat for about 8 minutes each side.

The polenta is ready to serve when it is golden brown on
either side. Serves 4.

PER SERVING	
Energy Kcals	234
Protein g	7.8
Fat g	11.8
Polyunsaturated fatty acids g	0.88
Saturated fatty acids g	1.06
Carbohydrate g	23.6
Calcium mg	31

For a complete meal stir-fry vegetables and strips of chicken or pork and add this to the noodles.

Sesame Noodles

Suitable as an accompaniment to Chinese meat dishes and stir-fry vegetables.

9 oz	medium egg noodles	250 g
2 tbsps	sesame oil	2 tbsps
2 tbsps	sesame seeds	2 tbsps
5	spring onions, finely chopped	5

Bring a large pan of water up to a rolling boil. Add the noodles and ensure they are fully covered in water.

Boil for about 4 minutes (or until just cooked). Strain the noodles.

Pour sesame oil into the pan, add sesame seeds and spring onions, stir over medium heat for several minutes to heat through.

Return the noodles to the pan and stir thoroughly.

Serve immediately. Serves 4.

PER SERVING	
Energy Kcals	354
Protein g	9.4
Fat g	15.8
Polyunsaturated fatty acids g	4.64
Saturated fatty acids g	1.52
Carbohydrate g	46.9
Calcium mg	67

Sicilian Caponata

This is a sweet and sour type of ratatouille. It can be served hot, at room temperature or cold. Leaving it to stand allows the flavours to develop. Delicious with Italian bread such as the Foccacia on page 209 for a light meal. Alternatively serve with rice, polenta or pasta.

2 tbsps	olive oil	2 tbsps
1	red onion, chopped	1
3	cloves garlic, crushed	3
1	red chilli, de-seeded and finely chopped	1
1	red pepper, de-seeded and cut in long strips	1
1	yellow pepper, de-seeded and cut in long strips	1
1	large aubergine, cut in 2.5 cm (1 inch) strips	1
1	400 g tin chopped tomatoes	1
1 tbsp	tomato purée	1 tbsp
5 fl oz	vegetable stock	150 ml
1 tbsp	white wine vinegar	1 tbsp
1 tbsp	sugar	1 tbsp
15	pitted olives, sliced	15
1 tbsp	drained capers	1 tbsp
	salt and freshly ground pepper	
2 tbsps	chopped fresh basil	2 tbsps

In large pan heat 1 tablespoon of olive oil, fry onion and garlic for about 2 minutes.

Add chilli, peppers and aubergine, stir well for about 4 minutes.

Add tinned tomatoes, purée, stock, vinegar and sugar and simmer for about 25 minutes or until aubergine and peppers are tender.

Add olives and capers, season well.

Just before serving mix in fresh chopped basil and the remaining tablespoon of olive oil. Serves 4.

PER SERVING	
Energy Kcals	180
Protein g	4.0
Fat g	10.3
Polyunsaturated fatty acids g	1.43
Saturated fatty acids g	1.49
Carbohydrate g	19.1
Calcium mg	53

Take care not to overcook basmati rice as it goes very mushy. Brown long grain rice is also very good cooked this way.

The spiced rice re-heats well at a later date either covered with cling film and microwaved or covered in foil and baked in the oven.

Spiced Rice

This rice dish has been one of my family's favourites for a long time. When making the spiced onion mixture it will taste surprisingly strong before the rice is added, do not be alarmed, once the rice has been added the taste will be much more subtle. I often serve this dish with barbecues; with a tomato relish and lamb kebabs, accompanied by a cucumber and yoghurt salad.

12 oz	basmati rice	350 g
2 tbsps	sunflower oil	2 tbsps
2	medium onions, very finely chopped	2
3 tsps	ground cumin	3 tsps
1 tsp	curry powder	1 tsp
2 tsps	garam masala	2 tsps
1/2 tsp	turmeric	1/2 tsp
1 tsp	salt	1 tsp

Put rice in a large pan of boiling salted water. Cook until just tender, drain well and set aside.

In a large frying pan heat the oil and gently fry the onions for about 12 minutes until tender and just turning golden.

Turn the heat up and add spices and salt, stir well and cook for further minute.

Tip the rice into the spiced onions and mix together well. Heat through to serve. Serves 4-6.

PER SERVING

Energy Kcals	297
Protein g	6.7
Fat g	3.3
Polyunsaturated fatty acids g	1.47
Saturated fatty acids g	0.28
Carbohydrate g	61.0
Calcium mg	72

You can make a batch and leave some to cool, freeze them for another time.

Use this recipe to make toad in the hole, cook sausages first in a roasting tin, then pour batter around the tin and bake.

Yorkshire Puddings

I was surprised at how good these were, it was fairly hard to tell that they were not made with cow's milk.

3 oz	plain flour	75 g
	pinch of salt	
1	egg	1
4 fl oz	soya milk	125 ml
	salt and freshly ground pepper	
2 tbsps	beef dripping or just plain	2 tbsps
	sunflower or olive oil for the roasting tin	

You will need a Yorkshire pudding tin with about 12 individual holes or 8 larger ones.

Alternatively make one large one in a roasting tin, which will need to be baked for longer.

Pre-heat the oven to 220C, 425F, gas 7. Make the batter; sift the flour and salt into a bowl. Make a well in the centre of the flour and crack the egg into it. Beat the egg into the flour, then slowly beat in the soya milk until all the flour is incorporated, an electric whisk may be used.

Fill the pudding tin with oil in each section.

Put in the oven for about 5 minutes until very hot and sizzling. Pour batter into tin.

Bake for about 15 minutes in the hot oven until well risen, crisp and golden.

Serve as soon as possible. Serves 4.

PER SERVING	
Energy Kcals	149
Protein g	2.9
Fat g	9.7
Polyunsaturated fatty acids g	0.66
Saturated fatty acids g	4.25
Carbohydrate g	16.8
Calcium mg	34

Savoury Sauces and Accompaniments

Aioli Sauce

Basil and Nut Pesto

Chilli Bean Salsa

Creamy Cider and Wholegrain Mustard Sauce

Creamy Curried Coconut Sauce

Creamy Minted Yogurt Sauce

Creamy Peanut and Coconut Chilli Sauce

Roasted Sweetcorn and Lime Salsa

Roasted Tomato Sauce

Tangy Gooseberry and Ginger Sauce

Tangy Mayonnaise

Tomato and Mint Salsa

Tomato and Red Pepper Coulis

Tomato and Sweet Chilli Relish

Veloute Sauce

Bread Sauce

Onion Marmalade

Quick and Easy Homemade Soya Cheese

Spiced Walnuts

Cajun Spice Mix

Flour Tortillas (Tortillas de Harina)

If the sauce curdles, remove from the heat and try whisking in a little cold water.

You can now buy concentrated fish stock from supermarkets in liquid form. Vegetable bouillon could be used instead of fish stock.

Aioli Sauce

This is a lovely creamy garlic sauce, which is very simple and perfect for the lactose-intolerant diner as it uses mayonnaise. It compliments many types of fish such as white fish, skate or salmon.

14 fl oz	fish stock	400 ml
2	cloves garlic, crushed	2
1 tsp	arrowroot or other thickener	1 tsp
6 tbsps	mayonnaise	6 tbsps
1 tbsp	finely chopped parsley	1 tbsp

Bring the stock and the crushed garlic to the boil.

Add the arrowroot and whisk until the mixture begins to thicken.

Remove from heat and allow the pan to cool several minutes before you whisk in the mayonnaise; if the sauce becomes too hot it will curdle.

When the mayonnaise is all whisked in add the parsley and season.

Warm over a very low heat. Spoon over the fish to serve. Serves 4.

PER SERVING	
Energy Kcals	172
Protein g	0.8
Fat g	18.0
Polyunsaturated fatty acids g	1.92
Saturated fatty acids g	2.61
Carbohydrate g	1.7
Calcium mg	9

Try different variations with
different herbs such as fresh
coriander and different nuts.

Basil and Nut Pesto

Most bought pesto contains cheese usually in the form of
Parmesan; the only one suitable for vegans that I have
discovered has been from the health food shop, it was very tasty,
but quite pricey. I have included a successful version of my own
which proved to be equally if not more delicious with a fresher
taste. It may be stored in the fridge for up to two weeks.
Serve with a bowl of pasta for a delicious supper.

7 fl oz	virgin olive oil	200 ml
2 oz	cashew nuts	50 g
2 oz	brazil nuts	50 g
2	cloves garlic, peeled and roughly chopped	2
3 oz	basil and flat leaf parsley, large stalks removed	75 g
1	heaped teaspoon maldon salt	1
2 tbsps	cider vinegar	2 tbsps
1 tbsp	lemon juice	1 tbsp
	freshly ground pepper	

Place all the ingredients in a food processor and whiz for 30
seconds, scrape around inside with spatula and whiz again for a
further 30 seconds, and taste for seasoning.
Scrape out and store in a screw top jar.
Use as required. Makes approx. 425 ml (15 fl oz). Serves 10.

PER SERVING	
Energy Kcals	250
Protein g	1.8
Fat g	26.4
Polyunsaturated fatty acids g	3.99
Saturated fatty acids g	4.23
Carbohydrate g	1.4
Calcium mg	12

This salsa makes a delicious meal with chunks of tinned tuna.

Chilli Bean Salsa

Salsa in Mexico means salad, yet we tend to think of them more as sauce accompaniments. This version is also a lovely salad in its own right. Varying the types of beans or the peppers gives the salsa more of a colourful look. Serve with the Spicy Chicken Quesadillas (see page 59).

1	400 g tin of borlotti, haricot, butter or pinto beans, drained weight about 290 g (or equivalent cooked from raw)	1
1	green pepper, de-seeded and finely diced	1
1	red chilli, seeds removed, finely chopped	1
2	spring onions, finely chopped	2
1 tbsp	fresh chopped coriander	1 tbsp
1 tbsp	lemon juice	1 tbsp
2 tbsps	olive oil	2 tbsps
	salt and freshly ground pepper	

Mix all the ingredients together in a bowl and season well. Serve chilled. Serves 4.

PER SERVING	
Energy Kcals	151
Protein g	5.4
Fat g	8.0
Polyunsaturated fatty acids g	0.79
Saturated fatty acids g	1.20
Carbohydrate g	15.5
Calcium mg	78

This sauce would also go very well with chicken, pork and gammon dishes.

Creamy Cider and Wholegrain Mustard Sauce

This mouth-watering sauce is adapted from the sauce I make with sugar-baked Suffolk ham. This version is slightly richer and creamier. Serve hot with the Pork Steaks with a Hazelnut and Sage Crust on page 88.

2 tsps	vegan margarine	2 tsps
2 tsps	plain flour	2 tsps
7 fl oz	dry cider	200 ml
3½ fl oz	chicken or vegetable stock	100 ml
2 tsps	runny honey	2 tsps
2 tsps	soy sauce	2 tsps
1 tbsp	wholegrain mustard	1 tbsp
5 fl oz	soya cream	150 ml
	freshly ground pepper	

Melt the margarine in a large frying pan, add flour and cook several minutes until flour is cooked.

Gradually stir in cider and stock until smooth.

Bring to the boil stirring well for 3 minutes until sauce thickens.

Stir in the honey, soy sauce and mustard.

Finally, pour in soya cream, season with freshly ground pepper. Gently warm to serve. Serves 4.

PER SERVING	
Energy Kcals	330
Protein g	5.2
Fat g	28.9
Polyunsaturated fatty acids g	16.82
Saturated fatty acids g	4.7
Carbohydrate g	9.25
Calcium mg	11

For a quick chicken curry, fry strips of chicken breast and add to the sauce.

Creamy Curried Coconut Sauce

I originally made this to go with kedgeree. However, I now often serve it with salmon or smoked haddock fishcakes for a light supper.

1 tbsp	groundnut oil	1 tbsp
1	medium onion, very finely chopped	1
2 tsps	madras curry powder	2 tsps
2 tsps	cumin powder	2 tsps
1 tsp	ground turmeric	1 tsp
1 tbsp	plain flour	1 tbsp
½ pt	vegetable stock	275 ml
1	400 ml tin coconut milk	1

In a medium size pan, heat oil and slowly fry onion for about 8 minutes until soft.

Add curry powder, cumin and turmeric and fry for 1 minute stirring continuously.

Add flour and stir well, slowly incorporate stock until smooth.

Bring to the boil stirring well, cook for about 1 minute. Add coconut milk, heat well and serve.

Serve warm with Kedgeree on page 227. Serves 4-6.

PER SERVING	
Energy Kcals	330
Protein g	5.2
Fat g	28.9
Polyunsaturated fatty acids g	16.82
Saturated fatty acids g	4.7
Carbohydrate g	9.25
Calcium mg	11

Creamy Minted Yoghurt Sauce

This is similar to the sauce found in Indian restaurants served with popadoms. It cools down any hot curry dishes and is ideal as a creamy accompaniment to dry spicy vegetable curries. I have served it with the Tandoori Rainbow Trout on page 89.

3 tbsps	plain soya yoghurt	3 tbsps
3 tbsps	mayonnaise	3 tbsps
1	heaped teaspoon runny honey	1
2 tbsps	chopped fresh mint	2 tbsps
	salt and freshly ground pepper	

In a liquidizer or food processor, mix all the above ingredients. Whiz for about 1 minute until well blended, chill. Serve at room temperature. Serves 4.

PER SERVING	
Energy Kcals	93
Protein g	0.7
Fat g	9.0
Polyunsaturated fatty acids g	5.21
Saturated fatty acids g	1.32
Carbohydrate g	2.5
Calcium mg	1

If the sauce becomes too thick, thin down with a drop of water and mix well. This sauce thickens on cooling, so it needs to be heated through thoroughly before serving.

Creamy Peanut and Coconut Chilli Sauce

This is great for the lactose-intolerant person who feels they have been deprived of rich fattening sauces. It is really a satay-style sauce and goes well with chicken or pork kebabs. I have served it with the Chicken Sticks on page 42.

2 tsps	groundnut oil	2 tsps
1	medium onion, very finely chopped	1
1	clove garlic, peeled and crushed	1
1	red chilli, de-seeded and finely chopped	1
5 fl oz	vegetable or chicken stock	150 ml
2 tbsps	crunchy peanut butter	2 tbsps
5 fl oz	coconut milk	150 ml
1 tsp	soy sauce	1 tsp
1 tbsp	chopped fresh mint or coriander	1 tbsp
	freshly ground black pepper	

Heat the oil in a small pan and sauté the onion, garlic and chilli for about 5 minutes until soft.

Pour in the stock, simmer for several minutes.

Next stir in the peanut butter and mix well.

Pour in coconut milk. Simmer for a few minutes during which time the sauce should become slightly thicker.

Stir in the soy sauce and mint, mix, and season with pepper.

Serve warm. Serves 4.

PER SERVING	
Energy Kcals	94
Protein g	2.6
Fat g	7.3
Polyunsaturated fatty acids g	2.5
Saturated fatty acids g	1.4
Carbohydrate g	5
Calcium mg	14.8

Roasted Sweetcorn and Lime Salsa

This is one of my favourite styles of salsa, grilling the sweetcorn gives a more intense nutty sweetness. This makes a great salad or a delicious accompaniment to Mexican empanadas, enchiladas or tortilla crisps for a snack. It can also be served with barbecued burgers.

2	fresh corn on the cob	2
1	small red onion, finely chopped	1
4	small tomatoes, seeded, finely chopped	4
1	small red chilli, seeded, finely chopped	1
2 tbsps	fresh lime juice	2 tbsps
3 tbsps	olive oil	3 tbsps
2 tbsps	coarsely chopped fresh coriander	2 tbsps
	salt and freshly ground pepper	

Pre-heat the grill. Place the cobs under the grill and toast for about 10 minutes, turning occasionally, until the outside is brown.

When cool scrape off all the kernels using a sharp knife.

Combine the kernels in a bowl with remaining ingredients, leave in the fridge for about an hour to allow the flavours to develop.

Season with salt and freshly ground pepper. Serve chilled. Serves 4.

PER SERVING	
Energy Kcals	174
Protein g	2.8
Fat g	12.6
Polyunsaturated fatty acids g	1.87
Saturated fatty acids g	1.78
Carbohydrate g	13.4
Calcium mg	11

Add ham and leeks for a delicious pasta sauce.

Roasted Tomato Sauce

This is a rich tomato sauce that goes really well with Italian pasta dishes. Also delicious served with Herb Crumbed Sardine Fillets on page 37.

6	medium tomatoes, quartered	6
4	cloves garlic, peeled and left whole	4
1 tbsp	red wine vinegar	1 tbsp
1 tsp	brown sugar	1 tsp
1	medium onion, roughly chopped	1
2 tbsps	olive oil	2 tbsps

Pre-heat the oven to 190C, 375F, gas 5. Mix all the ingredients in baking dish.
Roast uncovered about 30 minutes until the onions are soft.
Blend or process tomato mixture until smooth, if necessary thin down with dash of water or tomato juice.
Pass the sauce through a sieve. Warm gently to serve.
Serves 4.

PER SERVING	
Energy Kcals	131
Protein g	2.5
Fat g	8.3
Polyunsaturated fatty acids g	1.12
Saturated fatty acids g	1.30
Carbohydrate g	12.5
Calcium mg	29

Try with roast pork to replace apple sauce.
When gooseberries are out of season, use apples instead.

Tangy Gooseberry and Ginger Sauce

The sharpness of gooseberries cuts the acidity of oily fish. Serve with Crunchy Oat-coated Mackerel Fillets on page 98. When gooseberries are in season and are plentiful, it is worth making this and freezing it for a rainy day.

8 oz	ripe gooseberries	225 g
5 fl oz	water	150 ml
2 oz	caster sugar	50 g
2 tbsps	lemon juice	2 tbsps
1 oz	crystallized ginger	25 g

Top and tail and wash the gooseberries. Put all the ingredients except the ginger in a saucepan.
Gradually bring to the boil and simmer until the gooseberries pop open and change to a yellow colour.
Push the fruit through a sieve. Finely chop the ginger and mix into the sauce.
Warm to serve. Serves 4.

PER SERVING	
Energy Kcals	83
Protein g	0.8
Fat g	0.4
Polyunsaturated fatty acids g	0.02
Saturated fatty acids g	0.03
Carbohydrate g	20.7
Calcium mg	25

Liquidize for a smoother sauce.

Tangy Mayonnaise

This is really similar to Tartare sauce and is delicious with most fried fish dishes or fishcakes. Delicious served with the Smoked Fish Cakes on page 102.

2 oz	cornichons (small gherkins)	50 g
2 tbsps	drained capers	2 tbsps
7 oz	mayonnaise	200 g
1 tbsp	chopped fresh dill	1 tbsp
1 tbsp	lemon juice	1 tbsp
	freshly ground pepper	

Finely chop the cornichons and the capers. Combine all the ingredients together in a bowl.

Cover and refrigerate until required. Serve chilled. Serves 4-5.

PER SERVING	
Energy Kcals	292
Protein g	0.5
Fat g	31.7
Polyunsaturated fatty acids g	3.40
Saturated fatty acids g	4.64
Carbohydrate g	0.4
Calcium mg	11

It lasts up to a day in the fridge, any longer and the tomatoes tend to lose some of their brightness and the salsa goes watery.

Tomato and Mint Salsa

Most salsas require fresh coriander, however I have masses of lovely home grown mint in the summer and often make this to accompany barbecued lamb dishes. Again, like most salsas, it can be a refreshing salad.

8	ripe tomatoes	8
1	large red onion	1
1-2	red chillies	1-2
3 tbsps	olive oil	3 tbsps
	juice from 1 lime	
1 tsp	sugar	1 tsp
	bunch of fresh mint	
	salt and pepper	

Finely dice tomatoes into bowl. Personally I don't fuss about skinning and de-seeding the tomatoes as those bits are the best.

Finely chop red onion then de-seed and finely chop the chilli.

In a medium bowl combine the tomato, onion and chilli.

Stir in the olive oil, lime juice, sugar and plenty of freshly chopped mint.

Season with salt and pepper. Refrigerate until required. Serve chilled. Serves 4-6.

PER SERVING	
Energy Kcals	145
Protein g	2.4
Fat g	9.8
Polyunsaturated fatty acids g	1.55
Saturated fatty acids g	1.50
Carbohydrate g	12.7
Calcium mg	31

If you prefer, use fresh red peppers. Remove the skins by grilling the peppers until charred all over, then allow them to cool slightly before removing the skins and halving the peppers to remove the seeds.

Tomato and Red Pepper Coulis

My children prefer smooth sauces like this with no bits of onions to pick out. This sauce would be a suitable accompaniment to vegetarian roasts, rissoles and stuffed vegetables. It is also delicious with meatballs, meat loaves and pasta dishes.

2 tbsps	olive oil	2 tbsps
2	medium onions, finely chopped	2
2	cloves garlic, crushed	2
1	400 g tin chopped tomatoes	1
1 tbsp	tomato purée	1 tbsp
1	(approx. 350 g jar/tin) red pimientos, drained weight about 200 g	1
1 tsp	sugar	1 tsp
	salt and freshly ground pepper	
1 tbsp	chopped fresh basil, if available	1 tbsp

Heat the olive oil in a saucepan and cook onions and garlic for about 5 minutes until soft.

Add tomatoes, tomato purée, drained pimientos and sugar, cook for a further 5 minutes.

Liquidize, season well and stir in the chopped fresh basil. Serve hot. Serves 6.

PER SERVING	
Energy Kcals	140
Protein g	2.4
Fat g	9.4
Polyunsaturated fatty acids g	0.90
Saturated fatty acids g	1.33
Carbohydrate g	12.5
Calcium mg	33

Sweet chilli sauce containing vinegar, chillies, sugar, garlic and salt is used in Thai cooking. I find it a useful ingredient to keep in the fridge.

PER SERVING	
Energy Kcals	77
Protein g	1.5
Fat g	4.3
Polyunsaturated fatty acids g	0.64
Saturated fatty acids g	0.69
Carbohydrate g	8.5
Calcium mg	20

Try this sauce with plain white fish on a bed of steamed spinach, for a healthy tasty meal.

Add a tablespoon of soya cream to make the sauce slightly richer and creamier.

PER SERVING (FOR 6 PEOPLE)	
Energy Kcals	95
Protein g	0.8
Fat g	7.7
Polyunsaturated fatty acids g	2.04
Saturated fatty acids g	2.31
Carbohydrate g	6.0
Calcium mg	11

Tomato and Sweet Chilli Relish

A quick and easy sauce to serve cold with barbecued burgers or sausages. Also great with vegetarian burgers, rissoles or the Sweet Potato and Chick Pea Cakes on page 69.

4	ripe tomatoes, finely diced	4
1	small red onion, finely chopped	1
1 tbsp	olive oil	1 tbsp
1/2 tbsp	lemon juice	1/2 tbsp
2 tbsps	sweet chilli sauce	2 tbsps

Mix all the ingredients together and taste, adjust seasoning if necessary.
Served cold. Serves 4.

Veloute Sauce

This is a slightly lower fat sauce, as it uses stock where many sauces use milk and cream. It goes well with grilled or pan-fried fish such as sole, plaice, cod, haddock etc.

171/2 fl oz	good quality fish stock	480 ml
2 oz	vegan margarine	50 g
11/2 oz	plain flour	35 g

Bring the fish stock to the boil. Meanwhile melt the margarine in another pan, add flour and cook gently for about 1 minute.
Leave to cool slightly then slowly add the hot stock, stirring well, until smooth.
Return to the heat and simmer for about 20 minutes, stirring occasionally to avoid sticking.
Serve hot, add chopped fresh tarragon, dill or chives for a varied flavour.
Alternatively substitute some wine for the stock, add before stock and boil for several minutes. Makes about 400 ml.

Bread Sauce

This sauce was one that I thought I had better include as it is traditionally served with roast chicken and turkey. Made substituting oat milk, it was hard to tell it was not the real thing. I challenge anyone at Christmas to tell the difference.

¹/₂ pt	oat drink	275 ml
1	onion, chopped in quarters	1
6	cloves, or ¹/₂ teaspoon powdered cloves	6
2	bay leaves	2
6	black peppercorns	6
	pinch of nutmeg	
	salt	
2 oz	fresh white breadcrumbs	50 g
1 oz	vegan margarine	25 g
2 tbsps	soya cream (optional)	2 tbsps

Pour oat drink into a saucepan, add the onion, cloves, bay leaves, peppercorns, nutmeg and salt.

Heat over a low heat for about 10 minutes, to infuse the flavours into the oat drink.

Bring it up to a higher temperature, but not boiling, remove from heat and leave to stand for a further 5 minutes.

Strain the milk onto the breadcrumbs and mixing well add the margarine and soya cream, check for seasoning.

If it appears too thick, add a little more oat drink.

Serve warm or cool. Serves 4.

PER SERVING	
Energy Kcals	206
Protein g	4.0
Fat g	13
Polyunsaturated fatty acids g	5.07
Saturated fatty acids g	2.75
Carbohydrate g	20
Calcium mg	39

A nice filling for baked potatoes or with smoked ham.
  Make with red onions for a bit more depth in colour.

Onion Marmalade

I sometimes make a batch of this marmalade as it stores well in a jar in the fridge for several weeks. It is delicious served with the smoked duck salad on page 43. It is also particularly good with cold meats or pâtés as light lunch. Or for anyone who can eat goat's and sheep's cheese, the marmalade makes a delicious combination with either cold or grilled cheese.

5	large onions, each weighing about 225 g (8 oz), halved and sliced in half rings	5
1 tbsp	sunflower oil	1 tbsp
5 fl oz	red wine	150 ml
5 fl oz	balsamic vinegar	150 ml
2 oz	light brown sugar	50 g
4 tbsps	water	4 tbsps
1/2 tsp	salt	1/2 tsp

In a large frying pan or saucepan, heat oil and add the onions.
Fry over a gentle heat for about 10 minutes, stirring continuously until the onions are almost soft, make sure they do not burn.
Reduce the heat, add red wine, vinegar, sugar, water and salt.
Stir well, cover pan and simmer for about 30 minutes, add a few spoons of water if it dries out.
Remove lid and stirring occasionally cook for a further 5 minutes.
The marmalade should still be moist with a tiny bit of thick liquid.
Fill a large jar with boiling water, leave for few minutes and empty.
Fill with onion marmalade and close lid firmly.
Leave to cool and then refrigerate. Makes appox. 725 ml (1 1/4 pint).

PER 30 ML SERVING	
Energy Kcals	34.54
Protein g	0.59
Fat g	5.08
Polyunsaturated fatty acids g	0.31
Saturated fatty acids g	0.05
Carbohydrate g	6.07
Calcium mg	13.62

For other flavours add vegan bouillon or a small teaspoon mustard powder.

Soya flour is available from most health food shops.

Quick and Easy Homemade Soya Cheese

Although this does not have the same texture as processed soya cheese, making it is a lot cheaper and as you can see very simple and quick.

4 oz	firm vegan margarine such as Tomor	110 g
1	heaped teaspoon yeast extract	1
4 oz	soya flour	110 g

Gently melt the margarine, taking care not to overheat and burn.

Add the yeast extract and stir until melted. Mix in the soya flour and stir well.

Tip into bowl or square container and refrigerate.
It should become firm within a couple of hours. Grate or sprinkle as required. Makes 225 g (8 oz).
Serves 4.

PER SERVING	
Energy Kcals	326
Protein g	10
Fat g	28.9
Polyunsaturated fatty acids g	9.1
Saturated fatty acids g	7.7
Carbohydrate g	6.7
Calcium mg	58.9

Spiced Walnuts

This recipe works equally well made with whole almonds or cashew nuts and served as a great little snack. Also try mixing lots of varieties of spiced nuts in a large bowl when friends come round for drinks. Serve with smoked duck salad starter on page 43.

1 tbsp	olive oil	1 tbsp
1 tsp	Chinese five-spice powder	1 tsp
1 tsp	garam masala	1 tsp
7 oz	walnut halves	200 g
1½ tsp	caster sugar	1½ tsp
1 tsp	fine salt	1 tsp

Heat the oil in a large frying pan on medium heat.
Add the spices, stirring well and cook for 30 seconds.
Stir in the walnuts, followed by the sugar and salt.
Shake the pan continuously and cook for further minute over a low heat.
Leave to cool. Serves 4.

PER SERVING	
Energy Kcals	376
Protein g	7.3
Fat g	36.7
Polyunsaturated fatty acids g	23.95
Saturated fatty acids g	3.16
Carbohydrate g	4.3
Calcium mg	47

Delicious with chicken and fish dishes.

Cajun Spice Mix

Since I have included a few Cajun dishes in this book, I thought I would include a recipe for Cajun Spice Mix. It can be bought from most supermarkets but this homemade version tastes better and has no salt.

1 tbsp	garlic powder (if unavailable use 4 cloves fresh garlic, crushed)	1 tbsp
1 tbsp	onion powder	1 tbsp
2 tsps	cracked black pepper	2 tsps
1 tsp	dried cumin	1 tsp
1 1/2 tsps	cayenne pepper	1 1/2 tsps
1/2 tsp	allspice	1/2 tsp
1 tsp	dried oregano	1 tsp
1 tsp	dried thyme	1 tsp

Mix the spices together and store in a jar. If you use fresh garlic, you will need about 4 cloves crushed to a paste, the spice mix will then become a paste rather than a powder, in which case store it in the fridge.

Use as required in Cajun recipes. Fills a small jar.

PER QUANTITY	
Energy Kcals	102
Protein g	7.2
Fat g	2.8
Polyunsaturated fatty acids g	0.85
Saturated fatty acids g	0.42
Carbohydrate g	19.0
Calcium mg	320

A friend of mine recently used tortillas as pancakes, this was a great idea as once smothered in a sauce, they resembled ordinary pancakes with slightly more texture.

Flour Tortillas (Tortillas de Harina)

I find that the tortillas in the supermarket seem to contain so many unnecessary ingredients and E numbers. The homemade variety is not only healthier, but also a lot cheaper and fun to make. The other type of tortillas are the corn tortillas, however the main ingredient masa harina is quite hard to find (I searched in health food shops and delicatessens and had no luck). If you do find masa harina, which is special maize flour specially treated for tortillas, then make with 150 g (5 oz) masa harina, pinch salt and 100 ml (4 fl oz) warm water, make pliable dough, rest for 20 minutes then treat as with flour tortillas.

10 oz	plain white flour	275 g
2 tsps	salt	2 tsps
4 oz	white flora or lard, cut into small pieces	110 g
3½ fl oz	warm water	100 ml

Sieve the flour and salt into large bowl. Rub in the fat until the mixture resembles breadcrumbs.

Gradually add the warm water, until you have pliable dough. Knead for 5 minutes.

Divide into 12 balls and cover them with a damp cloth.

On a floured surface, roll each ball into a circle of approximately 23 cm (9 inches). The dough should be very thin.

Heat a large heavy frying pan over a medium heat and cook each tortilla, turning once.

Count to about 40 as you cook each side. Tortillas should be lightly spotted with brown.

Stack the cooked tortillas with greaseproof paper between each one.

Warm as recipe instructs before using. Makes 12.

PER TORTILLA	
Energy Kcals	160
Protein g	2.2
Fat g	9.4
Polyunsaturated fatty acids g	1.02
Saturated fatty acids g	3.79
Carbohydrate g	17.8
Calcium mg	32

Salads and Dressings

Chicken, Avocado and Watercress Salad

Bulgar Wheat Salad

Carrot and Sesame Salad

Celeriac, Walnut and Apple Salad with a Mint Tofu Mayonnaise

Crisp Chinese Salad

Cucumber, Mint and Soya 'Yogurt' Salad

Red Cabbage and Pumpkin Seed Coleslaw

Roasted Fennel and Beetroot Salad

Roasted Vegetable and Tuna Rice Salad

Warm Sweet Potato and Artichoke Salad

Tarragon French Dressing

Creamy Lemon Dressing

Creamy Tahini Dressing

Harissa Dressing

Lime and Coriander Dressing

Oriental Sesame Dressing

Sun-dried Tomato, Basil and Garlic Dressing

Tofu Mayonnaise

Even better, if you can buy smoked chicken, this would be delicious. For a vegetarian alternative omit chicken and add a handful of walnuts.

Chicken, Avocado and Watercress Salad

This makes a quick and tasty lunch if you have any spare chicken in your fridge, but prepare it just before serving as the avocado will start to discolour. Delicious served with brown rice or crunchy bread. Also try it as a filling for hot pitta bread or baguette for a lunchtime sandwich. Baby spinach would be equally as tasty as watercress.

8 oz	cooked chicken, diced	225 g
2	spring onions, thinly sliced	2
1	large ripe avocado	1
1/3 pt	Creamy Tahini Dressing (see page 161)	190 ml
	salt and freshly ground pepper	
3 oz	watercress	75 g

Mix chicken, spring onions and avocado, stir in the dressing. Season with salt and pepper and serve on a bed of watercress. Serves 4.

PER SERVING	
Energy Kcals	605
Protein g	18.7
Fat g	57.8
Polyunsaturated fatty acids g	26.79
Saturated fatty acids g	8.01
Carbohydrate g	2.6
Calcium mg	99

Check the preparation instructions on the packet of bulgar wheat as brands may vary.

Bulgar Wheat Salad

This refreshing summer salad is a variation of the traditional Middle Eastern salad, Tabbouleh. It may seem that there is a lot of mint and parsley in the recipe; this adds to the character of the salad.

8 oz	bulgar wheat	225 g
1 tsp	salt	1 tsp
1 pt	boiling water	570 ml
4 tbsps	olive oil	4 tbsps
3 tbsps	lemon juice	3 tbsps
1/2	cucumber	1/2
3	firm tomatoes	3
1	red pepper, de-seeded	1
4	spring onions	4
3 tbsps	chopped fresh mint	3 tbsps
4 tbsps	chopped fresh parsley	4 tbsps
	salt and pepper	

Mix the bulgar wheat with the salt and boiling water. Leave it for about 20 minutes until the wheat is tender. Drain off any excess water and leave to dry out.

Mix the bulgar wheat with the lemon and olive oil, refrigerate for several hours if possible at this point to allow the wheat to soak up the flavours.

Just before serving, chop the cucumber, tomatoes and pepper into small dice.

Finely chop the spring onions and include the green parts.

Mix the chopped vegetables and herbs with the bulgar wheat. Season with salt and pepper. Serve chilled. Serves 6-8.

PER SERVING	
Energy Kcals	222
Protein g	4.3
Fat g	9.5
Polyunsaturated fatty acids g	1.15
Saturated fatty acids g	1.29
Carbohydrate g	30.7
Calcium mg	59

Substitute 1 tablespoon of the oil for sesame oil to give a fuller flavoured dressing.

Any left over salad could be used in a sandwich with hummus or in pitta bread.

Carrot and Sesame Salad

A quick and easy salad to prepare. The carrots and sesame seeds mixed with a tahini dressing are a delightful combination. Serve as part of a buffet.

1 lb	carrots	450 g
2	sticks celery, chopped	2
3	spring onions, finely sliced	3
2 tbsps	lemon juice	2 tbsps
3 tbsps	groundnut oil	3 tbsps
1 tsp	tahini	1 tsp
1/2 tsp	runny honey (optional)	1/2 tsp
2 tbsps	toasted sesame seeds	2 tbsps
	salt and freshly ground pepper	

Peel carrots and grate into a bowl. Mix with the celery and spring onions.

In a separate bowl combine the dressing ingredients with 1 tablespoon of the sesame seeds.

Season with salt and pepper. Add dressing to carrot, celery and spring onion.

Mix well and serve chilled sprinkled with remaining sesame seeds. Serves 4-6.

PER SERVING	
Energy Kcals	159
Protein g	1.9
Fat g	12.5
Polyunsaturated fatty acids g	2.36
Saturated fatty acids g	1.84
Carbohydrate g	10.4
Calcium mg	103

This could also be made with egg-based mayonnaise.

Celeriac, Walnut and Apple Salad with a Mint Tofu Mayonnaise

Celeriac gives the salad an interesting crunchiness. The salad should be made just before serving to prevent the apple and celeriac from discolouring. Serve with hot bread or new potatoes for a delicious nutritious lunch.

1/2	celeriac, peeled and cut into small chunks	1/2
2-3	sweet eating apples, cored and cut into small chunks	2-3
4 oz	walnuts, roughly chopped	110 g
1 tbsp	chopped fresh mint	1 tbsp
1 tbsp	chopped fresh parsley	1 tbsp
	salt and freshly ground pepper	
1/4 pt	Tofu Mayonnaise (see page 164)	150 ml

Mix all salad ingredients with tofu mayonnaise. Serve chilled. Serves 6.

PER SERVING	
Energy Kcals	86.7
Protein g	1.9
Fat g	8.6
Polyunsaturated fatty acids g	1.9
Saturated fatty acids g	1.02
Carbohydrate g	0.5
Calcium mg	108.1

Try using Chinese leaves, cabbage, cauliflower or broccoli.

Crisp Chinese Salad

This is a very colourful salad, which can be made with a variety of raw vegetables.

2	large carrots, peeled	2
1/2	cucumber	1/2
6	spring onions	6
1	red pepper	1
8 oz	bean sprouts	225 g
	Oriental Sesame Dressing (see page 163)	

Cut the carrot and cucumber into thin julienne strips, similar in length to the bean sprouts.

Discard the outer leaves of the spring onion, keeping as much of the green as possible, shred the spring onion into similar strips.

Cut the red pepper in half and remove seeds, cut this into thin strips.

Mix everything with the bean sprouts.

Chill and toss with the dressing just before serving.
Serves 4-6.

PER SERVING	
Energy Kcals	184
Protein g	4.1
Fat g	13.0
Polyunsaturated fatty acids g	4.78
Saturated fatty acids g	2.16
Carbohydrate g	13.3
Calcium mg	124

Cucumber, Mint and Soya 'Yoghurt' Salad

This refreshing salad is based on Greek Tzatziki. It is ideal as a salad or as an accompaniment to certain dishes such as Sweet Potato and Chick Pea Cakes (page 69) or served with spicy dishes and barbecues.

11 oz	soya yoghurt (Yofu is excellent)	310 g
1/2	cucumber, chopped into small cubes	1/2
2 tbsps	chopped fresh mint	2 tbsps
1/2 tsp	runny honey	1/2 tsp
	salt and freshly ground pepper	

Mix all the above ingredients and season well.

Refrigerate before serving. Serves 2 as a salad or enough for 4 as accompaniment.

PER SERVING	
Energy Kcals	134
Protein g	8.5
Fat g	6.6
Polyunsaturated fatty acids g	3.72
Saturated fatty acids g	0.93
Carbohydrate g	10.7
Calcium mg	23

Red Cabbage and Pumpkin Seed Coleslaw

A lovely crisp salad full of goodness.

8 oz	red cabbage	225 g
6 oz	carrots, peeled	175 g
4 oz	fennel bulbs	110 g
1	red dessert apple	1
2 tbsps	pumpkin seeds (could use sunflower seeds)	2 tbsps
6 tbsps	Tarragon French Dressing (page 159)	6 tbsps
2 tbsps	soya yoghurt	2 tbsps

Wash and prepare the cabbage; remove tough outer leaves and central core if it is too tough and shred finely.

Shred the fennel, discarding the tough outer leaves.

Grate carrot and mix in large bowl with cabbage and fennel.

Wash and quarter apple, core and cut into small dice, leaving skin on for colour.

Add pumpkin seeds to bowl. Toss everything together with dressing and yoghurt.

Chill and serve. Serves 4-6.

PER SERVING	
Energy Kcals	150
Protein g	2.09
Fat g	11.9
Polyunsaturated fatty acids g	7.2
Saturated fatty acids g	1.5
Carbohydrate g	9.4
Calcium mg	44.5

Roasted Fennel and Beetroot Salad

Roasting fennel and beetroot is one of the best ways to cook these vegetables. If you are not keen on either vegetable you may be pleasantly surprised. The roasting juices from the tomatoes combined with the beetroot, olive oil and vinegar make a delicious red dressing. Serve warm with steamed couscous and nut burgers or tofu fritters. Alternatively serve with hot bread.

2	large beetroot, about 450 g (1 lb) total weight	2
1	large or 2 small fennel, about 200 g (7 oz)	1
2 tbsps	olive oil	2 tbsps
2	medium tomatoes, cut into 8 wedges	2
4	spring onions, cut into 1 cm (1/2 inch) slices	4
1 tbsp	balsamic vinegar	1 tbsp
	salt and freshly ground pepper	
3	sprigs fresh thyme	3
1 tbsp	fresh parsley	1 tbsp

Pre-heat the oven to 200C, 400F, gas 6. Peel the beetroot and cut into segments about 1 cm (1/2 inch) across.

Top the fennel and cut into segments similar size to beetroot. Place the beetroot and fennel in a large baking dish, pour over olive oil and shake well in the oil to get a good coating.

Roast in the hot oven for about 25 minutes until the vegetables are beginning to brown at the edges.

Add tomato wedges, onions and balsamic, mix well.

Return to oven for about 15 minutes, remove from oven.

Season with salt and pepper and sprinkle over the thyme leaves and chopped parsley.

If required drizzle extra olive oil over the salad.

Serve warm or chilled. Serves 4.

PER SERVING	
Energy Kcals	147
Protein g	3.5
Fat g	8.0
Polyunsaturated fatty acids g	0.90
Saturated fatty acids g	1.16
Carbohydrate g	16.1
Calcium mg	104

Right:
Blueberry Muffins and Banana Oat Shake (pages 225 and 229)

Substitute pasta instead of rice for a delicious pasta salad.

Roasted Vegetable and Tuna Rice Salad

This is perfect for a tasty summer lunch eaten outdoors. The vegetables should all slightly caramelise, giving an added natural sweetness. Serve with some salad leaves or watercress and the Sun-dried Tomato, Garlic and Basil Dressing .

1	large red pepper	1
1	medium red onion	1
1 tbsp	olive oil and extra to drizzle	1 tbsp
1	clove garlic, crushed	1
	salt and pepper	
4 oz	baby corn	110 g
1 lb	brown short grain rice, cooked	450 g
1	tin tuna steak, drained weight 150 g	1
	double the quantity of Sun-dried Tomato, Basil and Garlic Dressing (see page 163)	

Heat the grill, when it is hot, place the whole red pepper underneath and leave for about 4 minutes before turning. Repeat until completely blistered and black (about 4 turns). Place the pepper in small plastic bag.

Peel when cool enough to handle, remove seeds and stalk, cut into chunks, leave to one side.

Peel the red onion, cube and pull layers apart, mix with the olive oil, garlic, salt and pepper in an oven dish.

Leave a gap on one side and lay the baby corn out next to the onions, drizzle over a little more olive oil.

Grill for about 5 minutes turning from time to time, add the peppers and mix with the onions, continue grilling for a further 5 minutes until the baby corn is golden brown and the onions are soft and beginning to caramelise at the edges.

Leave to cool.

In a large bowl mix the rice with the peppers, onions, baby corn and tuna chunks, season well with salt and freshly ground pepper.

Refrigerate until needed.

To serve toss with the dressing. Serves 4.

PER SERVING	
Energy Kcals	307
Protein g	5.3
Fat g	13.2
Polyunsaturated fatty acids g	1.41
Saturated fatty acids g	1.63
Carbohydrate g	44.7
Calcium mg	30

Left:
Rich Chocolate Brownies (page 184)

Marinated artichoke hearts are found in most supermarkets and have a wonderful rich flavour.

Warm Sweet Potato and Artichoke Salad

This is an unusual salad, which served with warm crusty bread makes a delicious light lunch. Alternatively it could be served alongside grilled meat or fish.

1 lb	sweet potatoes, peeled but left whole	450 g
1 tbsp	olive oil	1 tbsp
	salt and freshly ground pepper	
8 oz	artichoke hearts marinated in oil (weight out of oil)	225 g
4 oz	watercress, washed and thick stalks removed	110 g
4 oz	crisp cos lettuce, broken up	110 g
2 tbsps	pine nuts	2 tbsps
1½ tbsps	balsamic vinegar	1½ tbsps

Boil or steam the sweet potatoes for about 10 minutes, until firm but almost tender.

Slice into 2 cm (³/₄ inch) thick discs. Coat in the olive oil and season well.

Heat a griddle pan and griddle the potato slices in batches for about 2 minutes either side, until charred.

Slice the artichoke hearts in quarters and quickly warm in the griddle pan.

Lay the leaves in a large salad bowl.

Toss the warm potato, artichoke hearts and pine nuts together and tip over the leaves.

Mix 4 tablespoons of the artichoke oil from the jar with the balsamic vinegar, season with salt and freshly ground pepper, whisk well and drizzle over salad before serving. Serves 4.

PER SERVING	
Energy Kcals	232
Protein g	4.2
Fat g	13.5
Polyunsaturated fatty acids g	4.03
Saturated fatty acids g	1.64
Carbohydrate g	25.6
Calcium mg	92

Add any other fresh herbs or garlic for a different flavour.

Tarragon French Dressing

This produces a slightly white and creamy dressing which should stay thick and not need shaking before serving. The dressing lasts for up to a week in the fridge. Serve with crisp mixed leaf salads.

2 tbsps	Dijon mustard	2 tbsps
2 tbsps	cider vinegar	2 tbsps
$^1/_2$ tsp	salt	$^1/_2$ tsp
7 fl oz	sunflower oil	200 ml
1-2 tbsps	water	1-2 tbsps
2 tbsps	chopped French tarragon	2 tbsps
	freshly ground pepper	

In a medium bowl whisk the mustard, vinegar and salt together.

Gradually add the oil, beating well to form emulsion as if making mayonnaise.

When all the oil has been added it will appear quite thick.

Stir in the water to thin the dressing down, followed by the tarragon and freshly ground pepper.

Store in a sealed jar in the fridge until required. Makes about 250 ml (9 fl oz).

Dressing serving size = 20 ml unless otherwise stated.

PER SERVING	
Energy Kcals	153
Protein g	0.2
Fat g	16.9
Polyunsaturated fatty acids g	10.59
Saturated fatty acids g	2.01
Carbohydrate g	0.3
Calcium mg	2

I have also made this with limes before, which is great with Thai fish dishes such as Thai fishcakes. Try using runny honey instead of sugar.

Creamy Lemon Dressing

This will have a milky white appearance and a delicious slightly creamy tangy flavour that adds a special touch to many fish dishes such as fish mousses, crab rösti or just fresh crab or lobster.

2	large lemons	2
1	level tbsp sugar	1
1/2 tsp	salt	1/2 tsp
10 fl oz	plain tasting oil such as sunflower or vegetable	275 ml
	freshly ground pepper	

Using a sharp knife cut top and bottom off the lemons, then moving from top to bottom cut the lemon skins off and cut out the individual segments, ensuring there are no pips or pith remaining.

Process the lemon segments, sugar and salt in a blender, until smooth and slightly white.

Slowly add the oil while machine is running.

Taste and season with pepper and add more oil if necessary (depends on size of lemons). Makes about 350 ml (12 fl oz).

Dressing serving size = 20 ml unless otherwise stated.

PER SERVING	
Energy Kcals	157
Protein g	0.0
Fat g	17.0
Polyunsaturated fatty acids g	8.22
Saturated fatty acids g	1.77
Carbohydrate g	1.0
Calcium mg	0

Creamy Tahini Dressing

This dressing is quite similar to Tarragon French Dressing, but the addition of mayonnaise and tahini make it suitable for salads such as rice, beans and pasta salads.

2 tbsps	mayonnaise	2 tbsps
1 tbsp	cider vinegar	1 tbsp
1 tbsp	tahini	1 tbsp
1/4 pt	sunflower oil	150 ml
4 tbsps	cold water (or more for a thinner dressing)	4 tbsps
	salt and freshly ground pepper	

Whisk mayonnaise in a bowl with vinegar and tahini.
Gradually add the sunflower oil, whisking well until thick and smooth.
Thin down with the water and season with salt and pepper.
Chill to serve. Makes about 250 ml (9 fl oz).

Dressing serving size = 20 ml unless otherwise stated.

PER SERVING	
Energy Kcals	138
Protein g	0.3
Fat g	15.1
Polyunsaturated fatty acids g	9.33
Saturated fatty acids g	1.88
Carbohydrate g	0.1
Calcium mg	11

Harissa Dressing

Harissa is a fiery North African paste made from a mixture of chillies, tomato and garlic with various spices. Here I have made it into a dressing using sun-dried tomato paste which I think adds a richer flavour. The dressing is delicious with roasted vegetables and couscous. Also great served with the Moroccan Lamb Burgers on page 51 and Spiced Rice on page 129.

1 tbsp	tomato purée	1 tbsp
1 tbsp	sun-dried tomato paste	1 tbsp
1	clove garlic, crushed	1
1 tbsp	ground cumin powder	1 tbsp
1 tsp	ground coriander powder	1 tsp
1/2 tsp	chilli powder	1/2 tsp
2	limes, squeezed	2
4 tbsps	olive oil	4 tbsps

Dressing serving size = 20 ml unless otherwise stated.

PER SERVING	
Energy Kcals	89
Protein g	0.4
Fat g	9.3
Polyunsaturated fatty acids g	0.79
Saturated fatty acids g	1.33
Carbohydrate g	0.8
Calcium mg	7

Mix all the above ingredients well before serving. Makes about 150 ml (1/4 pint).

Fish sauce is a Thai alternative to soya sauce or salt, made from anchovy extract; if you are unable to get hold of it substitute a light soya sauce instead.

Lime and Coriander Dressing

This is a delicate Thai-style dressing which goes very well with fish dishes. Serve with Monkfish and king prawn kebabs or just plain grilled fish and salad. Prepare dressing up to three days in advance.

3	limes	3
	groundnut oil	
	handful of fresh coriander	
1 tbsp	fish sauce (nam pla)	1 tbsp
1 inch	fresh ginger, peeled and finely chopped	2½ cm
1	red bird's eye chilli, de-seeded and finely chopped	1
2 tsps	sugar	2 tsps

Using a vegetable peeler, remove about 6 strips of lime zest, cut these into thin strips, then chop finely.

Squeeze the juice from the limes and pour it into a bowl with an equal amount of groundnut oil.

Remove leaves from the coriander, cut the stalks finely and chop the leaves.

Mix all the remaining dressing ingredients, including the zest.

Stir thoroughly, taste and adjust seasoning if necessary, dressing should be quite tangy, with enough sugar to cut acidity.

Refrigerate until required. Serves 4.

Dressing serving size = 20 ml unless otherwise stated.

PER SERVING	
Energy Kcals	244
Protein g	1.0
Fat g	23
Polyunsaturated fatty acids g	7.06
Saturated fatty acids g	4.51
Carbohydrate g	8.9
Calcium mg	23

If you don't have rice vinegar, cider or white wine vinegar will be fine.

Dressing serving size = 20 ml unless otherwise stated.

PER SERVING	
Energy Kcals	106
Protein g	0.9
Fat g	10.2
Polyunsaturated fatty acids g	4.00
Saturated fatty acids g	1.61
Carbohydrate g	2.9
Calcium mg	24

Oriental Sesame Dressing

This is a delicious dressing which will jazz up any crisp vegetable salad. The addition of sesame seeds and honey add a lovely nutty sweetness.

2 tsps	runny honey	2 tsps
2 tbsps	rice vinegar	2 tbsps
3 tsps	sesame oil	3 tsps
2 tbsps	groundnut oil	2 tbsps
2 tbsps	soy sauce	2 tbsps
2 tbsps	toasted sesame seeds	2 tbsps

Thin the honey down with the rice vinegar until smooth. Add the oils and soy sauce and taste.
Before serving mix in toasted sesame seeds. Makes about 100 ml (4 fl oz).

The dressing may appear to separate slightly from the oil, just mix well before serving.
 For a super vegan starter serve with crisp French bread croûtons topped with griddled slithers of mixed vegetables, such as asparagus, peppers, courgettes and aubergine.

Dressing serving size = 20 ml unless otherwise stated.

PER SERVING	
Energy Kcals	98
Protein g	0.5
Fat g	10.1
Polyunsaturated fatty acids g	0.83
Saturated fatty acids g	1.43
Carbohydrate g	1.2
Calcium mg	15

Sun-dried Tomato, Basil and Garlic Dressing

Great served with roasted vegetables. It has a delightful Italian flavour which makes any salad more interesting. Serve with the Fresh Tuna and Potato Niçoise on page 60.

1 tbsp	sun-dried tomato paste	1 tbsp
1	clove garlic, crushed	1
1 tbsp	red wine vinegar	1 tbsp
2 tbsps	olive oil	2 tbsps
1 tbsp	fresh basil	1 tbsp
	salt and freshly ground pepper	

Mix sun-dried tomato paste, garlic and vinegar together.
Slowly beat in the oil, taste and season with basil and salt and pepper. Add more oil if necessary depending on taste.
Serves 2-3.

Store in sealed jar for several days in the fridge.

Tofu Mayonnaise

Although egg mayonnaise is acceptable for the lactose-free diet, this tofu mayonnaise is more nutritious and slightly lower in fat, especially good for a vegetarian diet.

1	pack (250 g) silken tofu	1
2 tsps	wholegrain or Dijon mustard	2 tsps
1	clove fresh garlic (optional)	1
1/2 tsp	salt	1/2 tsp
	freshly ground pepper	
1 tbsp	white wine vinegar or lemon juice	1 tbsp
6 tbsps	sunflower oil	6 tbsps

Blend tofu, mustard, garlic, salt, pepper and 1 teaspoon vinegar in a processor.

Gradually pour in the oil and continue blending until smooth and creamy.

Add remaining vinegar and mix thoroughly.

Taste for seasoning and serve. Makes about 300 ml (1/2 pint).

Dressing serving size = 20 ml unless otherwise stated.

PER SERVING	
Energy Kcals	69
Protein g	1.5
Fat g	6.9
Polyunsaturated fatty acids g	4.16
Saturated fatty acids g	0.81
Carbohydrate g	0.4
Calcium mg	86

Puddings and Sweet Sauces

Apricot and Almond Fool

Apricot Tart Tatin

Baked Apple Charlotte

Baked Chocolate and Almond Torte

Baked Orange Semolina Puddings

Banana and Cashew Nut Ice Cream

Banana Fritters

Blackcurrant Ice Cream

Caramelised Apple Flan

Chocolate, Prune and Whisky Bread and Butter Pudding

Coconut Crème Caramel

Coffee Zabaglione

Fresh Raspberry Tart

Grilled Honey Glazed Pineapple and
Fig Kebabs served with an Orange Sabayon

Mixed Berry and Peach Coconut Crumble

Pear and Ginger Upside Down Pudding

Raisin, Lemon and Almond Ground Rice Pudding

Rhubarb and Almond Tart

Rich Chocolate Brownies

Tangy Citrus Cheesecake

Chocolate Fudge Sauce

Crème Pâtissière

Custard

Fresh Raspberry Coulis

Rich Butterscotch Sauce

Rich Mocha Chocolate Sauce

Oat and Honey Cream

Tofu and Almond Cream

You could make this using either different dried fruit or fresh fruit.

Apricot and Almond Fool

This is a quick and simple vegan pudding. It contains bags of goodness in the almonds and the apricots. Try it on the children to jazz up soya yoghurt. Serve with crisp biscuits or macaroons.

8 oz	dried apricots, two reserved and chopped	225 g
½ pt	boiling water	275 ml
½ pt	natural soya yoghurt	275 ml
3 oz	almonds without skins	75 g
1 tbsp	maple syrup	1 tbsp
½ tsp	vanilla essence	½ tsp

Cover the apricots with the boiling water and soak overnight, alternatively simmer in the water until soft.

Purée the apricots in the soaking liquid until smooth and leave to cool, when cold, fold in the yoghurt.

Grind the almonds finely in a food processor or grinder, add enough water to make a thick cream and continue grinding until smooth.

Sweeten with maple syrup and vanilla essence.

Add apricot purée and blend until smooth.

Spoon into four small dishes. Decorate with chopped apricots.

Refrigerate before serving. Serves 4.

PER SERVING	
Energy Kcals	298
Protein g	10.8
Fat g	15.3
Polyunsaturated fatty acids g	4.76
Saturated fatty acids g	1.43
Carbohydrate g	31.2
Calcium mg	105

I have made this pudding with a variety of different fruits; apples, quinces, bananas, fresh or tinned pineapple and the other day I used pears with crystallized ginger, which was scrumptious.

Apricot Tart Tatin

This is one of my favourites as it can be prepared in advance and cooked before serving. The pastry is deliciously crisp. Serve it with soya ice cream or soya yoghurt. Otherwise for a more healthy option serve it with the Oat and Honey Cream or the Tofu and Almond Cream.

Pastry

6 oz	plain flour	175 g
1	level teaspoon ground mixed spice	1
3 oz	caster sugar	75 g
	pinch salt	
3 oz	vegan margarine	75 g
1	large egg, beaten	1

Filling

2 oz	vegan margarine	50 g
4 oz	soft muscovado sugar	110 g
8 oz	unsulphured apricots	225 g

Soak the apricots overnight or boil for about 20 minutes until soft then drain.

Pre-heat the oven to 190C, 375F, gas 5. Grease a 25.5cm (10 inch) round flan tin or dish. Do not use a loose base dish or the filling will ooze out.

To make the pastry, sift the flour and mixed spice into a bowl, add the caster sugar and the salt, and mix well.

In a small pan, gently melt the margarine, stir it into the flour mixing well, and then mix in the egg.

Press the pastry into a ball and cover in a bowl and place in the fridge for one hour.

For the filling; melt the margarine with the sugar.

Pour into the bottom of the flan dish, covering most of the base.

Lay the apricots over the top of this mixture.

Roll the pastry out on a floured surface to just larger than the flan dish. Don't worry if it breaks you can patch it up.

Carefully lift the pastry to cover the apricots, fold over the sides if it is too big.

Pierce a couple of holes in the pastry.

Cook for about 25 minutes until firm to the touch and golden.

Cool slightly, then carefully turn onto plate before serving. Serves 6.

PER SERVING	
Energy Kcals	357
Protein g	4.5
Fat g	9.0
Polyunsaturated fatty acids g	2.17
Saturated fatty acids g	2.35
Carbohydrate g	71.8
Calcium mg	85

Baked Apple Charlotte

The jam on the bread tends to stick slightly to the side of the dish, but gives it a nice crunchy texture. The walnut oil also provides an unusual taste rather than the usual margarine. The pudding is itself quite creamy and does not really require any further cream, although my children enjoyed a spoonful of soya ice cream with it.

1 lb 12 oz	cooking apples	800 g
1½ oz	caster sugar	35 g
5	slices white stale bread, crusts removed	5
4 oz	apricot jam, preferably without the bits	110 g
2 tbsps	walnut oil, plus extra for brushing	2 tbsps
1 tsp	dark brown sugar	1 tsp

Pre-heat the oven to 190C, 375F, gas 5. Peel, core and slice the apples and put them into a heavy pan.

Add the caster sugar and cook, without water, until very soft. Then using a potato masher mash the apples until they are smooth and creamy.

Oil a 1 litre (1¾ pint) Pyrex dish. Cut each slice of bread into 4 triangles.

Gently warm the jam with a dash of water and the walnut oil, stirring well.

Dip the pieces of bread into this jam mixture to coat each slice.

Arrange the triangles to fit the bottom and the sides of the dish, save about 6 to 8 triangles for the top.

Any left over jam mixture; mix with the apple and pour into the bread-lined dish, cover with remaining bread.

Brush with extra walnut oil and sprinkle the top with dark brown sugar.

Bake for about 30 minutes until crisp and golden.

Allow to cool slightly before serving. Serves 4.

PER SERVING	
Energy Kcals	219
Protein g	1.5
Fat g	13.2
Polyunsaturated fatty acids g	0.75
Saturated fatty acids g	1.32
Carbohydrate g	48.1
Calcium mg	29

If you do not want to use Amaretto liqueur, use a strong black espresso instead.

For anyone who wants a chocolate mousse cake , follow the recipe and stop before the final cooking stage. Pour the uncooked filling over the biscuit base and refrigerate, however, this would be unsuitable for pregnant or elderly people as the eggs would be uncooked. Delicious for anyone else.

Baked Chocolate and Almond Torte

This rich slightly gooey torte turned out to be a big success with my in-laws one cold rainy Sunday lunch. Serve with soya cream or be really naughty and have some soya ice cream with it.

Base

4 oz	dairy-free digestive biscuits	110 g
1 oz	flaked almonds	25 g
2 oz	vegan margarine	50 g

Filling

8 oz	dairy-free good quality dark chocolate	225 g
4	eggs, separated	4
2 tbsps	Amaretto (optional) or use dark black coffee	2 tbsps

Pre-heat the oven to 180C, 350F, gas 4. Crush the biscuits until smooth crumbs, slightly crush the almonds and mix with biscuits.

In a small pan, gently melt the margarine, pour into biscuit crumbs and mix well.

Tip into a greased china flan dish approximately 25.5 cm (10 inch) diameter, and pat the mixture down flat.

Bake in the oven for about 10 minutes until firm, allow to cool while you make the filling.

Break the chocolate into pieces and melt in a bowl over a pan of boiling water. When the chocolate is melted remove the bowl from the pan.

In a separate bowl, beat the yolks and whilst chocolate is still quite hot pour slowly over yolks, beating continuously.

Stir in the Amaretto and leave to cool.

In a large clean bowl, whisk the egg whites until they form a peak, fold the whites into the chocolate mixture.

Pour over base, turn oven down to 170C, 325F, gas 3.

Bake for about 15 minutes, don't overcook as it dries out.

The torte should be eaten when cool and it will be quite sticky still in middle. Serves 6.

PER SERVING	
Energy Kcals	376
Protein g	4.1
Fat g	28.3
Polyunsaturated fatty acids g	3.08
Saturated fatty acids g	8.83
Carbohydrate g	36.8
Calcium mg	42

Use lemons or limes for a different flavour.

Baked Orange Semolina Puddings

These add a new dimension to semolina as we remember it. The addition of eggs makes it into a soufflé-style pudding, well worth a try. Take care not too cook these too hot and long as they may curdle.

2-3	large juicy oranges	2-3
1 oz	granulated sugar	25 g
1 oz	semolina	25 g
3	free-range eggs, separated	3
	icing sugar for dusting	

Pre-heat the oven to 190C, 375F, gas 5. Grate rind and squeeze juice from 2 oranges, to make about 275 ml (1/2 pint). Use another orange if necessary.

Place orange juice, rind, sugar and semolina in a pan and simmer until thickened stirring continuously.

Cool slightly then stir in egg yolks.

Whisk whites until they are stiff, fold them into the orange mixture.

Spoon into 6 lightly oiled ramekin dishes.

Bake in the oven for 15-20 minutes until risen and golden, dust with icing sugar.

Serve immediately. Serves 6.

PER SERVING	
Energy Kcals	75
Protein g	1.5
Fat g	3.0
Polyunsaturated fatty acids g	0.3
Saturated fatty acids g	0.77
Carbohydrate g	18.0
Calcium mg	42.78

Remove from freezer 10 minutes before serving.
  Use almonds instead of cashew nuts for a variation.

Banana and Cashew Nut Ice Cream

This is an easy non-soya ice cream with lots of goodness found in the nuts, oats and bananas. It has a very creamy slightly coarse texture, which may not appeal to everyone, however, it has a lovely rich taste.

9 fl oz	oat or almond drink	250 ml
2 oz	fine porridge oats	50 g
4 oz	cashew nuts	110 g
2	just ripe bananas (weight about 225 g-285 g with skins on)	2
3 tbsps	maple syrup, runny honey or brown sugar	3 tbsps

  Soak the oats in the oat or almond drink for about 30 minutes.
  Blend the soaked oats and cashew nuts in a food processor or liquidizer for about 5 minutes or until smooth and creamy.
  Peel bananas and roughly chop, add to mixture along with the maple syrup, honey or sugar. Use slightly less sweetening if using almond drink which is slightly sweet already.
  Blend until bananas are puréed, taste for sweetness. Remember once frozen it will not taste as sweet.
  Pour into a container. Freeze, folding the ice cream every hour or so. After about 3 hours it should be ready to serve. Makes about 570 ml (1 pint). Serves 4.

PER SERVING	
Energy Kcals	291
Protein g	8.9
Fat g	15.8
Polyunsaturated fatty acids g	3.2
Saturated fatty acids g	2.9
Carbohydrate g	30
Calcium mg	32

Make sure the bananas are not too overripe for this recipe. For an equally delicious pudding use fresh pineapple or apple rings.

Banana Fritters

Delicious crisp fritters. The addition of coconut to the batter makes the dish more exotic. Serve with soya ice cream, soya yoghurt or even tofu and almond cream.

2 oz	plain flour	50 g
	pinch salt	
1	large egg	1
3½ fl oz	coconut milk	100 ml
1 tbsp	caster sugar	1 tbsp
4	firm bananas	4
	oil for shallow frying	
1 tsp	icing sugar mixed with 1 dessertspoon of desiccated coconut	1 tsp

Sift flour with salt in a bowl. Make a well in the centre. Drop in the egg, mix with wooden spoon, gradually incorporating all the flour then slowly add the coconut milk, stirring well.

A thick cream consistency should be reached. Stir in the sugar and allow the batter to rest for 20 minutes.

Peel bananas, cut in half lengthways and dip into the batter.

Heat 5 mm (¼ inch) deep oil in a frying pan. When hot fry the fritters for about 2 minutes on each side until golden brown.

Drain and dust with icing sugar and coconut mix.

Serve immediately whilst the fritters are still crisp. Serves 4.

PER SERVING	
Energy Kcals	219
Protein g	1.4
Fat g	8.5
Polyunsaturated fatty acids g	0.60
Saturated fatty acids g	2.25
Carbohydrate g	40.1
Calcium mg	33

Use other seasonal fruit for a different style ice cream.

For a soya-free ice cream use oat cream on page 191 instead of the soya cream.

Blackcurrant Ice Cream

I thought I would include a fruity ice cream as you can already buy good chocolate and vanilla soya ice creams in most health food shops and supermarkets. This custard-based ice cream was made when I had a surplus of blackcurrants and the result was great, it went wonderfully with hot apple tarts and crumbles.

1 lb 4 oz	blackcurrants	560 g
1/2 pt	elderflower cordial	275 ml
3	eggs	3
4 oz	caster sugar	110 g
3 oz	cornflour	85 g
7 fl oz	soya cream	200 ml

You will need a 2 litre (3½ pint) freezer container. Top and tail just 110 g (4 oz) of the blackcurrants. Take the 450 g (1 lb) of blackcurrants which you haven't top and tailed. Rinse them thoroughly in a sieve.

Place these blackcurrants in a saucepan with the elderflower cordial, cover and bring to the boil, simmer for 2 minutes.

Sieve, pushing all the purée through into a clean bowl.

Separate the eggs, reserve the whites in the fridge. If possible, using an electric beater, whisk the egg yolks with sugar until creamy.

Next, add the cornflour and whisk until smooth then slowly beat in the soya cream.

Pour into a saucepan and whisk over a gentle heat until the mixture thickens to a custard.

Stir the blackcurrant purée into the custard mixture plus the remaining top and tailed whole blackcurrants, mix well, allow this to cool thoroughly.

Whisk the egg whites until they form a peak. Fold the whites into blackcurrant mixture.

Pour into container and freeze, gently stirring the ice cream occasionally, for about 3 hours.

Remove from freezer 5 minutes before serving. Makes about 1.2 litres (2 pints). Serves 8.

PER SERVING	
Energy Kcals	190
Protein g	3.4
Fat g	6.63
Polyunsaturated fatty acids g	2.9
Saturated fatty acids g	1.27
Carbohydrate g	38.5
Calcium mg	47

This is also good with pears, bananas or fresh apricots.

Caramelised Apple Flan

This is based on the French 'Tarte Tatin' recipe. I have included it as it is a super fast recipe for anyone wanting to produce a quick pudding for their lactose-free guest. Serve with soya yoghurt, oat cream, soya ice cream or tofu and almond cream.

2 tbsps	dark brown sugar	2 tbsps
1 tbsp	walnut oil	1 tbsp
1 tsp	ground cinnamon	1 tsp
1 lb	Bramley apples, peeled, cored and very thinly sliced	450 g
8 oz	puff pastry	225 g

Pre-heat the oven to 200C, 400F, gas 6. Oil a 25.5 cm (10 inch) round oven dish, which is at least 2 cm (3/4 inch) high. Sprinkle sugar on the bottom of dish and drizzle over oil and cinnamon.

Lay apples in a neat circle over the sugar, ensure all the base is covered, if necessary layer more apples on top of apples.

Roll out pastry and cut into a circle about 2 cm (3/4 inch) larger than round base, cover the apples with the pastry, pressing it down gently, fold the edges back over.

Bake in the oven for about 20-25 minutes until well risen, crisp and golden.

Turn out onto a warm plate to serve. Serves 4.

PER SERVING	
Energy Kcals	319
Protein g	2.9
Fat g	21.2
Polyunsaturated fatty acids g	0.12
Saturated fatty acids g	0.01
Carbohydrate g	40.5
Calcium mg	60

If you don't have whisky use a brandy or liqueur, otherwise soak the prunes in orange juice.
 Try using coconut cream instead of soya cream for a more exotic pudding.

Chocolate, Prune and Whisky Bread and Butter Pudding

This is a good dinner party pudding, your friends will not believe it is lactose-free, and it is a great way of using up any excess bread. Prunes not only increase the nutritional value of the dish they also make a wonderful combination with chocolate. Serve with soya cream or soya ice cream.

3 oz	pitted prunes, cut into 4 pieces	75 g
2 tbsps	whisky	2 tbsps
6	slices of thick sliced white bread	6
1 oz	vegan margarine	25 g
3 oz	dark dairy-free chocolate, cut into small pieces	75 g
1 oz	cocoa powder	25 g
10 fl oz	oat or soya milk	275 ml
3 oz	caster sugar	75 g
3	eggs	3
6 tbsps	soya cream	6 tbsps
	sprinkling of demerara sugar	

Pre-heat the oven to 180C, 350F, gas 4. You will also need an ovenproof dish with a base measurement of 20 x 15 cm (8 x 6 inch) and 4 cm (1$\frac{1}{2}$ inch) deep, lightly greased.
About 2 hours before you start, pour whisky over the prunes in small bowl and leave to soak.
Remove the crusts from the bread and lightly spread the slices with the margarine. Cut each slice of bread into 4 squares, lay half over bottom of the ovenproof dish.
Cover with the prunes, whisky and chocolate chunks, then lay the remaining bread over the top, overlapping slightly, margarine side up.
Sieve the cocoa in a medium mixing bowl and gradually add the oat or soya milk, making sure cocoa is mixed in thoroughly.
Beat in the eggs, caster sugar and soya cream.
Pour this cocoa mixture over the bread. Press the top gently with a fork to ensure all the bread is coated.
Sprinkle on a little demerara sugar.
Bake for approximately 30-40 minutes. The pudding will rise slightly and the surface should be crisp and golden. Serves 4-6.

PER SERVING	
Energy Kcals	249
Protein g	4.5
Fat g	16.4
Polyunsaturated fatty acids g	2.8
Saturated fatty acids g	4.3
Carbohydrate g	36.1
Calcium mg	36

Coconut contains a high proportion of saturated fats. It is a good addition to the vegetarian dairy-free diet, although those with a meat centred diet should limit their intake.

Coconut Crème Caramel

When I tried to make a crème caramel with soya milk, the result was very watery and not particularly successful. Made with coconut milk, however, the result was a creamy light pudding with a delicate coconut flavour.

1	400 ml tin of coconut milk	1
3	medium eggs	3
6 oz	caster sugar	175 g

Pre-heat the oven to 150C, 300F, gas 2. Put 75 g (3 oz) of the sugar in a heavy pan over a low flame.

Stir and let the sugar caramelise. When melted and golden brown (not burnt) pour the caramel equally into four ramekins.

In a small pan, heat the coconut milk over a low heat until warm.

In a bowl beat the eggs with the remaining sugar until light and creamy.

Gradually add the coconut milk, beating as you do so.

Strain the custard into a jug and pour into ramekins. Put the ramekins in a baking pan, pour enough hot water around them so it comes halfway up the cups.

Bake for 30-40 minutes, until the coconut caramels are set. When cool, refrigerate in the ramekins.

To serve, run a knife around the edges of the bowls and invert onto plates. Makes 4 individual pots.

PER SERVING	
Energy Kcals	325
Protein g	2.7
Fat g	18.7
Polyunsaturated fatty acids g	8.9
Saturated fatty acids g	2.3
Carbohydrate g	47
Calcium mg	25.5

Note that any liqueur can be used, such as Amaretto or a chocolate liqueur (as long as it contains no cream).

Coffee Zabaglione

This pudding is surprisingly creamy and light and is excellent served warm with a crisp biscuit. This dish can also be frozen and served as zabaglione ice cream.

4	egg yolks	4
2 oz	caster sugar	50 g
4 tbsps	strong black coffee	4 tbsps
2 tbsps	coffee liqueur (such as Tia Maria)	2 tbsps
	cocoa powder for decoration	

Combine egg yolks and sugar in a bowl. Whisk for several minutes with an electric beater until pale and frothy.

Place the bowl over a saucepan of simmering water and gradually beat in half the coffee and half the liqueur.

Beat constantly for about 10 minutes over heat until thick and creamy.

Then whisk in the remaining coffee and liqueur. If the mixture adheres to side of pan, quickly remove from heat and beat vigorously with wooden spoon, especially around base.

Pour into individual dishes.

Sprinkle with cocoa powder before serving. Serves 4.

PER SERVING	
Energy Kcals	138
Protein g	2.9
Fat g	6.3
Polyunsaturated fatty acids g	0.53
Saturated fatty acids g	1.62
Carbohydrate g	16.5
Calcium mg	25

When making flans or tarts, metal tins are preferable as they conduct heat better and the result will be a crisper pastry case. The pudding could be also made using any ripe seasonal fruit such as strawberries, blackcurrants, blackberries, peaches or nectarines. Or why not try it with a mixture of berries?

Fresh Raspberry Tart

This is a lovely summer pudding. It can be finished an hour or so before serving and refrigerated. The sweet pastry base retains its crispiness well.

10 oz	Sweet Pastry (page 222)	275 g
½ pt	Crème Pâtissière (page 187)	275ml
1 lb	firm ripe raspberries	450 g
1 tbsp	red currant jelly (or any other fruit jelly) to glaze	1 tbsp

Pre-heat the oven to 200C, 400F, gas 6. On a floured surface, roll out the pastry thinly and line a greased flan ring approximately 23 cm (9 inch) diameter and 5 cm (2 inch) deep with fluted edges. Trim the top and prick the base.

Fill with greaseproof paper and dried beans and bake blind for about 10 minutes.

Remove beans and paper and reduce oven temperature to 180C, 350F, gas 4, return to oven for about 7 minutes to dry out.

Remove from the oven and leave to cool.

Fill the pastry case with cooled crème pâtissière, smooth down well.

Lay the raspberries around the top to cover completely, it doesn't matter if they slightly overlap.

Mix the jelly with a fork to let it loosen slightly (if necessary warm slightly) and brush over the tart to cover the raspberries completely.

Refrigerate before serving. Serves 6.

PER SERVING	
Energy Kcals	484
Protein g	5.78
Fat g	22.2
Polyunsaturated fatty acids g	5.1
Saturated fatty acids g	6.4
Carbohydrate g	70
Calcium mg	117

For the non-alcoholic version, substitute Amaretto with extra orange juice.

Grilled Honey Glazed Pineapple and Fig Kebabs served with an Orange Sabayon

This is a relatively healthy pudding that leaves you feeling you've had something wicked! For those not so keen on a sabayon-style sauce, the kebabs would be great with soya ice cream or if you feel very virtuous, oat and honey cream.

Kebabs

1/2	a medium, ripe pineapple	1/2
3	ripe figs, quartered	3
2 tbsps	runny honey	2 tbsps
4	long skewers	4

Sabayon

3	egg yolks	3
1 oz	caster sugar	25 g
4 tbsps	orange juice	4 tbsps
	zest of one orange	
2 tbsps	Amaretto (optional)	2 tbsps

Peel the pineapple and remove any brown bits. Remove core and cut into 16 equal sized cubes.

Alternate pieces of pineapple and fig so you have 4 pieces of pineapple and 3 pieces of fig on each skewer, spoon over and cover well with the runny honey and lay skewers on an ovenproof dish.

Preheat grill. Grill for about 3 minutes, turn skewer and grill 3 minutes on the other side, they should be beginning to caramelise.

For the Sabayon; put all the ingredients in a pudding basin and set over a pan of simmering water. Whisk until light and fluffy, it will take about 5 minutes.

Serve immediately with the grilled kebabs. Serves 4.

PER SERVING	
Energy Kcals	185
Protein g	3.2
Fat g	3.9
Polyunsaturated fatty acids g	0.60
Saturated fatty acids g	1.02
Carbohydrate g	36.7
Calcium mg	65

Vary the fruit in this crumble according to availability, for example use blackcurrants or blackberries.

Mixed Berry and Peach Coconut Crumble

Crumbles are simple to make and a wonderful way of using seasonal fresh fruit. The topping for this crumble has the unusual addition of coconut, oats and almonds which complement the hot fruit perfectly. Serve with soya ice cream, soya yoghurt or soya custard.

4 oz	blueberries	110 g
4 oz	red currants, stalks removed	110 g
2	fresh peaches	2
3½ fl oz	blackcurrant cordial or blackcurrant syrup	100 ml

Topping

2 oz	plain flour	50 g
2 oz	ground almonds	50 g
2 oz	vegan margarine	50 g
2 oz	desiccated coconut	50 g
1 oz	caster sugar	25 g
1 oz	fine oats	25 g

Pre-heat the oven to 180C, 350F, gas 4. You will need a 1 litre (1¾ pint) pie dish.

Remove the stones from the peaches and cut flesh into small chunks.

Lay the berries, currants and peaches in the pie dish.

Pour over the blackcurrant cordial (I often buy syrup de cassis from France as it does not contain any of the artificial sweeteners our squashes contain. Alternatively you could use elderberry cordial).

For the topping, put the flour and almonds in a bowl and rub in the margarine until the mixture resembles breadcrumbs.

Stir in the coconut, sugar and oats. Spread evenly over the top of the fruit.

Bake in oven for about 30 minutes, until the top is golden. Serves 4.

PER SERVING	
Energy Kcals	472
Protein g	7.3
Fat g	28.4
Polyunsaturated fatty acids g	5.27
Saturated fatty acids g	11.45
Carbohydrate g	50.2
Calcium mg	87

Pears could be substituted with pineapple or apples.

Pear and Ginger Upside Down Pudding

This is a favourite pudding of mine which keeps well and may be easily reheated. It is also nice eaten cold as a cake. Serve hot with soya ice cream, soya cream or soya custard.

2 oz	vegan margarine	50 g
3 oz	light muscovado sugar	75 g
2-3	large firm but ripe pears, peeled, cored and cut into eighths	2-3
2	eggs, beaten	2
2 tbsps	black treacle	2 tbsps
3 oz	vegan margarine, melted	75 g
5 oz	light muscovado sugar	150 g
3 oz	crystallized ginger roughly chopped	75 g
3½ fl oz	oat drink	100 ml
2 tsps	ground ginger	2 tsps
½ tsp	ground cinnamon	½ tsp
6 oz	self-raising flour	175 g

Pre-heat the oven to 180C, 350F, gas 4. Grease a circular oven dish 25.5 cm (10 inch) across and 5 cm (2 inch) deep.

To make the topping, cream together the margarine and muscovado sugar.

Smear this mixture over base of dish and lay the pears neatly in a circle tips touching in centre of dish.

Beat together eggs, treacle, melted margarine, sugar, crystallized ginger and oat drink.

Sift the spices and flour into the egg mixture and mix thoroughly.

Pour over the pears, smooth down and bake for about 40 minutes until cooked through.

Leave for a few minutes, using a knife go around the edge of the tin then turn out onto a warm plate. Serve hot. Serves 6.

PER SERVING	
Energy Kcals	383
Protein g	2.9
Fat g	18.6
Polyunsaturated fatty acids g	4.64
Saturated fatty acids g	5.09
Carbohydrate g	59.8
Calcium mg	141

Egg yolks were used to increase the protein content of the pudding. However if you are cooking for a vegan omit the egg yolks and the pudding will still be delicious.

Raisin, Lemon and Almond Ground Rice Pudding

This is a tasty, nursery-style pudding which the kids will love. The raisins swell up and become really juicy giving the pudding added natural sweetness. I added the almonds to give the pudding a creamy texture as well as increase the calcium content.

1 pt	vanilla rice milk	570 ml
2 oz	ground rice powder	50 g
2 oz	raisins	50 g
1 oz	ground almonds	25 g
1 tsp	vanilla essence	1 tsp
2 tsps	runny honey	2 tsps
1	good sized lemon, grated	1
2	egg yolks	2

In a large saucepan whisk the rice milk slowly into the ground rice powder until smooth.

Add the raisins and ground almonds.

Cook over a medium heat until the sauce thickens. Reduce the heat and simmer for about 6 minutes, stirring occasionally.

Stir in the vanilla essence, honey and grated rind, remove from heat and leave to cool slightly (about 5 minutes).

Beat in the egg yolks, return to heat and cook gently for about 5 minutes, take care not to boil and curdle the yolks.

Serve hot in individual bowls. Serves 4.

PER SERVING	
Energy Kcals	260
Protein g	4.5
Fat g	8.5
Polyunsaturated fatty acids g	1.83
Saturated fatty acids g	1.26
Carbohydrate g	42.9
Calcium mg	67

Also delicious with gooseberries, apples, plums or fresh apricots, whatever is in season.

Tip: metal tins help make the flan pastry crisp.

Rhubarb and Almond Tart

This is an easy tart to prepare as the pastry does not require pre-cooking. The tart is then filled with an almond mixture with the uncooked rhubarb laid on top. It may be left in the fridge at this stage and put in the oven an hour before serving. Serve warm with soya cream or soya ice cream.

8 oz	Shortcrust Pastry (see page 223)	225 g
2 tbsps	raspberry jam	2 tbsps
4 oz	vegan margarine	110 g
4 oz	soft brown sugar	110 g
2	eggs, beaten	2
4 oz	ground almonds	110 g
1 oz	plain flour	30 g
1	orange	1
12 oz	rhubarb, cut in 1½ cm (½ inch) pieces	340 g
	redcurrant jelly for glazing	

Pre-heat the oven to 350F, 180C, Gas 4. On a floured surface, roll the pastry out thinly and line a greased 23 cm (9 inch) flan dish.

Prick base with a fork and smear over the jam.

Beat margarine and sugar until light and creamy then gradually add the eggs, beat well. Grate the zest from the orange, and squeeze the juice of half.

Stir in the almonds, flour, orange zest and juice.

When well blended, pour into the flan dish and smooth down.

Arrange the rhubarb neatly over the top, push down slightly into the almond mixture, but do not completely submerge.

Bake in the oven for about 40-50 minutes until firm to the touch and golden.

Glaze with jelly. Serve warm or chilled. Serves 6.

PER SERVING	
Energy Kcals	536
Protein g	7.5
Fat g	37.5
Polyunsaturated fatty acids g	8.5
Saturated fatty acids g	9.1
Carbohydrate g	50.6
Calcium mg	160

Cut into smaller squares and serve for a picnic or buffet.

Rich Chocolate Brownies

Serve with chocolate sauce and vanilla soya ice cream for a very indulgent yummy pudding. Alternatively serve cold as a tea-time treat.

Store in an airtight container for up to 6 days.

10 oz	dark dairy-free chocolate	275 g
8 oz	vegan margarine	225 g
10 oz	soft brown sugar	275 g
4	eggs, beaten	4
1 tsp	vanilla essence	1 tsp
4 oz	self-raising flour	110 g
1/2 tsp	bicarbonate of soda	1/2 tsp
	pinch salt	
1 tbsp	cocoa powder	1 tbsp
6 oz	chopped hazelnuts	170 g

Pre-heat the oven to 170C, 325F, gas 3. Line the base of a baking tin approximately 20 x 30 cm (8 x 12 inch) and 5 cm (2 inch) deep with greaseproof paper.

Put the chocolate in a bowl over a pan of boiling water, and stir until melted.

Cream the margarine and sugar by hand or in food processor until well blended.

Gradually add the eggs and vanilla essence, mixing well.

Pour the chocolate onto the eggs slowly, beating constantly. Sieve the flour, bicarbonate of soda, salt and cocoa.

Fold the flour and chopped hazelnuts into chocolate mixture, until well combined.

Pour into the lined baking tin and smooth down. Bake on the centre shelf for about 35-40 minutes.

It should be firm, slightly dry around the edges and a skewer should come out almost clean when put into the brownie.

Cut into squares and serve warm. Serves 12.

PER SERVING	
Energy Kcals	467
Protein g	5.3
Fat g	33.2
Polyunsaturated fatty acids g	5.86
Saturated fatty acids g	9.48
Carbohydrate g	47.4
Calcium mg	90

For a different flavoured cheesecake try using other fruit purées such as raspberry or strawberry.

Tangy Citrus Cheesecake

This is an extremely successful pudding. The addition of tofu and cashew nuts not only makes this pudding quite nutritious, it contributes to the realistic creamy cheesecake texture. Serve decorated with seasonal fresh berries or Fresh Raspberry Coulis (see page 188). For a vegan cheesecake, instead of gelatine, use Gelo following the manufacturers instructions.

Base		
6 oz	sweet wheat biscuits (check they are lactose free)	175 g
3 oz	vegan margarine	75 g
Filling		
1	lime	1
1	lemon	1
1-2	oranges	1-2
3 oz	cashew nuts	75 g
4 oz	firm tofu	110 g
3½ fl oz	soya milk	100 ml
2 oz	caster sugar	50 g
2	sheets gelatine (or equivalent in gelatine powder)	2

To make the base; crush the biscuits to fine crumbs. Melt margarine in small pan, take care not to overheat.

Stir the melted margarine into the biscuit crumbs, mixing well.

Press into a lightly oiled 20 cm (8 inch) cake or flan tin with loose base. Refrigerate to harden.

For the filling; grate the zest from all the fruit.

Squeeze the lime, lemon and oranges until there is 200 ml (7 fl oz) of juice altogether.

In a liquidizer or food processor, blend the cashew nuts, tofu, soya milk and sugar until it becomes smooth and silky.

Reserving 4 tablespoons of citrus juice to one side, pour remaining juice into the food processor and continue processing.

Soak the gelatine in a bowl of cold water until it becomes soft. Heat the reserved citrus juice until warm, add softened gelatine, and melt over a warm heat until dissolved.

Pour the melted gelatine into the cheesecake mixture, stirring well. Pour the filling over the base and leave to set in the fridge. Serve chilled. Serves 6.

PER SERVING	
Energy Kcals	353
Protein g	7.8
Fat g	24.3
Polyunsaturated fatty acids g	4.5
Saturated fatty acids g	4.6
Carbohydrate g	27.4
Calcium mg	157

If the sauce solidifies when cold, reheat slowly to sauce consistency.

Chocolate Fudge Sauce

This sauce is easy to do with a result that is as good as any chocolate fudge sauce made using butter. Perfect for serving warm or cold as an accompaniment to ice creams or sponge puddings.

2 oz	plain dark dairy-free chocolate	50 g
4 oz	dark brown sugar	110 g
1 oz	cocoa powder sifted	25 g
2 tsps	vanilla essence	2 tsps

Place all the ingredients in a saucepan, along with 275 ml (1/2 pint) cold water, slowly bring to the boil, stirring occasionally.

Boil for 2-3 minutes, stirring constantly, remove from heat. Serve hot. Serves 4.

PER SERVING	
Energy Kcals	195
Protein g	2.1
Fat g	5.6
Polyunsaturated fatty acids g	0.21
Saturated fatty acids g	3.28
Carbohydrate g	37.6
Calcium mg	30

Use in profiteroles as a filling topped with a coffee glacé icing (made with hot coffee and icing sugar). It could also be flavoured with cocoa to make a delicious chocolate filling.

Another idea is to mix this with fruit purées such as apple and blackberry and pour into individual pots or glasses as a tasty fool-style pudding. Try this for your children.

Crème Pâtissière

Crème Pâtissière is the delicious custard-like filling that fills many French tarts. It can be used as a creamy filling for many puddings and is excellent served with stewed fruit. I have used it to fill a Fresh Raspberry Tart (see page 178).

1/2 pt	plain soya milk	275 ml
2	large egg yolks	2
2 oz	caster sugar (or vanilla sugar and omit essence)	50 g
3/4 oz	plain white flour	20 g
3/4 oz	cornflour	20 g
1/2 tsp	vanilla essence	1/2 tsp
2 tbsps	soya cream	2 tbsps

Heat the soya milk until fairly hot but not boiling. Cream the yolks and sugar until pale, whisk in the sieved flours.

Gradually pour in the milk and stirring well. Return the mixture to the milk pan.

Slowly bring up to the boil, stirring continuously. It will begin to go thick and lumpy, don't worry just stir well until smooth.

Allow to cool slightly, then add the vanilla essence and soya cream.

Use chilled as required. Makes 275 ml (1/2 pint) quantity. Serves 6.

PER SERVING	
Energy Kcals	80
Protein g	2.2
Fat g	2.5
Polyunsaturated fatty acids g	0.70
Saturated fatty acids g	0.58
Carbohydrate g	13.1
Calcium mg	14

Tip: If you are not serving the custard immediately, lay greaseproof paper over to cover the top and this will prevent a skin forming.

PER QUANTITY	
Energy Kcals	424
Protein g	21.5
Fat g	20.14
Polyunsaturated fatty acids g	7.29
Saturated fatty acids g	4.32
Carbohydrate g	4.4
Calcium mg	118.05

This can be made using fresh strawberries or blackcurrants.

PER QUANTITY	
Energy Kcals	195
Protein g	4.3
Fat g	0.9
Polyunsaturated fatty acids g	0.3
Saturated fatty acids g	0.3
Carbohydrate g	45.7
Calcium mg	78.1

Right:
Rice and Honey Pudding
(page 203)

Custard

In my household, custard, when on offer, has to be the number one favourite, especially with hot puddings. The yolks give the custard a higher protein content and also adds creaminess. Serve straight away or use to top trifle.

1 pt	plain soya or oat drink	570 ml
2 dsps	custard powder	2 dsps
2	egg yolks	2
	sugar to taste	
1 tsp	vanilla essence or fresh vanilla pod	1 tsp

Warm the soya milk over a medium heat, taking care not to let it boil.

In a bowl, mix the custard powder with 1-2 tablespsoons of the soya milk until smooth, blend in the egg yolks and vanilla essence.

Next, pour the warm milk over the custard mixture, beating well.

Return to the pan and stir over a low heat until it thickens, take care not to cook too quickly and curdle eggs.

Sweeten with sugar to taste.

Serve hot. Makes just over 570 ml (1 pint).

Fresh Raspberry Coulis

Serve with soya ice creams, fresh fruit tarts, cheesecakes or even fresh fruit salad.

11 oz	fresh raspberries or frozen	310 g
2-3 tbsps	icing sugar	2-3 tbsps

Defrost the raspberries if frozen. Push the fruit through a sieve to remove seeds.

Sift in the icing sugar and mix well.

Taste for sweetness and add more sugar if necessary.

If the coulis is too thick, dilute with water or apple juice.

Serves 4-6.

Rich Butterscotch Sauce

Butterscotch sauce would usually be made with condensed milk, this version using coconut milk works very well and is almost as delicious. Serve with soya ice creams, bananas, meringues, sponge puddings or even try it with pineapple, banana or apple fritters.

7 fl oz	water	200 ml
4½ oz	dark brown sugar	125 g
7 fl oz	coconut milk	200 ml
½ tbsp	arrowroot	½ tbsp

Place the water and sugar in a small saucepan over a low heat. Stir until dissolved, then bring to boil and simmer for 15 minutes.

Remove from heat and leave for several minutes, add coconut milk and stir well.

Mix arrowroot with a tablespoon of water until smooth.

Pour the arrowroot into the sauce and stir over a gentle heat to thicken slightly.

Serve hot or cold. Makes just over 275 ml (½ pint). Serves 6.

PER SERVING	
Energy Kcals	85
Protein g	0.1
Fat g	0.1
Polyunsaturated fatty acids g	0
Saturated fatty acids g	0.07
Carbohydrate g	23.2
Calcium mg	21

Left:
Cheesy-Style Macaroni
(page 200)

Try making this sauce with coconut milk or coconut cream instead of the soya cream.

Rich Mocha Chocolate Sauce

This rich chocolate and coffee sauce is perfect served hot with chocolate brownies, soya ice cream, profiteroles and many other puddings.

5 oz	dark dairy-free chocolate, broken into chunks	150 g
5 fl oz	strong hot espresso coffee	150 ml
5 fl oz	soya cream	150 ml

Bring a pan of water to the boil. Put the chocolate chunks into a bowl and suspend over the water.

Melt the chocolate and stir until smooth. When thoroughly melted, remove the bowl from pan.

Slowly pour some of the hot coffee into the chocolate, stirring gently. Initially the chocolate will appear the go thick and solid.

Do not worry, just continue stirring and adding hot coffee slowly.

Eventually after about 150 ml (5 fl oz) of coffee it will become smooth and silky.

Finally add the soya cream and mix well, the result should be a smooth pouring chocolate sauce.

This can be allowed to cool and then reheated either in a microwave or over a pan of boiling water.

Serve hot. Makes about 275 ml (1/2 pint).

Serves 4.

PER SERVING	
Energy Kcals	251
Protein g	2.83
Fat g	16.8
Polyunsaturated fatty acids g	4.47
Saturated fatty acids g	6.92
Carbohydrate g	23.4
Calcium mg	14

For a better result, make sure you buy the fine porridge oats rather than Jumbo oats.

Oat and Honey Cream

I have to say I was very impressed when I created this cream, it has a lovely consistency. However, the cream will have a slightly grainy taste, because the oats have been broken down during the processing. This does make it very nutritious as hardly any parts of the oats have been removed.

Serve as very low fat cream with hot puddings. Delicious with stewed fruits such as pear and apple or even a warm apple flan. Use in the Banana Oat Shake on page 229 or the children's Chocolate Oat Dessert on page 201.

3 oz	fine porridge oats	75 g
11 fl oz	cold water (more water for a runnier cream)	300 ml
2 tbsps	runny honey	2 tbsps

Soak the oats in the water and honey for at least 2 hours. Blend in a food processor or liquidiser until smooth.

Sieve well and refrigerate until required.

This will keep well in the fridge for several days. Makes about 330 ml (12 fl oz).

PER QUANTITY	
Energy Kcals	405
Protein g	9.6
Fat g	7.8
Polyunsaturated fatty acids g	3.1
Saturated fatty acids g	1.36
Carbohydrate g	79.0
Calcium mg	46

To make an alternative to sour cream omit the vanilla and honey, and squeeze in a dash of lemon juice. Cashew nuts can also be used to produce a cream equally as delicious.

Once you start experimenting with this, there are many variations, by adding more nuts and less tofu, etc.

Tofu and Almond Cream

This makes a useful sauce to serve in place of dairy products like cream, Greek yoghurt and ice cream. Based on tofu and almonds, it is more nutritious and fairly low in fat compared to many creams.

2 fl oz	soya milk	55 ml
4 oz	firm tofu	110 g
2 oz	blanched almonds (flaked, ground or whole)	50 g
1 inch	vanilla pod (or 1 teaspoon vanilla essence)	2.5 cm
1 tsp	honey (more depending on taste)	1 tsp

Use a liquidizer or food processor to blend all the ingredients except honey, until smooth and creamy.

Add honey to taste, blend again to mix well.

Refrigerate until required.

This cream will last several days in the fridge. Makes about 250 ml (8 fl oz).

PER QUANTITY	
Energy Kcals	481
Protein g	24.5
Fat g	39.5
Polyunsaturated fatty acids g	11.68
Saturated fatty acids g	3.62
Carbohydrate g	6.3
Calcium mg	789

Children's Meals, Puddings, Sweets and Treats

Pasta with Bacon and Beans

Barbecued Chicken

Creamy Chicken Korma

Tasty Fish Pie

Quick Scone Pizza

Stir-fry Quorn and Vegetables with Noodles

Cheesy-Style Macaroni

Chocolate Oat Dessert

Easy Fruit Trifle

Rice and Honey Pudding

Chocolate and Brazil Nut Fudge

Fruity Slices

Honey and Sesame Corn Snaps

Try this recipe with drained tinned tuna and sweetcorn instead of the bacon.

Pasta with Bacon and Beans

Quick and simple to cook, providing a balanced, delicious meal for your children. It also makes a great meal for the whole family. The addition of hummus together with the sun-dried tomato paste gives the pasta a rich satisfying flavour.

6 oz	French beans	175 g
8-10 oz	dried penne or spiral pasta	225-275 g
4	rashers un-smoked back bacon	4
3 tbsps	crushed sun-dried tomato paste	3 tbsps
2-3 tbsps	hummus	2-3 tbsps

Top and tail the French beans and cut in half lengthways.

Bring a large pan of water to the boil, cook the penne for about 8-10 minutes.

After about 3 minutes throw in the beans and continue cooking.

Drain the pasta and beans when just cooked.

Remove the rind from the bacon rashers and chop into pieces. Heat a small frying pan and cook bacon for several minutes (this should not require extra oil).

In the large pasta pan toss the hot pasta and beans with sun-dried tomato paste, bacon and hummus.

Serve immediately. Serves 4.

PER SERVING	
Energy Kcals	481
Protein g	24.5
Fat g	39.5
Polyunsaturated fatty acids g	11.68
Saturated fatty acids g	3.62
Carbohydrate g	6.3
Calcium mg	789

If using chicken breast, marinate the chicken pieces in the sauce and then roast or barbecue them for 10-15 minutes. This will depend on the size and cut of the chicken. Kallo liquid seasoning is found in most supermarkets and health food shops and adds natural flavouring to many dishes.

Barbecued Chicken

This dish is very successful with older children who are beginning to enjoy more exciting styles of cooking. Using chicken legs and drumsticks enables it to be an economical dish especially if buying organic or free-range chicken. This is a great dish for all the family served with basmati rice and salad.

8	free-range chicken pieces (drum sticks and/or thighs)	8
1 tbsp	olive oil	1 tbsp
	freshly ground pepper	
2	large cloves garlic, finely chopped	2
1	medium onion, finely chopped	1
1 inch	fresh ginger, finely chopped	2.5 cm
1	heaped tablespoon soft brown sugar	1
1	heaped tablespoon tomato purée	1
2 tsps	Chinese five spice	2 tsps
1/4 pt	chicken or vegetable stock	150 ml
1 tbsp	cider vinegar	1 tbsp
1 tbsp	balsamic vinegar	1 tbsp
2 tbsps	dark soya sauce	2 tbsps
3 tbsps	light soya sauce	3 tbsps
1 tsp	kallo liquid organic seasoning	1 tsp

Pre-heat the oven to 200C, 400F, gas 6. Pat the chicken pieces dry. Rub with olive oil and freshly ground pepper.

Lay the chicken in a suitable oven dish. Roast in the oven for 20 minutes.

Meanwhile make the sauce. Mix all the sauce ingredients together in a bowl, stir thoroughly, alternatively liquidize to a smooth sauce.

Remove the chicken from the oven and pour over the sauce covering well.

Return to the oven and turn the heat down to 180C, 350F, gas 4.

Cook for a further 20-25 minutes, basting several times with the sauce. Serve hot. Serves 4-6.

PER SERVING	
Energy Kcals	373
Protein g	32.2
Fat g	25.6
Polyunsaturated fatty acids g	4.49
Saturated fatty acids g	6.61
Carbohydrate g	3.6
Calcium mg	22

Use cheaper cuts of chicken such as the legs and thighs. Pre-roast, remove meat from the bone then mix in the sauce and cook in the oven as with the chicken breast.

If possible make the sauce in large amounts and store in a jar in the fridge for up to one week. The sauce can also be frozen.

Creamy Chicken Korma

This is my daughter Harriet's favourite meal. It is a good beginners curry dish suitable also for those adults who only like a creamy mild flavour. Serve with basmati rice or hot naan bread.

1 tbsp	vegetable oil	1 tbsp
1	onion, chopped	1
2	cloves garlic, crushed	2
2 tsps	mild or medium curry powder	2 tsps
1 tsp	ground turmeric	1 tsp
3 tbsps	ground almonds	3 tbsps
5 fl oz	vegetable or chicken stock	150 ml
½ pt	coconut milk	275 ml
	salt and pepper (if desired)	
3	chicken breasts, each about 110 g (4 oz), boneless, skinless, each cut into 6 pieces	3

Garnish

	toasted flaked almonds and fresh coriander (optional)	

Pre-heat the oven to 200C, 400F, gas 6. Heat oil in a frying pan, sweat the onion and garlic for about 5 minutes, until softened.

Add curry powder and turmeric and stir over the heat for a further 30 seconds.

Tip the onions into a food processor with the ground almonds, stock, coconut milk and seasonings.

Whiz until you have a smooth liquid.

Lay chicken pieces in a suitable casserole dish. Pour over the sauce.

Bake uncovered for about 30 minutes, stirring occasionally, cover half way through the cooking if the curry begins to dry out.

Serve on warm plates, garnish with coriander and almonds. Serves 4-5 children or 3 adults.

PER SERVING	
Energy Kcals	327
Protein g	22.6
Fat g	25
Polyunsaturated fatty acids g	11.9
Saturated fatty acids g	3.8
Carbohydrate g	6.7
Calcium mg	29.7

For younger children take care to remove all bones. If your children like eggs, substitute some fish with hard-boiled eggs.

Tasty Fish Pie

Most children enjoy fish pie, and this is a simple version with the addition of peas which increase the nutritional value and make it a complete meal. Even my son Toby, who does not usually like fish, loved this dish.

1 lb	old potatoes	450 g
12 oz	white fish fillet (haddock, cod or coley)	350 g
3 oz	vegan margarine	75 g
1 oz	plain flour	25 g
5 fl oz	vegetable, chicken or fish stock	150 ml
1/4 tsp	Worcestershire sauce	1/4 tsp
5 fl oz	oat drink	150 ml
4 oz	frozen peas or petit pois	110 g
2 tbsps	oat drink	2 tbsps
	salt and pepper (if necessary)	

Pre-heat the oven to 200C, 400F, gas 6. Peel the potatoes and boil or steam until tender.

Lay the fish in a greased baking dish, season and dot with 10 g (1/2 oz) of the margarine.

Cover well with tin foil and bake for about 15-20 minutes. Remove from the oven and leave to cool slightly.

Remove the skin from the fish and flake flesh into fairly large pieces, reserve any cooking juices.

Melt 25 g (1 oz) of the remaining margarine in a saucepan, stir in the flour and gradually add the stock and Worcestershire sauce.

Allow sauce to come to the boil then slowly add 150 ml (5 fl oz) oat drink and frozen peas until well blended.

Mix the fish and any cooking juices into sauce and pour into the baking dish.

Mash the potatoes with the remaining margarine and 2 tablespoons of oat drink then season with salt and pepper.

Spoon the potato over the fish and smooth down evenly.

Bake in the oven for about 25 minutes or until heated through and browned.

Serve hot. Serves 4 hungry children.

PER SERVING	
Energy Kcals	354
Protein g	21.0
Fat g	18.3
Polyunsaturated fatty acids g	5.16
Saturated fatty acids g	5.15
Carbohydrate g	28.0
Calcium mg	44

If you have extra uncooked scone mixture, make into an instant teatime snack. The base is also ideal to freeze before adding the topping.

If children do not like soya cheeses, try dotting with tofutti (soya cream cheese) when the pizza is just cooked and piping hot. For a delicious adult pizza blanched spinach is delicious as a topping with the tofutti dotted on after cooking.

Quick Scone Pizza

By using a scone-type pizza dough this is a quick dish to prepare and many children may prefer it to a bread-based pizza base because it is less chewy. Add toppings of your choice: sliced mushrooms, peppers, garlic, cooked bacon, pepperoni, capers, olives, basil, chopped chillies, artichokes, sun-dried tomatoes, anchovies, drained tinned tuna fish, cooked ham.

Base

8 oz	self-raising flour	225 g
1/2	level teaspoon salt	1/2
2 fl oz	sunflower oil or olive oil	55 ml
3 1/2 fl oz	soya milk	100 ml

Topping

1/2	400 g tin of chopped tomatoes	1/2
1	heaped tablespoon sun-dried tomato paste	1
	pinch of salt	
	pinch of sugar	
	toppings of your choice (see above)	
4 oz	soya mozzarella	110 g

Preheat the oven to 200C, 400F, gas 6. Sift flour and salt, stir in the oil and soya milk and knead for several minutes until you have a smooth dough.

On a floured surface roll out into a 30 cm (12 inch) circle. Place on a greased, flat baking tray and bake in the oven for about 8-10 minutes until risen, firm and beginning to turn pale golden.

While the base is cooking prepare the topping.

Empty chopped tomatoes into a saucepan. Add sun-dried tomatoes and seasonings.

Simmer for about 15 minutes, allowing water in tomatoes to evaporate.

Using potato masher, mash slightly to become smoother.

Remove cooked base from the oven. Spread the tomato sauce over the pizza base.

Lay the various toppings on the tomato sauce, followed by the grated or thinly sliced soya mozzarella.

Cook in the oven for about 10 minutes until sizzling and golden.

Cut into slices to serve. Serves 4.

PER SERVING	
Energy Kcals	357
Protein g	6.8
Fat g	17.5
Polyunsaturated fatty acids g	2.18
Saturated fatty acids g	2.39
Carbohydrate g	45.9
Calcium mg	213

Non-vegetarian children may prefer strips of chicken breast or pork fillet instead.

Stir-fry Quorn and Vegetables with Noodles

Quorn is a vegetarian product readily available in chunks or minced form from health food shops and supermarkets. It is very low in fat and high in protein. Children love the chunks as they resemble chicken. It is useful to have tucked in the freezer as it can be cooked from frozen, which is handy when the fridge is bare. It is also good combined with other vegetables such as Chinese lettuce, broccoli etc. However I find this combination goes down best.

4 oz	French beans, top and tailed	110 g
6-7 oz	dried medium noodles	180-200 g
1 tbsp	groundnut oil	1 tbsp
2	cloves garlic, crushed	2
4	spring onions, cut into strips	4
7 oz	quorn chunks	200 g
2	small carrots, peeled and cut into thin straws	2
5 fl oz	vegetable stock	150 ml
4 oz	bean sprouts	110 g
2 tbsps	light or medium soya sauce	2 tbsps

Bring a pan of water up to boil for the noodles. When boiling put in the French beans and blanch for about 3 minutes, scoop out with slotted spoon so as not to waste the water, run cold water over the beans to retain their colour.

Return pan to heat, and when water re-boils, cook the noodles according to instructions, and drain when just cooked.

Meanwhile, heat oil in a large wok or frying pan.

Add garlic, spring onions and Quorn chunks, cook over medium heat for 3 minutes.

Add carrots, French beans and stock and cook for further 3 minutes.

Add bean sprouts, noodles and soy sauce and stir for several minutes to mix everything together well.

Serve straight away. Serves 4 children or 2-3 adults.

VEGETARIAN

PER SERVING	
Energy Kcals	222
Protein g	6.7
Fat g	7.1
Polyunsaturated fatty acids g	0.87
Saturated fatty acids g	0.55
Carbohydrate g	38.9
Calcium mg	47

Thin slices of bacon or ham could be added to the dish.

A couple of tablespoons of fine breadcrumbs could be sprinkled over the final dish for added texture. Then place under a hot grill to toast breadcrumbs.

Cheesy-Style Macaroni

I was a bit worried about trying to recreate a recipe that generally relies so much on all the cheese and milk in it. However it proved to be a success with the children. The addition of eggs in this recipe was a last minute idea to enhance the nutritional value of the meal.

8 oz	dried macaroni	225 g
2 oz	vegan margarine	50 g
1½ oz	plain flour	35 g
18 fl oz	good chicken stock (or vegetable if preferred)	500 ml
2 tsps	Dijon mustard	2 tsps
½ tsp	Worcestershire sauce	½ tsp
2	eggs, beaten	2

Bring a large pan of water to the boil and cook the macaroni until nearly cooked (cooking time varies on size, see instructions on back of pack), drain and put to one side.

In a saucepan melt the margarine, add flour and cook briefly, slowly add the chicken stock until the sauce is smooth, bring to the boil to thicken.

Add the mustard and Worcestershire sauce and season if necessary, allow to cool slightly.

Mix the eggs into the sauce and stir well, add the cooked macaroni.

Return the pan to a low heat and stir well for about five minutes until the macaroni is heated through and the eggs are cooked but take care not to scramble the eggs.

Serve immediately. Serves 4.

VEGETARIAN

PER SERVING	
Energy Kcals	336
Protein g	7.2
Fat g	15.4
Polyunsaturated fatty acids g	3.04
Saturated fatty acids g	3.45
Carbohydrate g	51.9
Calcium mg	33.2

Freeze for an iced version.

Chocolate Oat Dessert

I decided to try and create a custard-like pudding that contained no soya, as you can buy some chocolate soya-style puddings from most health food shops. I was a little doubtful about it, but when I made it for my two children, much to my surprise, they could not eat enough. Make it for your child, you never know, and it's not too unhealthy either.

12 fl oz	Oat and Honey Cream (see page 191)	330 ml
1	heaped tablespoon cocoa powder	1

Sieve the cocoa powder in a bowl.
Slowly beat in the oat and honey cream, mixing well to become a smooth chocolate dessert.
Sweeten as desired, pour into individual pots.
Serve chilled. Serves 3-4.

PER SERVING

Energy Kcals	108
Protein g	2.7
Fat g	1.9
Polyunsaturated fatty acids g	0.00
Saturated fatty acids g	0.03
Carbohydrate g	21.2
Calcium mg	12

If you want to make an adult version of this trifle, you could omit the jelly and use 150 ml of Sherry and 150 ml fruit juice poured over the sponge fingers, covered with fresh raspberries or peaches and then the custard. Everyone loves a trifle now and then.

Easy Fruit Trifle

This is a great pudding for a children's party or special occasion. I have checked out most bought trifle sponges and they all seem to contain whey, so I used sponge fingers as I found a variety from Waitrose which contained no whey, you need to look around. Otherwise use a Victoria sponge made with vegan margarine, see the Wicked Chocolate Cake recipe on page 221 and omit the cocoa powder. I like to use vegetarian jelly from the health shop. However, you could just as well use a standard jelly.

1	pack of raspberry jelly	1
1/2	175 g pack of sponge fingers	1/2
1 tbsp	good raspberry jam	1 tbsp
2	bananas	2
1 pt	custard see page 188 (alternatively 1 carton vanilla dessert)	570 ml
6	strawberries	6
	handful of flaked almonds for decoration, if desired	

Make jelly up to 570 ml (1 pint) with boiling water.

Spread the sponge fingers with the jam and lay them on the base of a serving bowl.

Pour the jelly over the sponge fingers and leave to set.

Slice the bananas and lay over the set jelly.

Pour over the slightly cooled custard and refrigerate.

Decorate with sliced strawberries and sprinkle over flaked almonds.

Chill to serve. Serves 6.

PER SERVING	
Energy Kcals	314.7
Protein g	7.3
Fat g	11.16
Polyunsaturated fatty acids g	3.15
Saturated fatty acids g	3.1
Carbohydrate g	43.3
Calcium mg	51.7

You could use Vanilla Rice Dream or Almond Drink which are both quite sweet, in which case omit the honey. Try making coconut rice pudding with half coconut cream, half rice drink.

Rice and Honey Pudding

The colour is not as white and creamy looking as with milk but it tastes surprisingly good. I tempted my children by smearing over some strawberry jam and needless to say they demolished the whole bowl.

1 tsp	vegan margarine	1 tsp
1 oz	pudding rice	25 g
1 pt	original Rice Dream	570 ml
1 tbsp	runny honey	1 tbsp
1/2 tsp	vanilla essence	1/2 tsp

Pre-heat the oven to 170C, 325F, gas 3. Rub the margarine round a pie dish.

Put the rice, Rice Dream, honey and vanilla essence in the dish, stir round to mix.

Bake for about 1-1 1/2 hours, by then it should be soft and creamy with a golden skin. Serves 2-3.

PER SERVING	
Energy Kcals	151.8
Protein g	0.76
Fat g	3.34
Polyunsaturated fatty acids g	0.76
Saturated fatty acids g	0.62
Carbohydrate g	30.27
Calcium mg	0.65

Another idea would be to dip whole brazil nuts or almonds into the fudge (without burning fingers). Then allow these to cool on greaseproof paper.

Chocolate and Brazil Nut Fudge

To find fudge without butter and cream seems to be an impossibility. I started making this to make a toffee sweet, however, the end result was a delicious buttery tasting fudge.

7 oz	caster sugar	200 g
1 tbsp	water	1 tbsp
1 tbsp	runny honey	1 tbsp
1 tbsp	malt extract	1 tbsp
1 tbsp	cocoa powder	1 tbsp
3 oz	brazil nuts, chopped	75 g
1 tsp	vanilla essence	1 tsp

You will need a small 10 x 15 cm (4 x 6 inch) tin, lined on the base with either greaseproof paper or rice paper.

Melt the sugar, water, honey and malt extract in a small pan over heat, without boiling, until the sugar is dissolved.

Bring to boil, stir constantly over heat until the liquid becomes golden brown.

Remove the pan from heat and stir in the cocoa powder, mixing well until dissolved.

Stir in chopped nuts and vanilla essence, return to heat if it cools down too quickly.

Pour into the prepared tin and leave to cool.

When the fudge is just firm carefully cut it into about 14 squares.

Could also be spooned into little cup cases. Makes 14 squares.

PER SQUARE	
Energy Kcals	107
Protein g	1.1
Fat g	4.4
Polyunsaturated fatty acids g	1.40
Saturated fatty acids g	1.13
Carbohydrate g	17.0
Calcium mg	12

Vary the nuts and fruit to find your favourite combination. Try adding a tbsp of honey and 55 g (2 oz) of rice crispies to make a crispier snack.

Fruity Slices

These are a healthy option for a quick treat, full of goodness and satisfying enough for that sweet craving. Surprisingly, my children enjoyed them too.

2 oz	dried apricots	50 g
2 oz	dried pear or apple	50 g
2 oz	dried banana or dates	50 g
2 oz	raisins or sultanas	50 g
2 oz	cashew nuts or hazelnuts	50 g
2 oz	ground almonds	50 g
2 tbsps	orange juice	2 tbsps
1½ oz	fine porridge oats	35 g

Pulse the dried fruit and cashew nuts in a food processor until fairly fine.

Mix in the ground almonds, oats and orange juice and quickly pulse again.

Spoon the mixture into a 18 cm (7 inch) square tin lined with greaseproof paper smoothing down well. Leave in the fridge to chill.

Turn out and cut into thin fingers. Makes about 16.

PER SLICE	
Energy Kcals	87
Protein g	2.1
Fat g	3.9
Polyunsaturated fatty acids g	0.79
Saturated fatty acids g	0.49
Carbohydrate g	11.6
Calcium mg	22

Honey and Sesame Corn Snaps

A great way to use up old cornflakes, and not as naughty as the chocolate version. Cooking them slightly, helps them hold together well in the cases.

2 oz	vegan margarine	50 g
3 oz	runny honey	75 g
2 oz	soft brown sugar	50 g
4 oz	cornflakes	110 g
1 tbsp	sesame seeds	1 tbsp
16	small paper cup cake moulds	16

Pre-heat the oven to 180C, 350F, gas 4. Melt the margarine, honey and brown sugar until runny and smooth.

Stir in the cornflakes and sesame seeds, mixing well. Spoon into the paper moulds.

Place the filled paper moulds on large baking tray.

Bake for about 8 minutes. Leave for 15 minutes to cool. Makes 16.

PER SERVING

Energy Kcals	53
Protein g	0.0
Fat g	3.4
Polyunsaturated fatty acids g	0.75
Saturated fatty acids g	0.86
Carbohydrate g	7.6
Calcium mg	2

Baking, Breakfasts and Beverages

Bacon, Onion and Sage Scones

Onion, Tomato and Rosemary Focaccia

Seedy Muffins

Polenta Bread Rolls

Carrot and Raisin Cake with Lemon and Orange Frosting

Chocolate and Almond Pithiviers

Coconut and Chocolate Flapjack

Currant and Peanut Cookies

Fresh Strawberry and Vanilla Roulade

Malted Tea Buns

Orange and Almond Shortbread

Spiced Apple and Walnut Cake

Wicked Chocolate Cake

Cornmeal Pastry

Crisp Sweet Pastry

Quick Flaky Pastry

Shortcrust Pastry

Wholemeal Pastry

Blueberry Muffins

Corn Griddle Cakes

Kedgeree

Porridge

Eggy Bread

Banana Oat Shake

Hot Chocolate

Summer Berry Fruit Crush

Tiger Nut Milk

These can be made with ham or pastrami for a slightly different flavour. Vegetarians should omit the bacon.

Bacon, Onion and Sage Scones

If I have run out of bread, I often make scones as they take so little time to prepare and bake, these scones are particularly good served hot from the oven with a steaming bowl of homemade soup. They are also delicious cold as a sandwich with Tofutti (soya cream cheese) and watercress or baby spinach leaves for a picnic or packed lunch.

1 tbsp	olive oil	1 tbsp
1	medium onion, finely chopped	1
4 oz	smoked back or streaky bacon, finely chopped	110 g
10 oz	self-raising flour	275 g
	pinch salt	
1 oz	vegan margarine	25 g
8	sage leaves, chopped	8
8 fl oz	oat drink	220 ml

Grease 2 large baking sheets. Pre-heat the oven to 220C, 425F, gas 7.

In a frying pan, heat the oil and sweat the onions for 5 minutes, add the bacon and continue cooking for several minutes until cooked through.

Sift the flour and salt into a large mixing bowl. Lightly rub in the margarine until the mixture resembles breadcrumbs.

Stir the onion and bacon mixture, sage and oat drink into the flour to form sticky dough.

Turn out onto floured surface.

Knead gently until smooth then press the dough out to 2.5 cm (1 inch) thick, stamp into small rounds.

Place scones on the prepared baking sheets.

Bake in the oven for about 15 minutes or until well-risen and golden brown.

Leave to cool on a wire rack, or serve hot from the oven. Makes about 12.

PER SERVING	
Energy Kcals	128
Protein g	4.6
Fat g	4.2
Polyunsaturated fatty acids g	1.04
Saturated fatty acids g	1.08
Carbohydrate g	19.3
Calcium mg	91

Try other versions using fresh chopped basil and black olives.

Fast action dried yeast makes baking quicker and simpler. Unlike some ordinary dried yeasts it does not need sugar or pre-mixing with warm water. If you wish to use ordinary dried yeast or fresh yeast, you will need to follow the manufacturers instructions.

Onion, Tomato and Rosemary Focaccia

The combination of the caramelised onions, sun-dried tomatoes and rosemary give this bread a wonderful flavour, particularly when still fresh from the oven. Serve with hot homemade soup or as part of a barbecue or buffet. I also recommend you try serving it with Sicilian Caponata (see page 128) to make an unusual starter or light meal.

2	medium onions, halved and thinly sliced	2
4 tbsps	olive oil	4 tbsps
1lb 10 oz	strong white flour	750 g
2 tsp	fine salt	2 tsp
1	7 g sachet fast action dried yeast	1
13½ fl oz	lukewarm water	450 ml
4 oz	sun-dried tomatoes in oil, drained and chopped	110 g
	large sprig of fresh rosemary, stalks removed and leaves chopped	
1 tsp	rock or maldon salt	1 tsp

Grease a large baking tray. Sweat the onions in 1 tablespoon of olive oil over a medium heat for about 8 minutes until tender but not too soft.

Sieve the flour and the fine salt into a bowl then stir in the dried yeast. Next pour in 2 tablespoons of the olive oil and then gradually work in the water a little at a time, until you have a manageable, soft dough which is not too sticky, you may not need all the water.

Tip the dough out onto a floured surface and knead for about 8 minutes until you have a silky dough.

Work in the chopped sun-dried tomatoes and chopped rosemary, and continue kneading until they are all well incorporated.

Work the dough into a large flat circle about 35 cm (14 inch).

Lay the dough on the prepared baking tray, then, using your fingers poke lots of holes over top, cover with onions, and drizzle with remaining 1 tablespoon of olive oil and sprinkle over the rock salt.

Leave in a warm place to rise slowly for about 45 minutes, until doubled in size.

PER SERVING	
Energy Kcals	408
Protein g	1.2
Fat g	13.2
Polyunsaturated fatty acids g	3.6
Saturated fatty acids g	1.6
Carbohydrate g	76
Calcium mg	146

While the dough is rising, pre-heat the oven to 220C, 425F, gas 7.

Bake in the oven for 15 minutes, check and turn tray around if the focaccia is cooking unevenly. Bake for further 7-8 minutes, until risen and golden brown with crisp darkening onions.

Lift the focaccia off the tray onto a cooling rack. Serve warm or at room temperature. Serves 6-8.

Store for several days in an airtight container. When using seeds check they are fresh, as the essential oils can quickly become rancid. For a fruity muffin use raisins and chopped apple.

Seedy Muffins

Seeds and malted wheat give an excellent texture and provide valuable vitamins and minerals. These muffins are fairly quick and easy to prepare and can be served either sweet with fruit jams or honey or savoury with Tofutti (soya cream cheese) and slices of ham, bacon, gravlax or smoked salmon.

3 oz	plain flour	75 g
4 oz	granary flour	110 g
1 1/2 tsps	baking powder	1 1/2 tsps
2 oz	soft brown sugar	50 g
1/2 tsp	salt	1/2 tsp
1 oz	sunflower seeds	25 g
1 oz	sesame seeds	25 g
1 oz	pumpkin seeds	25 g
2	eggs	2
1/4 pt	oat drink	150 ml
1 tbsp	sunflower oil	1 tbsp
1 tbsp	malt extract	1 tbsp

Pre-heat the oven to 200C, 400F, gas 6. Grease a 9-hole muffin tin or lay 9 paper muffin cup cases on a baking tray. In a large bowl, combine the flours and baking powder, brown sugar, salt and seeds, mixing well.

In a separate bowl beat the eggs, then whisk in the oat drink, sunflower oil and malt extract until well blended.

Pour this liquid over the dry ingredients and stir thoroughly. The mixture should have the consistency of a thick batter. Add more oat drink if necessary. Spoon the batter into the muffin tin.

Bake for about 20-25 minutes until risen, firm and golden. If using a tin, transfer the muffins to a wire rack, if using paper muffin cases, leave them in the cases and transfer them to the rack. Serve warm. Makes 9.

PER SERVING	
Energy Kcals	142
Protein g	3.1
Fat g	7.8
Polyunsaturated fatty acids g	2.35
Saturated fatty acids g	0.52
Carbohydrate g	23.8
Calcium mg	43

Just before shaping the rolls, knead in other ingredients such as sesame or sunflower seeds or currants for a different variation. Store in an airtight container for 2 days. Alternatively, they will freeze well when fresh.

Polenta Bread Rolls

Polenta flour gives these rolls an interesting slightly coarse texture and a golden colour. Serve with hot soups or as sandwiches with various fillings. They are also good halved when cold, spread with crushed garlic and chopped herbs then drizzled with olive oil. Wrap the rolls in tin foil and heat through in a hot oven for about 8 minutes for garlicky polenta rolls.

1 lb	strong white flour	450 g
8 oz	fine polenta flour	225 g
1	7 g pack fast action dried yeast	1
2 tsps	salt	2 tsps
13½ fl oz	warm water	400 ml
2 tbsps	olive oil	2 tbsps

Grease a large baking tray. In a large bowl, mix the flours and dried yeast together.

In a separate bowl, dissolve salt in warm water then add the olive oil.

Pour this liquid into the flour stirring well to form dough.

Tip the dough onto a floured work surface and knead for 5 minutes.

Shape into 16 equal size balls and lay them onto the prepared baking tray.

Sprinkle with a little extra polenta flour.

Leave to prove in warm place for about 40 minutes until doubled in size.

While the rolls are rising, pre-heat the oven to 220C, 425F, gas 7.

Bake in the hot oven for about 15 minutes, but turn the oven down slightly half way through the cooking.

The rolls should be risen and golden, and the underneath should sound hollow when tapped.

Turn the rolls onto a rack to cool. Makes 16 rolls.

PER SERVING	
Energy Kcals	160
Protein g	4.7
Fat g	2.1
Polyunsaturated fatty acids g	0.27
Saturated fatty acids g	0.24
Carbohydrate g	31.5
Calcium mg	40

If you have a juicer, you could use the left over carrot pulp instead of the grated carrot from making carrot juice (or carrot, ginger and apple – my favourite juice!)

Carrot and Raisin Cake with Lemon and Orange Frosting

This is a lovely nutritious cake with the tangy frosting making it a real treat. It would also be useful in packed lunch boxes or picnics.

Cake

6 fl oz	sunflower oil	175 ml
6 oz	light muscovado sugar	175 g
3	large eggs, beaten	3
4 oz	raisins	110 g
	grated zest from 1 lemon and 1 orange	
10 oz	carrots, peeled and grated	275 g
6 oz	plain flour	175 g
2	level teaspoons ground cinnamon	2
	good grating of nutmeg	
1	level teaspoon baking powder	1
1	level teaspoon bicarbonate of soda	1

Frosting

1 tbsp	lemon juice	1 tbsp
1 tbsp	orange juice	1 tbsp
7 oz	icing sugar, sifted	200 g

Grease and line a 18 cm (7 inch) square cake tin. Preheat the oven to 180C, 350F, gas 4.

In a large bowl, beat the oil and sugar together. Gradually beat in the egg, raisins, zest and grated carrot.

Sift the flour, cinnamon, nutmeg and raising agents into the bowl and fold the cake mixture well until well combined.

Tip the mixture into the tin, smoothing out the mixture and bake on the middle shelf of the oven for 35-40 minutes, until well risen and firm to the touch.

Leave to cool for about 10 minutes, then turn the cake out on to a rack and leave to cool completely.

To make the frosting; sift the icing sugar into a bowl and gradually beat in the lemon and orange juice until you have a smooth glossy icing.

Place the cake on a serving plate and pour the icing over allowing it to drizzle down the sides of the cake.

Once the icing has set serve the cake or cut it into 9 squares. Makes 9 squares.

PER SERVING	
Energy Kcals	441
Protein g	2.3
Fat g	21.7
Polyunsaturated fatty acids g	12.49
Saturated fatty acids g	2.41
Carbohydrate g	68.4
Calcium mg	64

Great for a messy children's treat, although make sure the filling has cooled properly.

Chocolate and Almond Pithiviers

This was inspired by a visit to the local French pâtisserie whilst on holiday, and is a crisp pastry with a gooey chocolate and almond filling. Most French-style buns and cakes such as croissants, pain au chocolat, pain au raisin, always contain butter so it was a good reason to try these pithiviers.

4 oz	vegan margarine	110 g
4 oz	icing sugar	110 g
4 oz	ground almonds	110 g
1 tsp	vanilla essence	1 tsp
6 oz	dark, dairy-free chocolate, chopped	175 g
8 oz	puff pastry (dairy-free)	225 g
	egg for glazing	
1 tbsp	icing sugar	1 tbsp
2 tbsps	flaked almonds, toasted	2 tbsps

Pre-heat the oven to 220C, 425F, gas 7. In a medium bowl, beat the margarine with the sifted icing sugar until soft and smooth.

Stir in the almonds and vanilla essence and beat to a smooth paste, then tip in the chocolate and mix well.

On a floured surface, roll out the pastry to about 3 mm ($1/8$ inch) thick.

Cut out 12 rounds going round a small bowl about 12 cm ($4^1/2$ inch) in diameter.

Spoon a sixth of the chocolate paste in the centre of 6 of the circles, leaving at least 1 cm ($1/2$ inch) round the edge, then brush the edge very lightly with water.

Then lay the 6 remaining circles over the top to cover evenly.

Using fork, press along edges, refrigerate for about 30 minutes to allow to set.

Glaze with beaten egg. Bake for about 12-15 minutes, until risen and golden.

Remove from the oven, allow to cool for about 5 minutes.

Mix 1 tablespoon of sieved icing sugar with 1 tablespoon water until smooth.

Top the pithiviers with a spoonful of this icing and followed by a sprinkling of flaked almonds. Makes 6.

PER SERVING	
Energy Kcals	311
Protein g	2.1
Fat g	34.5
Polyunsaturated fatty acids g	4.81
Saturated fatty acids g	9.53
Carbohydrate g	20.5
Calcium mg	20

As the flapjacks cool they will become firm – if you can wait! Store in a sealed container for 2-3 days.

Coconut and Chocolate Flapjack

The coconut and chocolate together makes a delicious combination, the chocolate should remain as chunks when you bite into the flapjack. These flapjacks are gluten free as well as dairy free.

6 oz	vegan margarine	175 g
6 oz	golden syrup	175 g
8 oz	porridge oats	225 g
4 oz	desiccated coconut	110 g
4 oz	dark dairy-free chocolate, cut into small chunks	110 g

Pre-heat the oven to 180C, 350F, gas 4. Grease a shallow, oblong baking tin measuring about 20 x 25.5 cm (8 x 10 inch).

Melt the margarine and golden syrup, stirring well, in a heavy pan over a medium heat until dissolved.

Stir in the oats and coconut, allow this to cool then stir in chocolate chunks.

Pour into the baking tin and smooth down flat.

Bake for about 30 minutes until golden.

Leave to cool slightly for 5 minutes then cut into squares, the flapjacks should become firm on cooling.

Turn out onto wire rack to cool completely. Makes about 12.

PER SERVING	
Energy Kcals	326
Protein g	3.3
Fat g	21.6
Polyunsaturated fatty acids g	3.34
Saturated fatty acids g	9.99
Carbohydrate g	31.5
Calcium mg	20

Make sure you don't give these to children with a nut allergy. Try using dark chocolate, or stoned chopped dates for different variations.

Currant and Peanut Cookies

These would be ideal to take on a picnic or put in packed lunch boxes.

4 oz	soft vegan margarine	110 g
4 oz	soft brown or caster sugar	110 g
1	egg, beaten	1
5 oz	self-raising flour	150 g
1	level teaspoon mixed spice	1
4 oz	currants	110 g
4 oz	peanuts in skins, chopped	110 g

Preheat the oven to 190C, 375F, gas 5. Beat together all the ingredients, except the currants and nuts, until well blended.

Mix in currants and nuts, then, using a dessertspoon, spoon onto greased baking sheets. Flatten them out into circles.

Bake for about 10-15 minutes until golden brown around edges.

Cool slightly before lifting on to wire rack to cool completely. Makes about 15.

PER SERVING	
Energy Kcals	131
Protein g	1.0
Fat g	9.9
Polyunsaturated fatty acids g	1.60
Saturated fatty acids g	1.83
Carbohydrate g	19.5
Calcium mg	4.4

This should be eaten soon after rolling, as it will not store too well. Try making it with fresh raspberries.

Fresh Strawberry and Vanilla Roulade

I have used a whisked sponge for this roulade which is much easier to roll up than a victoria sponge. The soya cream cheese is used as a substitute for double cream which combines wonderfully with the sweetened strawberries. This may be served as a cake at teatime or as a pudding.

Sponge

3	eggs	3
3 oz	caster sugar	75 g
1/2 tsp	vanilla essence	1/2 tsp
3 oz	plain flour	75 g
	pinch of salt	

Filling

6 oz	Tofutti original (soya cream cheese)	175 g
1 tbsp	soya cream	1 tbsp
1 tbsp	caster sugar	1 tbsp
1/2 tsp	vanilla essence	1/2 tsp
10 oz	fresh strawberries, hulled and sliced	275 g

Pre-heat the oven to 180C, 350F, gas 4. Grease a flat rectangular tin about 30 x 20 cm (12 x 8 inch) and 2.5 cm (1 inch) deep.

Cut a piece of greaseproof allowing for an extra 5 cm (2 inch) on each side, push the paper into the tin and grease well with oil, dust with flour and caster sugar.

Place eggs, sugar and vanilla essence in a bowl and fit it over (not in) a saucepan of simmering water.

Whisk the mixture until light, thick and fluffy (if using an electric mixer no heat is required).

Remove the bowl from the heat and continue whisking until cool.

Sift the flour and salt, and, with a large metal spoon, gently fold into the mixture, taking care not to beat out any of the air.

Carefully pour the mixture into the prepared tin, tip the tin so the mixture fills all the corners and bake in the middle of the oven for about 15 minutes.

The sponge is cooked if it has shrunk slightly and the edges look crinkled. When pressed gently it will feel firm but spongy.

PER SERVING	
Energy Kcals	214
Protein g	3.1
Fat g	11
Polyunsaturated fatty acids g	6.1
Saturated fatty acids g	2.05
Carbohydrate g	31.6
Calcium mg	31

Lift the paper with the sponge in it and cover with clean slightly damp tea towel and leave to cool.

In a small bowl, mix the Tofutti cream cheese with the soya cream beating well until smooth, add sugar to taste and the vanilla essence.

Spread this cream mixture over roulade and top with sliced strawberries, keep about 20 slices to decorate.

Keeping longest edge nearest you, hold each front edge of greaseproof and slowly roll away pulling greaseproof away from sponge as you roll.

It may not roll that easily, just try and push it into a swiss roll shape.

Alternatively cut the rectangle into 2 equal squares and fill with the filling.

Place on a serving plate and decorate with sieved icing sugar and remaining strawberries.

Refrigerate before serving. Serves 6.

Malt extract can be found in most health food shops. Store these buns in an airtight container.

Malted Tea Buns

As these are not yeasted buns they are fairly quick and easy to make. Best eaten fresh, otherwise halved and toasted for tea or breakfast.

5 fl oz	oat drink	150 ml
3 tbsps	malt extract	3 tbsps
2 tbsps	molasses	2 tbsps
1 tbsp	sunflower oil	1 tbsp
	pinch salt	
4 oz	mixed fruit (dates, apricots or raisins)	110 g
8 oz	self-raising white flour	225 g
4 oz	wholemeal flour	110 g
2 tsps	ground cinnamon	2 tsps
1/2 tsp	baking powder	1/2 tsp
1 tbsp	apricot jam (avoid bits)	1 tbsp

Pre-heat the oven to 200C, 400F, gas 6. Heat the oat drink in a small pan, with malt extract, molasses, oil and salt, until warm.

If using dates or apricots, chop into small pieces.

In a large bowl mix the flours, cinnamon, mixed fruit and baking powder.

Stir in the milk mixture until a dough is formed.

Tip onto a floured surface and quickly knead to form a smooth dough.

Divide equally into 9 balls and place on a large greased baking tray.

Bake for about 20 minutes until risen and golden, and hollow sounding underneath when tapped.

Brush with jam when still warm.

Eat warm or when cool. Makes 9.

PER SERVING	
Energy Kcals	177
Protein g	0.7
Fat g	3.7
Polyunsaturated fatty acids g	0.75
Saturated fatty acids g	0.86
Carbohydrate g	38.3
Calcium mg	65

Wash the orange well, and if possible use an organic one.

Orange and Almond Shortbread

The orange zest gives these biscuits a delicious flavour. They would also be equally good using lemon zest and chopped hazelnuts.

6 oz	vegan margarine	175 g
3 oz	caster sugar	75 g
1	large orange for zest only	1
	few drops of almond essence	
2 oz	ground almonds	50 g
2 oz	ground rice	50 g
6 oz	plain flour	175 g

Pre-heat the oven to 190C, 375F, gas 5. Beat the margarine with the sugar until soft and creamy.

Using a vegetable peeler, peel rind carefully off the orange, trying just to get outer zest and not the pith, then cut the zest into little pieces.

Mix the orange peelings with the sugar mixture, along with the almond essence and finally the almonds, ground rice and flour.

Work it together to form ball, leaving the bowl clean.

Lay the dough on a large greased baking sheet and press into a square about 1 cm ($1/2$ inch) thick.

Prick the shortbread all over with fork and mark out into fingers, sprinkle with extra caster sugar.

Bake for about 20 minutes until a pale biscuit colour.

Leave to cool and become firm before transferring to a serving plate. Makes about 18-24.

PER SERVING	
Energy Kcals	128
Protein g	0.2
Fat g	9.6
Polyunsaturated fatty acids g	2.06
Saturated fatty acids g	2.36
Carbohydrate g	15.0
Calcium mg	14

If you don't like walnuts, hazelnuts or pecans are a suitable alternative. Use half wholemeal flour if preferred.

Spiced Apple and Walnut Cake

This cake is one of my favourites. Serve for tea or as a hot pudding with soya yoghurt or how about trying it with the oat cream recipe on page 191.

4 oz	vegan margarine	110 g
6 oz	soft brown sugar	175 g
2	eggs, beaten	2
8 oz	plain flour	225 g
1	level teaspoon ground mixed spice	1
1	level teaspoon ground cinnamon	1
	grated nutmeg	
2	level teaspoons baking powder	2
8 oz	peeled and finely chopped cooking apple	225 g
3 oz	walnuts chopped	75 g
3 fl oz	oat drink	75 ml

Pre-heat the oven to 180C, 350F, gas 4. Grease and line a deep 18 cm (7 inch) round cake tin with greaseproof paper.

In a large bowl, cream the margarine and sugar until pale and fluffy.

Add the eggs a little at a time, beating well.

Sift the flour, spices and baking powder into the bowl and stir into the mixture.

Fold in the chopped apples, walnuts and oat drink to make soft dropping consistency.

Pour the mixture into the prepared tin and bake for about 1 hour, check after about 40 minutes, if necessary turn down heat, when cooked the cake should be well risen and firm to touch.

Turn out onto a rack to cool. Makes about 8-10 slices.

PER SERVING	
Energy Kcals	359
Protein g	4.4
Fat g	20.3
Polyunsaturated fatty acids g	8.24
Saturated fatty acids g	4.09
Carbohydrate g	46.8
Calcium mg	77

For a lemon or orange layer cake, use same sponge recipe without cocoa but use orange or lemon zest. Then fill with lemon or orange curd and top with lemon icing.

Wicked Chocolate Cake

A fabulous birthday party cake that will not leave the children feeling they have missed out.

Decorate with shavings of dark chocolate, using a vegetable peeler.

Sponge

4 oz	soft vegan margarine	110 g
4 oz	caster sugar	110 g
2	eggs, beaten	2
4 oz	self-raising flour, sifted	110 g
1 tbsp	cocoa (omit cocoa for a plain sponge)	1 tbsp

Icing

2 oz	vegan margarine	50 g
3 oz	dark dairy-free chocolate, broken up	75 g
6 oz	icing sugar	175 g

Pre-heat the oven to 170C, 325F, gas 3. Line the base of two 18 cm (7 inch) sponge tins and lightly oil.

Cream together the margarine and caster sugar until light and fluffy, then gradually beat in the eggs.

Fold in the sifted flour and cocoa.

Pour evenly into the prepared tins and smooth the mixture down.

Bake for about 25-30 minutes.

Remove from the oven, loosen the edges and turn out onto rack, leave to cool.

Meanwhile, make the icing.

Put the margarine and chocolate in a bowl.

Place the bowl over a pan of hot water until the chocolate and margarine melts, mix well.

Beat in the sifted icing sugar and leave the icing to cool slightly.

To assemble the cake; lay one sponge on a plate, spoon over one third of the icing and smear over evenly.

Cover with the other half of cake and spoon over the remaining icing.

Using a knife smooth icing evenly around the sides of the cake. Serves 6-8.

PER SERVING	
Energy Kcals	389
Protein g	2.7
Fat g	13.9
Polyunsaturated fatty acids g	2.15
Saturated fatty acids g	4.88
Carbohydrate g	72.1
Calcium mg	74

Cornmeal Pastry

The result is a crisp pastry that makes a pleasant change to ordinary shortcrust pastry. I use this pastry to make the Mexican-style Avocado and Prawn Empanadas see page 32. Try all sorts of pasty fillings with this pastry for a picnic or crisp snack.

7 oz	plain white flour	200 g
5 oz	cornmeal	140 g
1 tsp	salt	1 tsp
6 tbsps	olive or vegetable oil	6 tbsps
1	egg, beaten	1
	dash of cold water	

Combine the flour, cornmeal and salt in a bowl.

Stir in the oil and beaten egg and enough water to make ingredients cling together.

Knead dough on lightly floured surface until it forms a smooth ball.

Cover and chill until required. Makes about 400 g (14 oz).

PER QUANTITY	
Energy Kcals	1,900
Protein g	13.0
Fat g	103.2
Polyunsaturated fatty acids g	56.97
Saturated fatty acids g	10.80
Carbohydrate g	253.5
Calcium mg	304

Crisp Sweet Pastry

Sweet pastry generally cannot be bought commercially without containing any dairy products. This variation is a lovely crisp, biscuity pastry, which will match up to any others of its kind, making it ideal for fresh fruit tarts (see page 178).

6 oz	plain white flour	175 g
	pinch of salt	
3 oz	firm vegan margarine	75 g
3	medium egg yolks	3
3 oz	caster sugar	75 g
	few drops vanilla essence	

Sift the flour and salt into a large bowl.

Cut the margarine into small chunks and using the tips of your fingers rub the margarine in the flour until the mixture resembles breadcrumbs.

Make a well in the centre of the flour and add the yolks, sugar and vanilla essence and using a knife work in all the surrounding flour, then gently knead until smooth.

Place in bag and chill for at least 30 minutes.

Use as instructed. Makes about 400 g (14 oz).

PER QUANTITY	
Energy Kcals	1,623
Protein g	7.4
Fat g	85.1
Polyunsaturated fatty acids g	20.06
Saturated fatty acids g	25.16
Carbohydrate g	220.5
Calcium mg	309

Jus-rol assures me that the following products are suitable for both vegetarians and vegans, not containing any dairy, milk or egg products:

Jus-rol Puff Pastry Sheets and Blocks
Jus-rol Shortcrust Pastry Sheets and Blocks
Jus-rol Vol-au-Vents (all sizes)
Jus-rol Filo Pastry Sheets

However, their Sweet Dessert Pastry is unsuitable as it contains dairy products.

PER QUANTITY	
Energy Kcals	1,928
Protein g	0.3
Fat g	141.4
Polyunsaturated fatty acids g	37.06
Saturated fatty acids g	42.50
Carbohydrate g	174.3
Calcium mg	322

The pastry would work with a soft margarine, although it will never be as firm and easy to roll out.

PER QUANTITY	
Energy Kcals	1,568
Protein g	0.1
Fat g	102.0
Polyunsaturated fatty acids g	17.27
Saturated fatty acids g	36.19
Carbohydrate g	173.1
Calcium mg	318

Quick Flaky Pastry

This is a fairly easy crispy light pastry that can be used to substitute puff pastry if you are unable to buy it.

6 oz	firm vegan margarine	175 g
8 oz	plain flour	225 g
1/2 tsp	salt	1/2 tsp
	cold water to mix	

Put the margarine in the freezer for about 1 hour.
Sift the flour and salt into a bowl.
Dip the margarine in the flour and quickly grate into the bowl.
Using a knife mix the fat into the flour. Gradually add some cold water a little at a time and using a knife mix to form dough that leaves the bowl clean.
Quickly bring together to form a ball with your hands.
Chill in the fridge for half an hour.
Use as required. Makes about 400 g (14 oz).

Shortcrust Pastry

For a good bought short crust pastry Jus Rol make a good frozen one in a 680 g (2 x 340 g) pack.

2 oz	firm vegan margarine	50 g
2 oz	white flora or lard	50 g
8 oz	plain flour, sifted	225 g
2 tbsps	cold water	2 tbsps
	pinch salt	

Rub the fats into the sifted flour and salt until the mixture resembles breadcrumbs.
Using a knife add the water and mix to form a firm dough.
Cover and refrigerate for at least 30 minutes before using.
Makes about 350 g (12 oz).

Take care not to over cook as it will burn easily, giving the pastry a bitter taste.

Wholemeal Pastry

For a more wholesome pastry use this recipe. This pastry rolls out quite thinly and does not require as much pre-cooking as short crust. The baking powder gives it a lighter texture.

The pastry should be left to rest longer than ordinary short crust, for the flour to absorb the liquid.

8 oz	wholewheat flour	225 g
2 tsps	baking powder	2 tsps
	pinch of salt	
2 oz	firm vegan margarine	50 g
2 oz	white flora or lard	50 g
1 tsp	brown sugar	1 tsp
2 tbsps	vegetable oil	2 tbsps
6 tbsps	cold water	6 tbsps

In a large bowl, mix the flour, salt and baking powder. Lightly rub in the fats until the mixture resembles breadcrumbs.

Combine sugar, oil and water and pour into flour.

Using knife blade, mix to light dough.

Cover and refrigerate for at least 1 hour before using.

Makes about 400 g (14 oz).

PER QUANTITY	
Energy Kcals	1,613
Protein g	24.4
Fat g	103.2
Polyunsaturated fatty acids g	17.93
Saturated fatty acids g	36.41
Carbohydrate g	156.3
Calcium mg	199

Try chocolate muffins for a special treat, by substituting dark chocolate chunks.

Blueberry Muffins

These are very quick and simple to make and a favourite with my children for breakfast or tea, I think it is because blueberries are not as sharp as some fruit such as blackcurrants. However you could use many types of fruit or even dried fruits instead of the blueberries.

10 oz	self-raising flour	275 g
5 oz	soft brown sugar	150 g
1	egg, beaten	1
7 fl oz	soya milk	200 ml
3½ fl oz	sunflower oil	100 ml
5 oz	blueberries, washed	150 g

Pre-heat the oven to 180C, 350F, gas 4. Use either large paper muffin cases or a tin with 180 ml (6 fl oz) capacity holes, well greased.

Sift the flour with the sugar, add the egg, milk and oil and beat well.

Stir in the blueberries.

Spoon mixture into prepared tin or the paper cases.

Bake in the oven for about 20-25 minutes until risen and golden.

Place onto a wire rack, serve warm. Makes about 8 big muffins.

PER SERVING	
Energy Kcals	306
Protein g	4.2
Fat g	13.5
Polyunsaturated fatty acids g	8.38
Saturated fatty acids g	1.66
Carbohydrate g	45.7
Calcium mg	142

If you have an Aga, cook straight on the lightly greased hot plate.

Corn Griddle Cakes

These are delicious served with crisp rashers of bacon and maple syrup for an American-style lactose-free breakfast.

4 oz	plain flour	110 g
1	level teaspoon baking powder	1
1/2 tsp	paprika	1/2 tsp
1/2 tsp	salt	1/2 tsp
1	egg, beaten	1
5 fl oz	soya milk	150 ml
4 oz	sweetcorn – either fresh off cob and quickly boiled, frozen or tinned and drained	110 g
1 tbsp	sunflower oil	1 tbsp
	extra oil for frying	

Sift the dry ingredients into a bowl. Beat in egg and then gradually add the soya milk until you have a smooth batter.

Stir in the sweetcorn and a tablespoon of oil.

Heat a large griddle pan or heavy frying pan, pour in about 1 teaspoon oil.

Spoon about 1 large heaped tablespoon of batter for each griddle cake at a time.

Cook until the bubbles show on the surface, then turn the cakes over and cook the other sides until golden brown (about 1 minute on either side).

Serve on warmed plates. Makes about 8 cakes, enough for 4.

PER SERVING	
Energy Kcals	231
Protein g	4.5
Fat g	12.8
Polyunsaturated fatty acids g	7.04
Saturated fatty acids g	1.42
Carbohydrate g	429.5
Calcium mg	59

Most smoked white fish would be suitable for this dish.

Kedgeree

Kedgeree makes a hearty filling breakfast, one that even the children should enjoy. We often have it as a light supper and any left over I heat up for a quick breakfast.

Alternatively serve hot for lunch or a light supper with the Creamy Curried Coconut Sauce (see page 136). It would also be an impressive starter for 8 if reheated in ramekins and turned onto small plates with the sauce poured around edge.

1 lb	smoked haddock fillet, or cooked fresh salmon if preferred	450 g
8 oz	basmati rice	225 g
1	medium onion, finely chopped	1
1 oz	vegan margarine	25 g
1 tsp	garam masala	1 tsp
1 tsp	ground cumin	1 tsp
1/2 tsp	ground turmeric	1/2 tsp
4	hard-boiled eggs, cut into quarters	4
	juice of half a lemon	
2 tbsps	freshly chopped parsley	2 tbsps
	salt and freshly ground pepper	

Pre-heat the oven to 190C, 375F, gas 5. Bring a pan half filled with water to the boil, simmer the haddock for about 10 minutes, do not overcook.

Drain the fish, saving the cooking water. Remove the skin and bones and flake the fish.

Add a little more water and cook the rice in the fish water until just tender, drain and leave to dry out a little.

Gently sauté the onion in the margarine for about 8 minutes until softened, add the spices and fry for a further 3 minutes. Remove from the heat.

In a large warm baking dish combine the rice with the spiced onion mixture, eggs, parsley, lemon juice and flaked fish, season with freshly ground pepper and salt only if haddock is not too salty.

Cover with tin foil and heat through in the oven for 15-20 minutes until piping hot. Serves 4.

PER SERVING	
Energy Kcals	365
Protein g	26.1
Fat g	12.8
Polyunsaturated fatty acids g	1.90
Saturated fatty acids g	1.99
Carbohydrate g	48.6
Calcium mg	50

For an even creamier porridge use all oat milk.
 For a special treat add 1 tablespoon soya cream at the end before serving.

PER SERVING	
Energy Kcals	217
Protein g	6.6
Fat g	5.0
Polyunsaturated fatty acids g	0.10
Saturated fatty acids g	0.02
Carbohydrate g	38.8
Calcium mg	29

Porridge

Eating oats is an ideal start to the day. Porridge was traditionally made using water, and served with salt in Scotland, but in the south milk and sugar were added. I find it delicious made with half water and half oat milk. Try it with oat cream drizzled over the porridge and sweetened with a sprinkling of brown sugar, maple syrup or runny honey.
 Also great with chopped dates or bananas.

17 fl oz	water	500 ml
17 fl oz	oat drink	500 ml
4 oz	fine porridge oats	110 g
	pinch of salt	

Mix all the ingredients in a saucepan well.
 Bring to boil, simmer, stirring occasionally for about 5 minutes until porridge thickens. Sweeten to taste.
 Serve immediately. Serves 2-3.

For a light supper, try adding chopped ham to the eggs before frying.

PER SERVING	
Energy Kcals	147
Protein g	3.2
Fat g	8.3
Polyunsaturated fatty acids g	4.79
Saturated fatty acids g	0.91
Carbohydrate g	16.0
Calcium mg	36

Eggy Bread

This is especially enjoyed in our house for breakfast or a quick children's supper with tomato ketchup. In America they stack it with crispy bacon and maple syrup.

3	eggs, beaten	3
1 tbsp	soya milk	1 tbsp
	pinch of salt	
4	thick slices of white or brown bread	4
2 tbsps	sunflower oil for frying	2 tbsps

Heat a large frying pan with half the oil over a medium heat. Mix the eggs with milk and salt.
 Dip the bread slices in the egg, allowing them to soak up as much as possible.
 Turn the bread over and soak the other side.
 Lift bread out of egg, allowing excess egg to fall back into egg mixture.
 Place in a hot frying pan, cook for about 1-2 minutes, turn over and repeat.
 The egg bread should be golden and cooked through. Serve immediately. Serves 4.

For an iced shake, try chopping up the banana and freezing it before blending. Try experimenting with other fruits such as strawberries, peaches or raspberries, etc.

PER SERVING	
Energy Kcals	345
Protein g	6.9
Fat g	4.1
Polyunsaturated fatty acids g	0.20
Saturated fatty acids g	0.20
Carbohydrate g	74.9
Calcium mg	32

Banana Oat Shake

This is a creamy alternative to a milkshake and a lot better for you! The shake would be good for babies or toddlers (omitting honey for very young babies).

2	large ripe bananas	2
12 fl oz	chilled Oat and Honey Cream (see page 191)	350 ml

Whiz the two ingredients together in a blender or processor. Pour into two glasses and serve immediately. Serves 2.

Hot Chocolate

It is quite hard to find drinking chocolate that does not contain milk powder. I have recently discovered an organic drinking chocolate without any milk products, it was, however, purely made up from cocoa powder and a lot of sugar. I therefore suggest you use cocoa and sweeten to taste.

If using vanilla rice milk, you will not need to sweeten the drink so much. Also avoid boiling if using soya or rice milk as these are more prone to curdle. Try using different types of honey for a varied flavour.

PER SERVING	
Energy Kcals	31
Protein g	1.9
Fat g	2.2
Polyunsaturated fatty acids g	0.06
Saturated fatty acids g	1.28
Carbohydrate g	1.2
Calcium mg	13

1 tsp	cocoa powder	1 tsp
1/2 pt	oat drink	275 ml

Mix the cocoa with some of the oat drink to form a smooth paste.

Gently heat the oat drink, until hot enough to drink.

Pour over the cocoa paste and mix well. Sweeten to taste with sugar or honey. Serves 1.

Supermarkets or farm shops sometimes stock frozen summer fruits that can be used for an economical alternative all year round.

PER SERVING	
Energy Kcals	91
Protein g	1.4
Fat g	0.3
Polyunsaturated fatty acids g	0.18
Saturated fatty acids g	0.06
Carbohydrate g	22.0
Calcium mg	32

Summer Berry Fruit Crush

This is pleasantly cooling and refreshing on a hot summers day. Experiment with all different fruits, depending on the season. Peaches, melons or any other soft fruit would also create a delicious fruit crush.

4 oz	strawberries	110 g
4 oz	raspberries	110 g
8 fl oz	apple juice	250 ml
4	ice cubes	4
	clear honey or sugar to taste	

Using a blender mix all the ingredients excluding the ice. Sieve the mixture to remove any pips. Blend with the ice cubes to crush them.
Serve immediately. Serves 2.

Tiger nuts may be hard to find. You can sometimes get them from health food shops. I buy them at the local market on the health food stand. They may seem fairly pricey, but they work out cheaper than buying soya milk and in my opinion the effort is well worth it. Another milk to try making is almond milk although almonds are more expensive.

PER SERVING	
Energy Kcals	202
Protein g	2.2
Fat g	11.9
Polyunsaturated fatty acids g	1.10
Saturated fatty acids g	2.00
Carbohydrate g	22.9
Calcium mg	24

Tiger Nut Milk

Tiger nuts, also known as chufa nuts, are chewy brown rhizomes. They produce a slightly sweet milk. This milk is delicious chilled as a drink, it has a slight natural sweetness and is as satisfying as a glass of cow's milk. It is also excellent poured over cereals or used in cold milky drinks.

8 oz	tiger nuts	250 g
1³/₄ pts	water	1 litre
	sweeten with honey if desired	

Wash the tiger nuts and leave to soak for 12 hours in some fresh water, to slightly soften skin.
Discard the soaking water, place the nuts in a liquidizer with one quarter of the water, blend until it becomes a pulp, add remaining water and blend well.
Leave to stand for a while before straining.
Refrigerate and shake well before serving as it may settle slightly at the bottom. Makes 1 litre, serves 4.

Useful Organisations

Action Against Allergy
PO Box 278
Twickenham
Middlesex TW1 4QQ
T. 020-8892 2711
Email: AAA@actionagainstallergy.freeserve.co.uk

Autism Unravelled
3 Palmera Avenue
Calcot
Reading
Berkshire, RG31 7DZ
T. 0118-961 5967
Email: bluecat@autism-unravelled.com
Web: www.autism-unravelled.com

The Anaphylaxis Campaign
PO Box 149
Fleet
Hampshire
GU52 6FA
T. 01252-542 029
Web: www.anaphylaxis.org.uk

The Asthma and Allergy Research Centre
12 Vernon Street
Derby DE1 1FT
T. 01332-362 461
Email: jmcmaara@globalnet.co.uk

British Allergy Foundation
Deepdene House
30 Bellegrove Road
Welling
Kent KT14 7ED
T. 020-8303 8583
Email: allergybaf@compuserve.com

British Association for Nutritional Therapists
(for a register of nutritional therapists)
BCMB
27 Old Gloucester Street
London WC1N 3XX
T. 0870-606 1284

British Dietetics Association
(for information on state registered dieticians)
5th Floor
Charles House
148-9 Great Charles Street
Birmingham B3 3HT
T. 0121-200 8080
Web: www.bda.uk.com

British Goat Society
34-36 Fore Street
Bovey Tracey
Newton Abbott
Devon TQ13 9AD
T. 01626-833 168
Web: www.allgoats.com

Diabetes UK
10 Queen Anne Street
London W1M 0BD
T. 020-7636 6112
Web: www.diabetes.org.uk

HealthScreening
(for allergy testing)
1 Church Square
Taunton
Somerset TA1 1SA
T. 01823-325 023
Email: allergyca@aol.com

Hyperactive Children's Support Group
71 Whyke Lane
Chichester
West Sussex PO19 2LD
T.01903-725 182
Email: web@hacsg.org.uk
Web: www.hacsg.org.uk

Irritable Bowel Syndrome
IBS Network
Northern General Hospital
Sheffield S5 7AU
T.0114-261 1531
Helpline: 01543-492 192
Web: www.ibsnetwork.org.uk

National Eczema Society
163 Eversholt Street
London NW1 1BU
T. 0870-241 3604   1-4 pm

Probiotics International
(makers of ProtexinLacta)
Matts Lane
Stoke cum Hamden
Somerset TA14 6QE
T. 01935-822 921
Email: info@protexin.com
Web: www.protexin.com

UK Supermarkets

ASDA – Customer Services
Asda House
Great Wilson Street
Leeds LS11 5AD
T. 0113-241 7730
Web: www.asda.co.uk

Co-op – Customer Services
CWS Ltd
Freepost MR9 473
Manchester M4 8BA
T. 0800-317 827
Email: customer.relations@co-op.co.uk
Web: www.co-op.co.uk

Marks and Spencer
Room 101
Michael House
47 Baker Street
London W1A 1DN
T. 020-7268 1234
Web: www.marks-and-spencer.com

Safeway – Customer Services
Beddow Way
Aylesford
Nr Maidstone
Kent ME20 7AT
T. 020-8848 8744
Web: www.safeway.co.uk

Sainsbury's – Customer Services Department
Stamford House
Stamford Street
London SE1 9LL
Helpline: 0800-387 504
Web: www.sainsburys.co.uk

Somerfield – Customer Relations
Somerfield House
Whitchurch Lane
Bristol BS14 0TJ
T. 0117-935 9359
Web: www.somerfield.co.uk

Tesco – Nutrition Advice Service
PO Box 18
Cheshunt
Herts EN8 9SL
T. 0800-505 55
Web: www.tesco.com

Waitrose – Nutritional Advice Service
Doncastle Road
Southern Industrial Area
Bracknell
Berkshire RG12 4AY
T. 01344-424 680
Web: www.waitrose.com

Index